The Daily Telegraph

GUIDE TO
PLANNING YOUR RETIREMENT

NIKI CHESWORTH

D0336110

MACMILLAN

First published 2003 by Macmillan
an imprint of Pan Macmillan Ltd
Pan Macmillan, 20 New Wharf Road, London N1 9RR
Basingstoke and Oxford
Associated companies throughout the world
www.panmacmillan.com

ISBN 1 4050 0638 2

1 3 5 7 9 8 6 4 2

A CIP catalogue record for this book is available from
the British Library.

Typeset by SetSystems Ltd, Saffron Walden, Essex
Printed and bound in Great Britain by
Mackays of Chatham plc, Chatham, Kent

The Daily Telegraph

GUIDE TO
PLANNING
YOUR
RETIREMENT

For Katie and Guy

Contents

Introduction

If you are looking forward to enjoying your retirement on a comfortable income then you may have to think again. There is a £27 billion savings gap – too few people are saving enough for their old age and unless they start making better provision for the future, millions will be living on reduced state benefits and be forced into poverty.

Action is needed, which is why the government has commissioned several independent reports, and a Green Paper on pension reform. This will simplify the pensions tax regime and give more flexibility on retirement, as well as more protection to scheme members.

However, it is vital that you understand that there will still be no room for complacency. Even those people in the best private pension schemes run by employers or the private sector are already finding that a comfortable retirement is looking less secure. The increasing cost of running these schemes is forcing employers to consider cutting benefits or to ask employees to join schemes which provide less generous benefits.

So that readers can understand just how serious the situation is for both state and private pensions this book starts by looking at the pension crisis. Chapter 2 guides readers through the main pension choices so you can then choose which types of pension to find out more about in later chapters. There is no point in reading about individual pensions, for example, if the questions you answer in Chapter 2 reveal that these are not the best option for you. The tax benefits of pensions and what the state has to offer as well as employer and individual pensions are then covered in detail in Chapter 3.

Once readers understand the pensions options on offer to them and the benefits of paying into a pension, they can check they are investing enough to meet their retirement needs. Chapter 8 allows you to calculate how much you need to invest, Chapter 9 looks at ways to boost your pension, while Chapter 10 shows you how to maximize your pension on retirement.

Special considerations for people running their own businesses and the impact of divorce on pensions are covered in detail in other chapters.

Recent falls in stock markets mean pensions are not the sound investment they once were. Investors – particularly those nearing retirement – could do better by looking at alternatives in addition to any pension provision they already have. These possibilities are covered in Chapter 12. We then look at how you should plan your retirement from aiming to retire early to considering retiring abroad, and follow with a checklist of things to do as retirement looms.

Although jargon is kept to the minimum and explained when used, pensions are complex long-term investments. The impact of a poor financial decision is something you may have to live with for 20 years once you retire. This book does not aim to replace the need for financial advice and aims simply to help you make an informed decision. So Chapter 15 looks at getting financial advice – what you need to know and the questions you should ask.

Although only 1 per cent of employees retire on the maximum pension allowed by the Inland Revenue, not all retire in poverty. Many do – and will still be able to – retire on a comfortable pension . . . but only if they start planning today.

Bear this in mind:

- The state pension is forecast to fall to only 10 per cent of average earnings over the next three decades.

- If you are 20 and delay starting a pension for ten years, you could cut your final pension pot by half.

Remember, retirement planning is not a one-off decision. You should review your pension provision regularly to check you are investing enough. This book can guide you all the way to retirement; although some pension rules may change, the basic principles are likely to remain the same.

THIS BOOK IS ALSO FOR YOUNG READERS

The solution to the £27 billion retirement savings gap is to encourage people to start investing in a pension at a young age, which is why increasing numbers of people in their 30s are taking pensions seriously for the first time.

If you start investing at 50 instead of at 30, funding a decent pension could cost you nearly five times as much – instead of a contribution of £200 a month you would have to pay almost £1,100. So do pass this book on to your children or your younger colleagues – they will benefit from planning their retirement today even though it may be 20, 30 or even 40 years away.

*

The information contained in this book is correct at the time of going to press. However, readers should be aware that major pension reform is planned by the government, and although the proposals for this are covered in this book, they are subject to parliamentary approval and could therefore be amended before becoming law. In addition, there could be further changes to the taxation of pensions in future Budgets. The general advice given in this book should remain unaffected by any changes, however, readers are still advised to seek advice before making any major financial decisions.

1 The Pensions Crisis

The pensions crisis is caused by a demographic time bomb. As we live longer, we need more to live on in retirement. Gone are the days when a worker would retire at 65 and die within just a few years. Today, retirement can last for 20 years or more. Or to put it another way, you could have a retirement half as long as your working life.

This has made pensions – from the state, provided by employers and arranged by individuals – more expensive. In simple terms, more needs to be invested to provide a sufficient income in retirement for everyone.

The problem has been compounded by falling stock markets which have hit the value of pensions and jeopardized the future of the best employer schemes, some of which are in deficit. Even when stock markets recover, growth is expected to be slow for the foreseeable future. Low interest rates have also taken their toll, hitting the value of pensions that can be bought on retirement (these so-called annuity rates recently hit a 40-year low).

The savings gap for retirement now stands at £27 billion and is rising, that is equivalent to more than 10p on the basic rate of income tax.

Where will the money come from to plug the gap? If it is from the state, it will mean much higher taxes – something that would be politically damaging. Employers will be reluctant to bridge the savings gap particularly as many of them are already raiding company profits to boost their company pension schemes and cutting the amount they pay towards their employees' pensions.

So that leaves . . . individuals. *You* will be the ones who will have to pay.

However, with pensions increasingly seen as poor value following stock market falls, individuals are increasingly reluctant to invest what is necessary, when only higher-rate taxpayers are being given real incentive to invest.

STATE PENSIONS

The Growing Cost of State Pensions

When the state pension was first introduced individuals paid their 'stamp' believing they were setting aside money for their future. Today, contributions paid in National Insurance simply go straight into existing pensioners' pockets, there is nothing invested for tomorrow – no National Insurance fund set aside to pay for the rising costs of the state scheme. As we live longer the problem is compounded, leaving more and more people drawing a pension but fewer and fewer people paying for it.

Today, 90 per cent of people live to claim their state pension, compared to two thirds in 1950. In addition, people are now claiming their pension for eight years longer than they were at the start of the 1950s, putting a further drain on the state.

At the same time, the workforce is falling. The UK's population is expected to grow by 4.4 million to 64 million over the next 25 years. However, the number of people aged 15 to 50 is projected to fall by 1.5 million in this period, and it is the elderly who will account for the population growth, with the number aged 50 or over forecast to increase by over 6 million.

Poverty in Retirement

Well, there is always the state pension to fall back on, isn't there? Sadly no. The value of the state pension has fallen in real terms – in terms of actual spending power. This is because it keeps pace with inflation not earnings which tend to rise more rapidly. In fact, in 2000 the state pension rose by just 75p a week. According to Help the Aged if the link to earnings had remained the state pension would now be well over £100 a week instead of £75.50 in 2002/ 2003. As a result, the value of the state pension is forecast to fall to only 10 per cent of average earnings over the next three decades.

If things look grim for tomorrow's pensioners they are just as bad for those who have already retired, according to one recent report which claimed that one in five pensioners in Britain is living in absolute poverty.

Instead of increasing the basic state pension the government has topped it up with benefits: the minimum income guarantee (MIG) and the pension tax credit. However, these are not given automatically but have to be claimed and are means tested. An estimated 770,000 pensioners are missing out by £1.9 billion a year as a result.

Less Help from the State Second Pension

While someone retiring in 2002 who had consistently earned around one and a half times the average male earnings and had contributed to the state second pension, SERPS, since its launch in 1978 would have received a maximum total state pension of £10,922 a year – including £6,996 of SERPS – future generations are likely to be less lucky.

The maximum they will receive from the new state second pension (S2P), when flat-rate contributions are introduced, will be just £44 a week. The maximum from SERPS is currently around £131 a week.

Fewer People Opting Out

Despite this reduction in benefits, the cost of providing state second pensions is growing and, as a result, the government wants more of us to opt out of the state top-up pension. This is called contracting out.

Effectively, this involves some of an individual's National Insurance contributions being diverted into a private pension plan or scheme. However, the cost of providing an alternative pension, combined with falling stock markets and low annuity rates, mean experts say more workers would be better off sticking with – or moving back into – the state scheme. To match the benefits of the state second pension, actuaries claim that in many cases private pensions would have to grow by 7 per cent a year – something they are unlikely to do in the foreseeable future.

This will do nothing to achieve the government's aim of reducing dependence on the state for pensions.

PRIVATE PENSIONS

Too Little Invested by Too Few

Only 40 per cent of people retiring have any form of private pension.

While employer pensions tend to be generous, the average person with a personal pension retiring today has just £25,000 with which to buy an income to last their entire retirement. They are unlikely to get more than £30 a week from this. Bearing in mind that the minimum income guarantee (the means-tested state benefit) will top-up their £75.50 state pension to £100 anyway, they will probably only be £2 or £3 a week better off than someone who has made no retirement provision at all – hardly an incentive to save for old age.

Four out of ten of people retiring today are purchasing an annuity with less than £10,000 – boosting their pension by £700 or £800 a year at most, or about £13.50 a week.

So the message coming across is – if you are poor, don't bother investing in a pension. All you will be doing is paying for an income that the state would provide anyway. Hardly an incentive to save for old age.

Problems with Personal Pensions

When personal pensions were introduced in 1988 to encourage greater private provision, there was an expectation that anyone without an employer's pension would be able to provide for themselves. However, personal pensions have failed to provide value for money in many cases and have also failed to attract investment from people on lower incomes. Investors who were seduced into saving in these schemes have been hit time and time again by stock market falls, annuity rates falling to a 40-year low, bonus-rate cuts and the Equitable Life scandal.

Few people with personal pensions continue to contribute to them until they retire. A third of those who bought personal pensions stopped paying into their plans within three years – often barely covering the costs of setting them up, let alone providing for their retirement.

People retiring today have been hit by a double whammy – the value of their pension fund may be only half the amount it was a couple of years ago and the income this will buy them (an annuity must be purchased to give them an income for life) could be half what they were led to expect when they first took out their pension.

New Stakeholders Fail to Impress

So the government reformed the system again and introduced stakeholder pensions in 2001. These too have failed to appeal to people on lower incomes and now further reform has already been proposed. Only 1 per cent of the 4.5 million investors with personal pensions bothered to switch to the new stakeholder scheme in the first year despite lower charges and nine in ten stakeholders set up by employers are empty with no money invested.

Employer Pensions in Deficit

Until recently, employer pensions (despite the Maxwell scandal in which the newspaper magnet raided the *Mirror* company pension scheme) have remained largely unaffected by the pensions crisis. They are now subject to more regulation and the recent changes to the tax credit system has left them £5 billion a year poorer, although most have, in the past, been in healthy surplus and many employers have even been able – until recently – to take contribution holidays.

Today, this situation has reversed. Some employer pensions are now in deficit with companies forced to raid profits to bolster their pension schemes. Falling stock markets and the need to pay pensions for longer, as life expectancy increases, means that employer after employer is abandoning final salary schemes, which pay pensions based on pay and years of service, for more risky money purchase schemes which rely on stock market and investment performance.

These problems have been compounded by a technical accounting rule change – FRS17 – which requires companies to highlight pension shortfalls based on current stock market values (which have plummeted) and consequently makes the firms look financially weaker than previously.

So benefits are being cut, employer pensions are unlikely to pay as generous a pension in future and – despite all the regulation – there is another major problem.

Pensions Can Vanish

Members of final salary schemes who believe they have the safest of all pensions will be shocked to discover that their pensions are not safe. If their employer goes bust they can find their company pension pays little more than half of what they had expected. This, in fact, happened to the employees of at least one large company, Allied Steel and Wire, in 2002. Meanwhile, people saving into personal pension schemes with Equitable Life have seen the value of their pension pots fall and face stiff exit penalties if they withdraw their funds early.

Investors with money purchase type pensions – either in employee schemes or personal or stakeholder pensions – saw the value of their pensions almost halve in the two years to the summer of 2002 as a result of stock market falls.

Complexity and Confusion

Whatever reforms are undertaken they need to simplify not confuse and be communicated to individuals in a clear and concise manner.

A recent survey by the National Association of Pension Funds (NAPF) found that the complexity of the UK pensions systems has taken its toll on consumers' understanding of their own pension arrangements. The poll found that while half the people surveyed acknowledged their pension saving was inadequate, three quarters still nonetheless expected to enjoy a comfortable income in retirement. Despite an awareness that greater life expectancy posed a growing threat to state pensions provision, the average age at which respondents expected to retire was 61.

While recent reports have suggested that people should be contributing 20 per cent of their income to a pension fund, only 15 per cent of respondents thought they were contributing this much, while a quarter had no idea what they were contributing, and a third thought it was nothing at all.

THE SEARCH FOR A SOLUTION

The government has commissioned several reviews and reports to look into the pensions crisis.

The Sandler Report

The review, led by former Lloyds of London chief Ron Sandler, was commissioned in June 2001 and reported its findings in July 2002. It called for sweeping reforms aimed at encouraging consumers to save more for their retirement.

The report found that:

- Pension products are far too complex.

- Products and advice do little to help consumer ignorance because pension providers tailor their products to suit advisers, who usually earn a commission on the sale, rather than tailoring them to suit the public.

It recommended the introduction of a new range of easy to understand products, which would be sold directly to consumers under a specific brand name. Charges would be limited and transparent. It also suggested that advisers should be paid hourly fees rather than commissions on sales so as to reduce the likelihood of bias creeping into supposedly independent advice.

In addition to making simple savings products more easily available it acknowledged that:

- The various pensions tax regimes need urgent consolidation.

- Small employers suffer undue regulatory burdens.

- Drastic cuts need to be made to the regulations governing the contracting out of state-pension provision.

Many of these proposals have been adopted in a new pensions Green Paper.

Public Sector Pension Reviews

A review of public sector final salary, index-linked pensions is being undertaken by two separate inquiries: that of the Office of the Deputy Prime Minister and the Government Actuary's Department.

These reviews will look at the rising cost of public-sector pensions and the problems of deficits in some schemes. The outcome is likely to be a recommendation that employees in the public sector either contribute more to their pension or that benefits are cut (or possibly both).

The Pickering Report

This report, *A Simpler Way to a Better Pension*, was published in the summer of 2002. Written by Alan Pickering, former head of the National Association of Pension Funds, the report warned it was 'the last chance for voluntarism in the pension industry' before ministers seriously considered compelling all employers and possibly employees to pay into occupational pension schemes. The report went on to say that there was little appetite among workers or employers for compulsion, which could be viewed as another form of tax, but unless the proposals in his report were broadly accepted, the government would be left with few other options if it was to wean all but the poorest people off state benefits and reach its target of raising the proportion of retired people with a private pension from 40 to 60 per cent.

Another proposal is that employers could make membership of the scheme compulsory. However, employees would benefit from rules allowing them to join a company scheme after their first week in employment and pensions would become more portable, being taken from one employer to another rather than being frozen as a deferred pension.

In the new pensions Green Paper, the government has decided against compulsory private pensions, but will allow individual employer schemes to make membership compulsory.

Other Proposals

A state retirement age of 67 or even 70. Already adopted in other countries (the US has increased its retirement age from 65 to 67), this is a long-term possibility; women in the UK have already seen their retirement age increase from 60 to 65. This proposal has been put forward by a number of organizations including the Pensions Policy Institute (PPI). In a paper entitled *Raising State Pensions Age: Are We Ready?* the group suggests that raising the retirement age from 65 to 70 would mean the government could increase the basic state pension from its current level of £75.50 to £110 a week. This has been rejected by the government which wants to increase the number aged 50 plus in the work place and give workers, the option of working past 65 – but not make this compulsory.

No earnings-related second pension. This is already on the cards – a flat-rate pension of £1 a week for each year of contributions to the new state second pension (S2P) will end the link with earnings so higher earners do not benefit more than those on low incomes.

One state pension worth £100 a week or 22 per cent of average earnings and rising in line with inflation. Instead of a confusing mixture of state pension and means-tested benefits several organizations have proposed one simple state pension for all. However, in the light of the government's introduction of an even more complex benefits system in retirement with a minimum income guarantee and pension credit, this is unlikely.

Higher National Insurance Contributions or collecting a compulsory pension contribution through the National Insurance system. This will be politically damaging as it will be seen as a tax increase. However, it would go a long way to solving the problem.

A compulsory private pension for all with employers being forced to contribute. This was achieved in Australia in 1986 when employers (only those who were part of negotiated pay settlement agreements) agreed to pay 3 per cent of wages into employee pensions and workers agreed to forgo a 3 per cent pay rise in return. Now every employer makes a contributions equal to 9 per cent of pay. This has been rejected by the government, but it is considering proposals that employers can make membership of the company scheme compulsory.

More generous tax treatment of pension savings before and after retirement. One recent survey by independent financial advisers R. J. Temple found that increased tax relief or the ability to receive their pension free of tax when they retire were the most popular solutions to encouraging people to save more for their retirement. People are aware of the need to save more – only 5 per cent of those surveyed said they would be happy to rely on the state pension – but they need more encouragement to make the commitment. Sadly, this will not be adopted by the government.

THREAT TO TAX BREAKS

Despite the pensions crisis, there are rumours that the government is going to clamp down on tax relief on pensions – one of the major incentives for investing in them in the first place.

However, two major tax breaks will remain:

- Tax-free lump sums on retirement.

- Higher-rate tax relief on contributions.

Instead, the government is planning to introduce one tax regime for all pensions, replacing the eight different regimes that currently exist. This will limit tax breaks, but only for a tiny percentage of the workforce.

THE PENSIONS GREEN PAPER

Proposals based on the Sandler Report and the Pickering Report were published at the end of 2002 in a Green Paper on pension reform which will be followed, after some initial consultation, by a Bill, and then an Act of Parliament.

However, even if this paper does lead to reform, people contributing to pensions today are still vulnerable. Legislation is unlikely until 2004 at the earliest. The document, *Simplicity, Security and Choice: Working and Saving for Retirement* contains the following proposals:

Tax Changes

• To replace the eight different tax regimes for pensions (within these there are different rules concerning levels of contributions and the levels of benefits).

• The complicated age- and earnings-related limits on how much you can put into your pension will be scrapped and replaced by a £200,000 annual cap and a £1.4 million lifetime limit.

Working Past Retirement

• The government plans to introduce measures to extend working lives, promoting working for the over 50s and those beyond retirment age.

• Although the government is not proposing an increase in the state retirement age it has set up an independent commission to monitor the progress of reforms and to ask whether there is a need to go beyond the voluntarist approach. This could mean compulsory contributions or a compulsory increase in the state retirement age in years to come if the current proposals fail to tackle the pensions crisis.

• There will be consultation about allowing individuals to continue working for a company while drawing their occupational pension from that company to encourage flexible retirement (for example, switching to part-time work while supplementing this reduced income with some of their occupational pension).

- For public service shcemes, an unreduced pension will be payable from age 65 rather than age 60 for new members.

- Incentives to work past 65 while delaying taking the state pension will be increased.

Retirement Age Changes

- You will no longer be able to retire at 50. From 2009, the minimum early retirement age will rise to 55.

Information Changes

- There will be an increase in the number of people receiving forecasts of their pension income with more people receiving combined pension forecasts including pensions from the state and private pensions.

- A new pension advice line and an improved web-based retirement planner will be set up.

Employer Pensions

- Greater protection for pensions scheme members will be introduced.

- Employers will be able to make joining their pension scheme a condition of employment for new recruits.

- Employers will have more rights if they leave a scheme – members will be able to enjoy the benefits of their employer's contributions from day one rather than having to wait two years (under the current system employer's contributions are lost if you move jobs within two years). When a member leaves, trustees will be able to transfer a *de minimis* amount to a stakeholder pension.

- The security of final salary pensions when a scheme is wound up will be improved by introducing a fairer system of distribution of assets between different scheme members instead of penalizing those who have yet to retire while those who have recently retired ususally escape with their pensions intact.

- The proposals state that members with the longest service are given priority along with those within 10 years of retirement and that a new class of creditor is introduced – placing pension scheme debt above any other unsecured creditors but below secured and prefential creditors such as the Inland Revenue and the banks.

- There are also proposals to introduce an insurance scheme to protect the pensions of members whose employer becomes insolvent.

- The minimum funding requirements of occupational schemes will be replaced with scheme-specific regulation to allow schemes greater flexibility. It will also make the funding position more transparent for scheme members. The changes will save companies £80 million a year and alow them to invest more appropriately given the characteristics of their own particular membership.

- A new pension regulator will focus on protecting the benefits of scheme members.

- Employers will be given the right to be consulted on changes to an employer's pension scheme to prevent firms changing closing schemes without dialogue with employees.

- Better investment by occupational pension schemes will be encouraged.

Annuities

- Annuities will still be compulsory (you will still have to buy an annuity to provide an income with the proceeds of your stakeholder, personal or occupational money purchase pension fund).

- However, there are proposals for limited-period annuities, which will allow someone to use part of their pension fund to provide an annuity for a predetermined period.

- The Green Paper will also introduce a new value-protected annuity so that if you die before age 75 some of the capital that has not yet been paid out can be paid to your dependants (instead of the annuity dying with you). This payment would be equal to the difference between the amount paid for the annuity and the stream of payments already made under the annuity.

Simpler Products

- There will be consultation on how to bring stakeholder pensions into the simple product suite proposed by the Sandler Report.

- Generic financial advice – for example, a financial health check that helps you decide which types of pension or investment are best for you – will be available to help consumers assess their financial position.

These proposals are consultative and will, at the earliest, take effect from 2004.

EVEN IF THE GOVERNMENT ACTS,
SO MUST YOU

A recent study suggested that young people in their mid 20s need to accumulate a pension fund of £500,000 to ensure a 'decent' income in retirement – defined as half of average earnings. People who delay pension saving until they are 40 will have to put aside nearly 30 per cent of their earnings each year to retire with an income of half average earnings at age 65.

These figures may shock those who have been lulled into a false sense of security because they are setting aside £50 or even £100 a month. However, they show that whatever the government proposes, it will be up to individuals to set aside increasing amounts if they want a comfortable, not a subsistence, retirement.

2 Your Pension Choices

Gone are the days when employees had a job for life, working for the same employer until they retired. Also gone is the certainty that came with this, that the employee would have the ability to build up a pension from an employer that would provide a decent income in retirement.

Those were not necessarily the good old days. After all, millions of employees – particularly the low paid and part-timers – benefited from no employer pension at all. However, even these workers had some certainty: they knew they would either have to save to supplement their retirement income or rely on the state. The second option was not such a bad deal as state pensions used to be worth a far higher proportion of national average earnings than today when the basic state pension is more of a subsistence income.

Today, life is far less certain and far more complicated. Workers are likely to have between five and nine jobs in their working life-times – if not more – and could have periods of unemployment and self-employment as well as career breaks to start a family. At the same time, relying on the state is no longer an option as over the decades the value of the basic state pension has been eroded because it has kept pace with price inflation not earnings inflation. This means that more people have to make decisions about their retirement income – they can no longer expect these decisions to be made for them either by their employer or by the state.

While it has never been more vital to be pro-active and plan your retirement, the options have never been more confusing.

So, to avoid confusion and information overload this chapter shows readers which pension options may be most suitable for you, rather than looking in depth at each type of pension. A series of question and answer sessions takes you through the different pension choices. When you have selected the most suitable options for your circumstances, you can then read more about what is relevant to you – state, employer and individual pensions are covered in greater depth in later chapters as well as the pension alternatives.

However, remember, your pension choices should change along with your circumstances. So you may have to repeat this process several times before retirement.

Remember also that the guidance in these question and answer sections is general. They are simply a means of getting you to the relevant information more quickly. Your age, attitude to risk, earnings, ability to save, plans for the future, past career history, existing pension provision and a whole range of factors should be taken into account before making a decision. Readers are therefore advised to seek independent financial advice before investing in, boosting or transferring a pension.

IF YOU ARE AN EMPLOYEE

Are you a member of your employer's pension scheme?

DON'T KNOW
Ask the personnel department or, if there isn't one, the payroll department.

YES
You will probably be better off sticking with your employer's scheme because your employer will usually contribute to the scheme and will pay the costs of running the scheme.

NO

Do you have the option of joining an employer pension scheme?

DON'T KNOW
Ask. An employer's pension is usually the best option unless you plan to move jobs in the near future (within two years). In future (from 2004 if new legislation is passed by then), all employees will be able to benefit from their employer's pension without waiting

two years – so even those planning to move jobs shortly may still be better off in an employer's scheme. All employers with five or more employees must offer staff access to a stakeholder pension unless they already offer some form of pension provision.

NO
You will have to make your own pension provision – a stakeholder pension is usually the best option but the decision will depend on your earnings, how much you can afford to invest and how near you are to retirement. People with very little disposable income only a few years from retirement may want to consider alternatives such as a tax-free cash savings account known as a cash ISA.

YES
Find out if you can join the scheme. Some employers require a minimum period of service before you can join. New employees are increasingly finding they cannot join the old-style final salary schemes, which paid a pension based on earnings at or near retirement. These tend to offer higher pensions than the newer type of scheme known as money purchase where your pension depends on how much has been invested and how these investments have grown as well as annuity rates on retirement. Even so, an employer's pension is usually worth joining because:

- The employer often contributes.

- The employer usually pays the cost of running the scheme.

- Many schemes offer additional benefits such as life insurance (death in service) and widow/widower's pensions.

The general advice is to stick with your employer's scheme.

However, see these decision trees later in this chapter: STARTING A NEW JOB; LEAVING A JOB; DO YOU HAVE A PENSION WITH A FORMER EMPLOYER? Also read Chapter 9: How To Boost Your Pension.

IF YOU ARE SELF-EMPLOYED

Do you have any private pension provision?

NO

Then consider starting right now. The self-employed do not qualify for the state second pension (although the government is considering allowing this), and may not always even qualify for the full basic state pension. Many people running their own business believe that their business is their pension, but, if you cannot sell the business or its assets at the right time and for the right price you may be left with little to live on in retirement. If your business fails you will have no 'pension' at all. The other advantage of pensions is that they are very tax efficient.

YES

Make sure you are investing enough to provide a comfortable retirement. The minimum investment recommended is around 10 per cent of your earnings. Remember that the self-employed do not qualify for the state second pension so you will have to invest more to make up for this shortfall.

Track down any past pensions with former employers and any paid-up personal pensions. Review your existing pension arrangements to make sure you are getting the best value for money. Stakeholder pensions are low charging. Also review your investments – in light of recent stock market falls you may be better off switching your investments to different funds.

See Chapter 8: How Much Do I Need to Invest? And Chapter 9: How to Boost Your Pension.

IF YOU ARE NOT WORKING

You can contribute to a stakeholder pension (or someone can do this on your behalf) and still receive tax relief (even if you are a non-taxpayer). You are advised to consider this. Also check that you are building up an entitlement to the basic state pension and the state second pension.

If you are unemployed, caring for a dependant or someone who is long-term disabled, read Chapter 4: State Pensions and Benefits for advice.

STARTING A NEW JOB

Do you have an existing pension?

NO
Skip to the question **Does your employer offer a pension?** on page 27.

YES

Is your pension with a former employer?

NO
Skip to the question **Do you have a personal or stakeholder pension?** below.

YES
Skip to the next question and answer session LEAVING A JOB.

Do you have a personal or stakeholder pension?

NO
This means you have no existing private pension arrangements. Your best option is to join your employer's scheme.

YES
If you have the option of joining your new employer's scheme you can either:

1. Leave the pension 'paid up'. In this case it will continue to grow although no extra contributions are made. You can start the pension up again if you leave your job.

2. Continue paying into the stakeholder or personal pension (but not in all cases).

3. Transfer the pension into your employer's scheme (again not in all cases).

1. If you are leaving a pension 'paid up' check:

    - There are no penalties (there may be with older-style personal pensions).

    - The charges (if stock market returns are low and charges are high they will eat into your pension fund).

    - If you are not happy with the answers to these questions you can switch your pension to a low-cost, flexible stakeholder pension.

2. In the past it was NOT possible to be both a member of an employer's pension scheme and pay into a personal pension unless you had earnings in addition to those from your main employment. However, since the introduction of stakeholder pensions, it is now possible to pay in up to £3,600, including tax relief, into a stakeholder in any tax year AND be a member of an employer's scheme, but only if you earn £30,000 or less a year (or have done so in any of the last five years) and/or are not a controlling director of the company.

    So you can continue paying into your stakeholder pension and be a member of an employer scheme to boost your total pension on retirement. This is advisable because:

    - Few employees earn the maximum allowable pension from their employer. Generally you need 40 years of continuous service to get this maximum pension – unlikely in an age when we job hop, take career breaks and may be made redundant at least once in our working lives.

    - Boosting your pension using an employer's top-up pension usually means you have to take your top-up pension at the same time as you retire and cannot take any of this extra pension as a lump sum. With a stakeholder you can retire when you like (from age 50 – or from age 55 after 2009) and take up to a quarter of the fund as a tax-free lump sum.

- Your stakeholder can move with you from job to job.

3. You could consider transferring your personal or stakeholder pension into an employer's scheme (if that is allowed). This can boost the pension you will get from your employer either by buying 'extra years' of service in a final salary scheme or boosting the total invested in a money purchase scheme. Check if there are any transfer penalties from your personal pension and note that not all employer schemes accept transfers. Also note that this option will restrict your choices in future. With a personal or stakeholder pension you can take your pension aged 50 (rising to 55 after 2009). With an employer's scheme you generally have to wait until age 65 (age 60 for older women).

Is this pension contracted out?

YES
If you have contracted out of the state second pension (SERPS before April 2002 now S2P) you will generally have to stop contracting out once you join an occupational scheme as most schemes are contracted out. You cannot contract out twice and get two lots of rebates. Inform your personal or stakeholder pension provider.

NO
There is no need to take any action.

Does your employer offer a pension?

NO
This means your employer has fewer than five staff. If that is not the case your employer should be offering you access to a stakeholder pension otherwise they are breaking the law.

If your employer does not have to offer any pension provision, make your own. Read Chapter 6: Individual Pensions later in this book. There is nothing to stop you from asking your employer if he would make contributions to your individual stakeholder or personal pension plan. The employer can tax-deduct these contributions.

YES

Can you join?

You may find that there are certain restrictions on new employees joining the main employer scheme, for example, you may have to complete at least two years' service before joining. Instead, you may be offered a stakeholder pension as another option.

If you can join the main occupational scheme, you will generally be advised to do so because your employer:

- usually contributes to the scheme

- pays the costs of running the scheme

- offers additional benefits such as life insurance (death in service) and widow/widower's pensions

Are you likely to move jobs within two years?

YES

If you move jobs within two years you lose the pension you have built up with your employer – unless your employer is very generous. (This rule is likely to change from April 2004 when 'immediate vesting' is due to be introduced, enabling staff to benefit from day one instead of waiting two years.) Under the current rules:

- You cannot take (transfer) any pension entitlement you have built up to a new employer's scheme or a stakeholder pension.

- You cannot leave your pension with your former employer who would – if you had been a scheme member for more than two years – have to pay you a pension when you reach retirement.

Any contributions you have made will be refunded minus the tax relief. You will not get a refund of any contributions made by your employer. As a result you may have been better off contributing to your own stakeholder pension because you would at least have built up some pension during these two years.

NO
See the next question.

What kind of scheme does your employer run?

There are several types – all benefit from generous tax breaks including tax relief at your highest rate on all contributions you make:

Final salary: this is generally regarded as the best. Your pension depends on your salary near retirement and the number of years you have been a member of the scheme not on stock market performance. However, these schemes are expensive to run and many employers are now closing them to new members. If you have the option of joining one you are generally advised to do so unless you are planning to move jobs within two years.

Money purchase: these tend to pay out less on retirement because the employer usually contributes less and the pension depends on stock market performance, how much is invested and annuity rates on retirement. However, as employers usually offer additional benefits and often contribute to these schemes they are worth joining unless you are planning to move jobs within two years.

Group personal or stakeholder pensions: these are the same as personal pensions bought by individuals but in this case it is the employer who arranges for them to be set up. Your contributions are usually deducted from your pay, and your employer may not always contribute. However, where the employer does contribute you are generally advised to join one of these schemes. Even if the employer makes no contributions, the schemes can be worth joining as the charges can be lower than if you arranged the pension yourself. Check that you can arrange life insurance (or that life insurance is arranged) through the scheme because you will get tax relief on your contributions.

Will your employer contribute to the plan?

YES
Then generally you should join the scheme.

NO
There are fewer reasons to join the employer scheme, however bear in mind:

- Your employer will set up the scheme (saving you the hassle).

- Your employer may pay the costs of the scheme or the costs may be lower than for a pension you could arrange for yourself.

- Your contributions will be deducted directly from your pay – so you may be forced to save for retirement.

Read Chapter 5: Employer Pensions for further questions to ask your employer before deciding whether or not to join the scheme.

What are the additional benefits?

Many employer schemes offer additional benefits such as life insurance (known as death in service). These are worth having because you do not have to pay for them.

However, some employees may find they are inflexible. For example, the scheme may only provide widows or widowers with a pension should you die. So if you are single, divorced or co-habiting you may find this perk is not worth having.

LEAVING A JOB

Do you have a pension with your former employer?

NO
Skip to **Do you have a personal or stakeholder pension?** on page 35.

YES

Were you employed for less than two years?

YES
You lose out. Your employer does not have to provide you with a pension when you retire and only has to refund you your contributions (not any employer contributions) less any tax relief you have been given. Some employers are more generous and will give you a transfer to another pension.

You may only get a fraction of the amount you paid in (your own contributions) because investment fees or an administration charge will also be deducted. If the scheme is contracted out of the state second pension (SERPS before April 2002 now S2P) a sum will be deducted to restore your state second pension entitlement.

Note: from April 2004 this is due to change and you will be able to benefit from your employer's contributions and transfer to a new scheme even if you have less than two years' service.

NO
If you were employed for more than two years you have the following options:

1. Leave your company pension where it is
   This will be an option if you:

   - are being made redundant and will be out of work

   - are becoming self-employed and do not yet know what kind of pension you will be able to afford

   - have been a member of a very good final salary scheme for a number of years – you will find this pension hard to beat in the current market

- are approaching retirement

If it is a final salary scheme, your pension will grow by 5 per cent a year or by the rate of inflation, whichever is the lower. This is known as a 'deferred pension'. With inflation at a low rate your deferred pension will hardly grow. However, at least it will not fall in value as it would have done if it had been invested in recent years in the stock market. Bear in mind that inflation does not usually keep pace with pay rises, so in terms of a percentage of final pay what you receive on retirement may not keep pace with your earnings.

In the past, employees were often advised to transfer their final salary pension into a personal or stakeholder pension where it could grow by more than 5 per cent a year. However, if you transfer out of a scheme you will not get the full amount as a transfer value and you will also have to pay charges on your new pension plan, and when you retire your income will depend on annuity rates (annuities must be bought with at last 75 per cent of your fund by age 75 to provide an income for life). Another option is a Section 32 buy-out (S32B) contract. This enables you to retain the benefits of a final salary scheme including the valuable guaranteed minimum pension with the maximum tax-free cash sum depending on your length of service and your final year's earnings with your old employer. Although the retirement age from the original company scheme is applied to the S32B plan, you can take the benefits earlier by transferring to a personal or stakeholder pension.

However, the general advice given to most employees – particularly those in their 40s and 50s – is to leave your pension in the final salary scheme, where you will take fewer risks. However, employees should still take independent advice to ensure that this decision is best for them. The city watchdog, the Financial Services Authority, will expect a good case to be made (in writing) for a transfer to take place.

If your employer's pension is a money purchase scheme your fund will continue to be invested and grow until you retire or until you transfer to another pension scheme. Your pension will therefore depend on the investment performance of the fund manager and the charges of the scheme. The case for leaving your pension in a money purchase scheme is less clear cut. Before transferring it to a new scheme check:

• Penalties – will you suffer by transferring your pension?

• Charges – will they be more or less expensive in the new pension?

• Fund performance – who is better at managing your money?

If your pension is a group personal or stakeholder pension you can simply take it with you and continue to contribute to it; you do not have to leave it behind. Alternatively you can transfer the pension to a new scheme.

2. Transfer your pension into a scheme run by your new employer
   If you are joining a company with a company scheme you can join and which accepts transfers, you can switch (transfer) the pension built up with your previous employer to the new scheme (unless you were in that former scheme for less than two years in which case you do not receive a penny although any contributions you had made will be refunded minus tax relief – this rule is set to change from April 2004 enabling all employees to take a transfer).
   Before doing this check:

• What type of scheme does the new employer offer? Does it offer as good or better benefits? Generally you should not switch from a final salary scheme to a money purchase scheme.

• What penalties will be charged? The transfer value can be substantially lower than the paid-up value (the value if you left your money in the scheme).

3. Transfer your pension to a stakeholder pension
   This will be an option if:

   - You are not eligible to join another employer's pension scheme.

   - You are becoming self-employed.

   - You expect to remain in your future jobs for only a few years at a time.

Although the charges are low with stakeholder pensions, if you are transferring from a final salary scheme you may find the penalties you pay for transferring do not outweigh the potential gains from stock market growth. Combine charges, penalties and falling stock markets, and in recent years you would have been better off leaving your final salary scheme as a deferred pension rather than transferring it to a stakeholder pension (unless your former employer went bust leaving a pension scheme deficit).

If you are planning to transfer your pension it will probably take four to six weeks for your employer to send you a transfer statement and then three or four months for the pension assets to be transferred to a new scheme.

Get impartial advice before making any decision. Check that your financial adviser has the right qualification – known as G60 – to handle transfer evaluations. Consider paying a fee (it could cost £500 or more) to an expert to evaluate the benefits of switching.

If you get advice from someone who earns a commission they may be under pressure to recommend a switch so they can earn their money (which can be as much as £1,000 or more in commission).

Can you boost your pension before you leave?

This should be considered particularly if you are being made redundant or approaching retirement and are a member of a final salary scheme. You can buy 'extra years of service' in some cases or make additional voluntary contributions (AVCs) to boost the pension your former employer will pay on retirement. Ask the trustees of the pension fund for details. Note: you must do this before you leave service – not afterwards.

Do you need to replace benefits provided by your old scheme?

Many employers' schemes provide extra benefits such as life insurance of up to four times salary. However, once you leave the scheme these 'death in service' benefits end. Consider replacing this life insurance. If you are planning to take out a stakeholder or personal pension you can pay up to 10 per cent of your contributions to provide life insurance cover and receive tax relief (at the highest rate you pay) on these premiums.

Do you have a personal or a stakeholder pension?

If you are leaving a job and have a personal or a stakeholder pension as part of a group scheme you can take this pension with you – even if it was a plan arranged by your former employer. If your former employer contributed to the plan, make sure that you make up for this shortfall in contributions.

DO YOU HAVE A PENSION WITH A FORMER EMPLOYER?

DON'T KNOW
This is not surprising. You may have worked for a company 20 years ago and cannot remember whether or not you had built up a pension entitlement. Contact your former employer to ask if you were a member of the scheme and if you had built up any pension entitlement.

If you cannot trace your former employers because they have:

- moved

- been taken over

- merged with another company

- gone out of business

then contact the Pension Schemes Registry which runs the Pensions Tracing Service by telephone on 0191 225 6316 or visit www.opra. gov.uk/registry and fill in the on-line tracing form.

YES

When did you leave your job?

Even if you were a member of a former employer's scheme you may not qualify for a deferred pension. The current rules require employers to give you a deferred pension only after two years' service. However, providing a preserved pension only became a legal requirement, subject to certain conditions, from 6 April 1975. Many pension schemes did not provide any preserved pension for members who left before this date. If the scheme required you to make contributions, you should have received a refund of these when you left the employment. If you did not have to make contributions there would obviously have been no benefit at all when you left your job. After 6 April 1975 you should have been offered a preserved pension if you had completed five years service. You may not have been able to transfer your pension if you left the scheme before 1 January 1986 as the trustees/scheme authorities did not have to offer you a transfer value as an alternative to a preserved pension.

The Pensions Act 1995 extended the right to a transfer value to those people whose pensionable service terminated before 1 January 1986 unless they were a member of a final salary scheme that protects the value of preserved pensions. So you may be unaware that you could have transferred your pension. However, if the scheme was contracted out of SERPS you should have some benefits in the scheme.

Since 6 April 1988 schemes have been required to provide you with a deferred pension (or a transfer) if you have completed two years of service. If you leave the scheme without completing two years service, you may (subject to the rules of the scheme) be able to obtain a refund of any contributions you have made. If you have more than two years service, the law does not allow you to have a refund. Instead, you will receive a transfer value or leave behind a deferred pension. From April 2004, all employees – not just those with two years' service – will be entitled to a transfer value.

Do you know where to write for details of your pension?

YES

Then you will need to supply your former employer with your full name, National Insurance number, address, pension scheme number (if you have this), date of starting employment and date you left the scheme.

If the company you worked for has been merged or taken over you will need to supply the details of who you worked for and, if you have this information, the name of the pension scheme of which you were a member.

NO

If you cannot track down your former employer's address contact the Pensions Tracing Service on 0191 225 6316 or visit www.opra. gov.uk/registry.

To trace a pension scheme you will need to provide as much information as possible so that the service can find an up-to-date contact address for the pension scheme. The information you should try to find includes:

- The full name and address of the employer who ran the occupational pension scheme you are trying to trace. Did the employer change names, or was it part of a larger group of companies?

- The type of pension scheme you belonged to, for example, was it an occupational pension scheme or a group personal pension scheme?

- The dates you belonged to this pension scheme.

- The name of your employer and if the company traded under a different name or changed its name.

- The type of business.

- Any other addresses.

For details on ways to boost your pension see Chapter 9: How To Boost Your Pension and for your choices on retirement see Chapter 10: Maximizing Your Pension On Retirement.

3 Tax and Pensions

Pensions – both occupational and private – offer generous tax breaks and should be a core part of your financial planning for retirement.

Tax relief is not only given on money paid in at the highest rate of tax the individual pays (which means 40p of every £1 invested is tax relief for higher-rate taxpayers), but pension funds also grow free of tax and – upon retirement – any lump sum paid is also free of tax. Investing in a pension plan – or benefiting from the fact that your employer does this for you – is one of the most tax-efficient ways to save and invest.

Not surprisingly, such generosity from the government does not go unchecked. There are limits on how much can be invested, and on retirement the bulk of the pension must provide an income which is taxed.

Pension tax relief is worth around £19 billion a year to private pensions. Half of this goes to the wealthiest 10 per cent of tax payers, of which 50 per cent goes to the wealthiest 2.5 per cent.

Although there have been rumours that the government plans to redirect this tax relief towards the low paid while restricting it for higher earners, the recent Green Paper on pension reform only proposes a single lifetime limit on the amount of tax-privileged pension saving with a lifetime ceiling of around £1.4 million and an annual limit of £200,000.

TAX RELIEF

Tax relief on contributions is given at the highest rate an individual pays. This means it only costs a basic-rate taxpayer paying tax at 22 per cent £88 for £100 to be invested in their pension. Or, for every

£1 contributed, the government pays in an additional 28p. For higher-rate taxpayers the relief is even more generous. Investing £100 in a pension only costs them £60 with the remaining £40 coming in the form of tax relief.

Full term relief is given on all contributions which from April 2004 can be up to £200,00 a year.

The way tax relief is given depends on the pension.

Occupational Pensions: Employee contributions to an employer's company pension scheme are taken out of the employee's salary before calculating tax. Contributions are therefore made from gross (untaxed) income effectively giving tax relief at source. So no tax relief needs to be claimed.

Individual Pensions: Basic-rate tax relief does not have to be claimed by people investing in stakeholder or personal pensions. They make contributions and the pension provider adds the tax relief. So anyone wanting to invest the maximum £3,600 allowed into a stakeholder pension need only part with £2,808. The pension provider claims the tax relief.

Note: maximum investment limits for pensions are currently under review, and in future an annual limit of £200,000 will be introduced.

However, higher-rate tax relief must be claimed. This is the additional 18 per cent tax relief (the difference between the basic rate of 22 per cent and the higher rate of 40 per cent).

Note that non-taxpayers can now receive tax relief even though they do not pay tax. When stakeholder pensions were introduced in April 2000, tax breaks were extended to non-taxpayers. With occupational and personal pensions contributions can only be made out of earned income, so non-earners could not invest in a pension and receive tax relief.

TIP

It pays to make additional contributions to your pension in years when
the individual is a higher-rate taxpayer – to maximize tax relief. If a
higher-rate taxpayer has missed out on a chance to make the most of
this higher-rate relief, all is not lost. Carry-back rules allow the individual to backdate contributions to the previous tax year.

Maximum Contributions

These generous tax benefits are not unlimited. Contributions can
only be made out of earnings up to an earnings cap of £97,200 (for
the 2002/2003 tax year). Higher earners can contribute from earnings above this cap but only to unapproved pensions which do not
qualify for tax relief. As from 6 April 2004, this cap is expected to
be removed and replaced with a £200,000 annual cap, subject to a
£1.4 million lifetime limit.

The tax rules have always stated that an individual cannot contribute to an occupational or company pension scheme and a personal pension at the same time, unless he has additional earnings
other than from employment. Even then, contributions made out
of these additional earnings are subject to maximum contribution limits (ranging from 17.5 per cent to 40 per cent). So if an
employee who is a member of an occupational pension scheme
earns an extra £1,000 a year from part-time lecturing or working
in a bar at weekends, only a percentage of these earnings (up to
the limits listed on page 44) can be invested in a personal pension
– no more.

However, the new stakeholder pension allows employees to get
round this rule. They can be a member of an occupational scheme
and contribute to a stakeholder plan, but only if they earn £30,000 a
year or less (or have done in any of the last five years, and/or are
not controlling directors.

It is not yet known how the reforms to pension contributions
will affect this situation but according to the consultative paper

Simplifying Taxation of Pensions, published at the end of 2003 at the same time as the Green Paper, the only limit will be on the annual contribution to pensions. So, as from 6 April 2004, it is likely that no maximum percentage of earnings will be imposed and no restrictions on where these contributions are made. An employee may pay into a stakeholder and an occupational pension at the same time with the only limit being on the maximum capital value in the pension fund.

Although, at £1.4 million, this may seem high, it will only provide a pension of about £65,000 a year – again a high income, but what could amount to a dramatic fall for a fat cat.

The current earnings cap – £97,200 is far below this. With tax breaks, an annual personal pension contribution for a top earner can be about £25,000 a year – a fraction of the new £200,000 total allowed as of 2004.

Anyone exceeding the £1.4 million cap will be heavily fined – if someone's pension is £1.8 million they will be fined at the rate of 30 per cent. The balance will then by taxed at 40 per cent giving an overall 60 per cent tax.

Occupational Pensions: Employees can only contribute up to 15 per cent of their annual earnings. In this case earnings are defined as annual salary, bonuses, commissions and the taxable value of most benefits in kind, such as company cars. So the maximum contribution for the last tax year was 15% x £97,200 = £14,580. Employer contributions do not count towards the 15 per cent of earnings contribution limit and are not taxable as a benefit in kind.

Employees can exceed this 15 per cent limit, however, if they earn £30,000 or less a year (or have earned less than this in any of the last five years) and are not controlling directors of their company, by investing in a top-up pension plan linked to their company pension scheme, a scheme known as an additional voluntary contribution (AVC), and up to a further £3,600 in a stakeholder pension. These limits will be scrapped from 6 April 2004.

Individual Pensions: There are two options for those people investing in personal or stakeholder pensions:

1. For people wanting to make the maximum contribution of up to £3,600 in a tax year, payments can be made out of any income, or savings or paid by another person. So non-earners, non-working wives and even children can now have a pension plan and receive tax relief. Individuals make contributions net of tax which means they only need pay £2,808 if they want to make the maximum contribution of £3,600. The remaining £792 is tax relief at the basic rate of 22 per cent (22% x £3,600 = £792).

2. Contributions over £3,600 can be made, but in this case the contributions cannot exceed a maximum percentage of 'net relevant earnings' up to an earnings cap of £97,200 for 2002/2003.

   - For employees, 'net relevant earnings' will usually be salary plus bonuses minus any expenses or payroll donations.

   - For the self-employed (and those in partnership), 'net relevant earnings' are usually the taxable profits of the business.

   - Although non-earners and low earners cannot contribute more than £3,600 a year to their pension as they do not have sufficient/any 'net relevant earnings' they may be able to get round this rule as contributions over £3,600 can continue to be made for up to five years after an individual's earnings have ceased. Simply nominate a basis year that is different from the current tax year when taking out your stakeholder pension. These limits will be scrapped from 6 April 2004 and the earnings cap abolished.

Note: The rules are different for pensions taken out before personal pensions were launched in the late 1980s. Old-style pensions (taken out before July 1988) are known as retirement annuity contracts and have lower contribution limits and the maximum lump sum that can be taken tax free on retirement is different.

Contribution Limits

Age at start of tax year	Maximum contribution as % of net relevant earnings	(Limits for retirement annuity contracts taken out before July 1988)
Up to 35	17.5%	(17.5%)
36 to 45	20%	(17.5%)
46 to 50	25%	(17.5%)
51 to 55	30%	(20%)
56 to 60	35%	(22.5%)
61 to 74	40%	(27.5%)
75 and over	nil	nil

Future Changes

The pensions Green Paper has proposed that in future individuals can decide how much they want to save and when – so no maximum percentage will apply from 6 April 2004.

Tax-Free Lump Sums

Although the bulk of a pension fund must be used to provide an income in retirement the tax rules allow that a certain amount can be taken as a tax-free lump sum.

Occupational Schemes: Employees can usually take up to one and a half times final salary on retirement as a tax-free lump sum. However, this reduces their pension income. This lump sum may be calculated as:

- Three-eightieths of final salary for each year of service up to a maximum of 40 years' service – giving 120/80 or 1.5 times final salary. So if your final salary is £30,000 you can take a maximum lump sum of £45,000.
  or

- 2.25 times the pension available before commutation (taking the lump sum), if this is greater. So if the annual pension is £5,000 you can take a lump sum of £11,250. The annual pension will then be reduced accordingly.

  or

- a set commutation factor may be used. For example, 12:1, which means you get £12 as a lump sum for every £1 per annum of pension which you give up in exchange

Individual Pensions: Up to 25 per cent of the stakeholder or personal pension fund can be taken as a tax-free lump sum on retirement. With retirement annuity contracts (old-style personal pensions) the maximum is three times the income from the remaining fund (what is left in the fund after you have taken a lump sum).

The remainder of the fund must be used to purchase what is known as a compulsory-purchase annuity. This is an investment plan which provides the retiree with an income for life.

Retirees will often be better off taking the maximum tax-free lump sum on retirement, rather than forgoing this and opting for a larger pension, but be aware that the larger the tax-free lump sum, the smaller the annual pension. However, while pension income is taxable, if they invest their tax-free lump sum in tax-free investments such as ISAs and certain National Savings products, the income can be earned tax free. Retirees should ensure that the income they earn from these investments is higher than the income that would have been paid out by an annuity.

Retirement Rules

Personal and stakeholder pensions can be taken at any time between the ages of 50 (55 from 2009) and 75. However, benefits can be drawn *even* if the individual does not retire, or can be taken well after retirement. This gives great flexibility. Someone planning to retire early can build up a decent pension without their employer knowing of their intentions, while someone who has built up an inadequate pension can continue to contribute after retirement or leave their pension fund to grow, so that when they do take their pension it is enhanced.

Those employees in occupational employer schemes can also retire from age 50 (55 from 2009), but only if the scheme rules allow. This is usually restricted to cases where the employee is forced to retire due to ill-health or is offered an early retirement incentive instead of taking redundancy. Most schemes require all staff to retire at age 65 (although women with pension rights built up before the 1990s can often take these benefits from age 60). With an employer's scheme you must retire to take your pension. Although you may return to the same employer later – for example, for part-time work – this could jeopardize any tax-free lump sum, although the pensions Green Paper proposes allowing this, enabling a phased retirement. It also proposes making it easier to work past 65.

The rules have changed to allow top-up pensions – additional voluntary contributions known as AVCs – to be taken from age 50 until age 75 even if they are linked to the main employer's scheme and to allow the pension from the AVC to be paid even if the employee has not retired. However, this still depends on the scheme rules.

Some employers are now offering more flexible retirement options for both the main scheme and AVCs.

Life Insurance Contributions

Anyone contributing to a personal pension or stakeholder pension can divert some of their contributions to pay for life insurance. For policies started before 6 April 2001, the maximum that can be used to buy life insurance is 5 per cent of contributions. For policies started on or after that date it is 10 per cent.

TIP

Buying life insurance through a personal or stakeholder pension is very cost effective because plan holders get tax relief on their life insurance premiums – a big saving, particularly for higher-rate tax-payers.

Maximizing Tax Relief

We waste, as a nation, some £977 million a year by failing to optimize the tax reliefs offered by company, personal and stakeholder pensions and AVCs.

The most obvious way to maximize tax relief – i.e. to get some money back from the Inland Revenue for a change – is to contribute more. The only snag is that investors cannot get their hands on this money until they reach 50 (with a personal pension or stakeholder pension), rising to 55 from 2009, or retire (if they are members of a company pension scheme).

 TIP

Higher-rate tax relief is not always given automatically. It needs to be claimed if you contribute to an individual or stakeholder pension. If the taxpayer receives an annual tax return, then he can claim tax relief by filling this in. Alternatively contact your tax office for form PP120.

 TIP

Employees contributing to personal pensions and stakeholder pensions can receive tax relief through their PAYE tax codes. This is a valuable tax benefit. Instead of waiting for up to 21 months (from the start of one tax year until the deadline for submitting tax returns) for tax relief, they will receive it instantly.

Carry Back

Anyone contributing to a personal or stakeholder pension or to a retirement annuity contract can ask for all or part of the amount they contribute to their pension to be treated for tax purposes as if they had made the contribution in the previous tax year. This can only be done if they have sufficient unused relief in that year, that is if they had not contributed the maximum allowed (for details, see the table on page 44). Carry back must be effected by 31 January the following year.

 TIP

Anyone who was a higher-rate taxpayer last year but is now a basic-rate taxpayer, should consider carrying back contributions to last year to receive tax relief at the higher rate. That way they will receive 40 per cent tax relief on their contributions instead of 22 per cent.

The option to use the carry-back facility must be made either before or at the time the contribution is paid. Investors who realize they have missed out on a valuable tax break and want to claim tax relief retrospectively cannot do so (it is not possible to decide to carry back after the event).

The rules for retirement annuity contracts are slightly different. To carry back a contribution for the 2001/2002 tax year, the contribution must be paid by 5 April 2003. However, unlike with personal pensions and stakeholder pensions, the decision to carry back can be made after the event. Investors then have until 31 January 2004 to decide if they want to carry the contribution back. Carry-back claims are only allowed once the tax for the year to which contributions are being carried back has been calculated and paid. Inland Revenue form PP43 can be used to carry back contributions.

TIP

Those with personal pensions can elect to use any of the last five years as their 'basis' year. So if their earnings were higher in one of those years they can base maximum contributions on that year's earnings. They must elect by 31 January following the end of the tax year to carry back contributions and must make the election at the same time as, or before, they make the pension payment.

TAX ON RETIREMENT

Pensions are taxable. When paid by an employer's scheme tax is deducted automatically because pension income is treated in the same way as salaries with tax deducted through the PAYE system.

As a result, it could be more tax efficient to take the maximum tax-free lump sum allowed out of the pension scheme and invest this in schemes that are tax free – such as individual savings accounts (ISAs) and certain National Savings products. Not only will the income from these schemes be tax free (unlike the remainder of the income paid by the company pension scheme), but the rate of return could be higher too – although as recent stock market falls show, you could lose thousands of pounds instead.

Pensions paid out of compulsory annuities, which must be purchased with the bulk of the fund from a money purchase scheme or personal or stakeholder pension, are paid with basic-rate tax deducted.

Tax Saving on Retirement

According to research from IFA Promotion, the organization promoting the benefits of independent financial advice, some £90 million could be rescued from the taxman by UK taxpayers transferring savings accounts to non-taxpaying spouses, where appropriate, so that the tax liability on the savings is lower, or even zero. So if your husband or wife is a non-taxpayer or pays tax at a lower rate than you do, consider transferring savings and investments to your spouse to:

- Cut your tax bill.

- Boost your income.

You cannot do much about your pension – it is taxable and you cannot transfer it, but you can transfer other investments.

The average deposit held by individuals in the UK is £8,461. If a higher-rate taxpaying spouse transferred two thirds of this sum – £5,641 – into their partner's name (assuming the partner currently has no income and therefore no tax liability) and if this sum was then invested in an instant access account paying 4 per cent gross, the couple could make a gross saving of £90 a year.

4 State Pensions and Benefits

Do not be tempted to skip this chapter because you believe what the state has to offer is irrelevant. Even if you have saved prudently for your retirement, recent falls in the stock markets, a reduction in the pensions paid by many private and employer pension schemes and tax and state benefit changes, mean that everyone approaching retirement needs to know what they are going to get from the state and how this will affect their financial position in retirement.

It is also important that you are aware of what is on offer from the state because:

- Some employer schemes, known as clawback or integration or abatement, pay a pension that takes into account what you get from the state. Say, for example, you are due to receive a retirement income of £200 a week but you receive £90 a week from the state. Half of this £90 could be deducted from your employer pension. Four in ten final salary schemes in the private sector operate a clawback, with some taking back up to 50 per cent of the state pension.

- It may not be worth your while making any private pension provision. Means tested state benefits can mean that your savings simply replace state benefits. In other words, if you do not save for your retirement you will be only marginally better off than if you scrimp and save.

- You may be able to top up your retirement income without the need for large contributions by opting out of or opting back into the state second pension (now S2P) at the most suitable time.

- You may be able to boost your pension by ensuring that you receive the full basic state pension. Contrary to popular belief not everyone qualifies for the full amount.

- If you are planning to retire abroad your state pension could be frozen at the value it was when you retired – or it could increase as though you remained in the UK. It all depends on where you live overseas.

As part of any pension planning process, you should check your entitlement from the state. This income can then be taken into account when assessing:

- How much extra you need to invest to fund the required income in retirement.

- What your tax position is likely to be once you retire.

- When you plan to retire. You can, for example, delay taking your state or other pension until you need it. You will then receive a higher amount.

- When you can retire. The state retirement age is increasing to 65 for women, bringing them into line with men.

- Where you retire – the entitlement to increases in the basic state pension depends on where you live overseas.

THE BASIC STATE RETIREMENT PENSION

How much is it worth?

The current basic state retirement pension is £75.40 for a single person and £123.80 for a couple for the 2003/2004 tax year. It rises each April in line with inflation. However, in future it will rise by at least 2.5 per cent a year even if inflation (measured by the Retail Price Index) is lower.

How do I qualify?

Contrary to popular belief not everyone is entitled to the full basic state pension.

The basic state pension is a contributory scheme that individuals pay for out of their National Insurance Contributions (NIC). To receive the full amount, individuals generally have to pay – or have been credited with – NICs for about 90 per cent of their working lives.

Anyone earning more than the National Insurance threshold and paying NICs, will be credited with NICs, and as from April 2000 people whose earnings fall between the lower earnings limit and the primary threshold (£4,004 to £4,628 a year for the 2003/2004 tax year), who do not actually pay NICs, are also credited with NICs even though no contributions are taken out of their pay.

Employees who earn less than the lower earnings limit (£3,900 in 2002/2003) do not pay any NICs. However, they may still be able to build up entitlement to the basic state retirement pension if they get certain benefits or are a carer who gets Home Responsibilities Protection (HRP).

Employees pay Class 1 NICs which are deducted from their salary through PAYE. The self-employed build up their entitlement to the basic state retirement pension through Class 2 NICs, which they pay at a flat rate. The self-employed earning less than the lower earnings limit can opt to pay voluntary NICs to build up their entitlement to a pension. Those people who are registered as unemployed will be credited with qualifying years.

The years in which an entitlement to the basic state pension is built up are known as 'qualifying years'. The amount of pension depends on the number of qualifying years built up before reaching state retirement age; the more qualifying years, the higher the pension.

Men: Need 44 qualifying years to get the full (100 per cent) pension.

Women: If they reach the age of 60 before 2010 need 39 qualifying years. However, when the state pension age is equalized at 65 from 2020 the number of qualifying years will increase to 44. During the phased increase of the state retirement age for women from 2010 the number of qualifying years will gradually increase.

How the Basic State Pension Is Reduced

The following is an example of how the basic state pension is reduced; the figures show the percentage of the full rate of basic pension that will be paid. The reduction depends on the number of qualifying years and the number of years in your working life. As the tables include so many variables we have assumed the number of years in your working life are 44.

Number of qualifying years	% of basic state pension	Number of qualifying years	% of basic state pension
6	nil	23	59
7	nil	24	62
8	nil	25	65
9	nil	26	67
10	25	27	70
11	29	28	72
12	31	29	75
13	34	30	77
14	36	31	80
15	39	32	83
16	42	33	85
17	44	34	88
18	47	35	90
19	49	36	93
20	52	37	95
21	54	38	98
22	57	39 → 44	100

So how much does it cost me?

Someone paying the maximum NICs of £41.66 a week (for the 2002/2003 tax year) could pay this amount for 44 years. In return, they get the basic state pension of £75.50 (2002/2003 tax year once again) for possibly only a few years.

It works out as being very expensive. However, it should be

taken into account that NICs do not only fund pensions but also other benefits such as the Jobseekers' Allowance.

What if I have no earnings?

People in receipt of the following state benefits are credited with NICs and therefore, even though they are not earning, build up qualifying years:

- Jobseekers' Allowance

- Incapacity Benefit

In addition, those out of paid work while looking after children and receiving Child Benefit or looking after a person with a long-term illness or disability, can qualify for Home Responsibilities Protection (HRP). This can reduce the number of qualifying years needed to earn the full basic state retirement pension. However, to get the full pension carers still need 20 qualifying years – on top of the years covered by HRP. From 2020 this will increase to 22 qualifying years.

Only the person who is the 'main payee' for Child Benefit can get HRP (if this is the case your name will be the first name on the order book or shown at the top of any letter from the Child Benefit Centre). You can change the main payee if you need to but note that as you only get HRP for full tax years (from 6 April to 5 April) and if you change the main payee name neither person will get HRP in that tax year. To change the main payee for Child Benefit contact the Child Benefit Centre on 0870 155 5540 from 8 a.m. to 5.30 p.m., Monday to Friday. You will need your Child Benefit reference number.

For more information ask for *State Pensions for Carers and Parents – Your Guide (PM9)* from the Department of Work and Pensions – call 0845 731 3233.

Can't married women rely on their husband's pension?

A married woman who does not have enough NICs to earn a basic state retirement pension of her own, can only claim a pension provided:

- She has reached state retirement age.

- Her husband has reached state pension age.

- Her husband has claimed his pension.

She can then receive a pension of up to 60 per cent of the full basic state retirement pension, currently (2002/2003) this is £45.20.

The rules mean that women who are older than their husbands can find they are left with no income until he reaches 65. So a wife five years older than her husband will have to wait until she is 70 to get any state pension.

You do not have to be living with your husband to get this pension.

Warning: Some married women who opted to pay reduced NICs do not qualify for the basic state pension although they will – as part of a married couple – qualify for a pension when their husband retires.

What if I am a wife who paid reduced NICs?

If you paid reduced NICs you will suffer as a result. Pensions paid to these women – some four million wives who contributed £8 billion between them – are pathetic, as little as 8p a week. Known as the married women's stamp, it turned out to be a con. Women were informed at the time of the consequences but the confusing jargon used meant few of them knew what they were signing up for.

Some 10,000 women are still paying NICs at the reduced rate of 4.85 per cent compared to 11 per cent for most workers. They could switch to full-rate Class 1 NICs if they wanted, but unless they pay these for at least 10 years they will not get a penny extra.

So, I will not suffer if I paid full-rate Class 1 NICs?

Sadly, you may still not qualify for the full basic state pension. Women coming up to retirement now who are unaffected by the equalization of the state retirement age need at least 39 years of Class 1 contributions to receive a full state pension from age 60.

However, many women will have had career breaks to start families and will only qualify for a reduced pension in their own right from the age of 60. If they have less than ten years contributions they will not get a penny because you need at least ten years of full contributions to get 25 per cent of the basic state pension.

Women in this situation will have to wait until their husband reaches 65 to get the married woman's pension.

Don't I get a full pension in my own right?

Only if you have paid enough NICs.

So many women who have paid NICs, but have not worked for enough qualifying years, can find they are no better off once their husband reaches 65 than women who paid the reduced rate or did not work at all. The maximum they will receive will be based on their husband's contributions and will, at most, be 60 per cent of the full state pension. As a married couple, they will receive £123.80 a week in 2003/4 with £46.35 of this for the spouse.

So I am still being treated as my husband's chattel?

Yes. It is amazing in today's age. However, it does mean married women get a pension even if they have not contributed enough NICs.

For further information ask for *Pensions for Women – Your Guide (PM6)* from the Department of Work and Pensions – call 0845 731 3233.

What if I am not married?

Then your contributions are what count. If you have paid Class 1 NICs for at least 39 years (44 when the state pension age for women increases to 65) you will get the full basic state pension.

What if I am a divorcee?

Divorced people can replace their own contribution record with their husband's or wife's record for the period the marriage lasted.

What if I am a widow?

Widows may be able to get a state pension based on their spouse's NIC record if they have no NIC record of their own, or may only qualify for a reduced pension. They can also inherit 50 per cent of the spouse's state second pension (this was formerly 100 per cent). See the section on THE SECOND OR ADDITIONAL STATE PENSION on page 64.

What about married men?

They cannot rely on their wife's contributions if they have not paid enough NICs to qualify for their own basic state pension. However, this will change from 2010 when the state pension ages start to be equalized.

So some people get no state pension at all?

Yes. If you have not paid or not been credited with enough contributions you will not get any pension. However, people aged 80 or over who are in this situation can claim a 'non-contributory' pension which is not based on NICs. It is 60 per cent of the basic state retirement pension and is paid to those who:

- are aged 80 or over

- are living in Great Britain when they claim and have lived here for a total of 10 years or more after their 60th birthday

- have no basic state retirement pension or are paid less than 60 per cent of the full rate

If you do not qualify for the basic state pension you will still usually be entitled to other state benefits.

What is the tax position?

The basic state retirement pension is taxable as income. There are no other tax breaks.

When can it be taken?

It can be claimed when you reach the state pension age, which is 65 for men and, currently, 60 for women. However, the state pension age for women is being gradually increased from 2010 so that from 2020 women will retire at the same age as men, that is at 65. Women born before 6 April 1950 are not affected – they will still retire at age 60. Women born after 6 April 1955 will have a state pension age of 65.

Women born on or after 6 April 1950 but before 6 April 1955 will see their retirement age gradually increase as follows:

Changes to State Retirement Ages for Women
Born Between 6 April 1950 and 6 April 1955

Date of birth	Pension age date	Pension age in years and months
6.4.50–5.5.50	6.5.2010	60.1–60.0
6.5.50–5.6.50	6.7.2010	60.2–60.1
6.6.50–5.7.50	6.9.2010	60.3.60.2
6.7.50–5.8.50	6.11.2010	60.4–60.3
6.8.50–5.9.50	6.1.2011	60.5–60.4
6.9.50–5.10.50	6.3.2011	60.6–60.5
6.10.50–5.11.50	6.5.2011	60.7–60.6
6.11.50–5.12.50	6.7.2011	60.8–60.7
6.12.50–5.1.51	6.9.2011	60.9–60.8
6.1.51–5.2.51	6.11.2011	60.10–60.9
6.2.51–5.3.51	6.1.2012	60.11–60.10
6.3.51–5.4.51	6.3.2012	60.12–60.11
6.4.51–5.5.51	6.5.2012	61.1–60.12
6.5.51–5.6.51	6.7.2012	61.2–61.0
6.6.51–5.7.51	6.9.2012	61.3–61.2
6.7.51–5.8.51	6.11.2012	61.4–61.3
6.8.51–5.9.51	6.1.2013	61.5–61.4
6.9.51–5.10.51	6.3.2013	61.6–61.5
6.10.51–5.11.51	6.5.2013	61.7–61.6
6.11.51–5.12.51	6.7.2013	61.8–61.7

Date of birth	Pension age date	Pension age in years and months
6.12.51–5.1.52	6.9.2013	61.9–61.8
6.1.52–5.2.52	6.11.2013	61.10–61.9
6.2.52–5.3.52	6.1.2014	61.11–61.10
6.3.52–5.4.52	6.3.2014	61.12–61.11
6.4.52–5.5.52	6.5.2014	62.1–61.12
6.5.52–5.6.52	6.7.2014	62.2–62.0
6.6.52–5.7.52	6.9.2014	62.3–62.1
6.7.52–5.8.52	6.11.2014	62.4–62.3
6.8.52–5.9.52	6.1.2015	62.5–62.4
6.9.52–5.10.52	6.3.2015	62.6–62.5
6.10.52–5.11.52	6.5.2015	62.7–62.6
6.11.52–5.12.52	6.7.2015	62.8–62.7
6.12.52–5.1.53	6.9.2015	62.9–62.8
6.1.53–5.2.53	6.11.2015	62.10–62.9
6.2.53–5.3.53	6.1.2016	62.11–62.10
6.3.53–5.4.53	6.3.2016	63.0–62.11
6.4.3–5.5.53	6.5.2016	63.1–63.0
6.5.53–5.6.53	6.7.2016	63.2–63.1
6.6.53–5.7.53	6.9.2016	63.3–63.2
6.7.53–5.8.53	6.11.2016	63.4–63.3
6.8.53–5.9.53	6.1.2017	63.5–63.4
6.9.53–5.10.53	6.3.2017	63.6–63.5
6.10.53–5.11.53	6.5.2017	63.7–63.6
6.11.53–5.12.53	6.7.2017	63.8–63.7
6.12.53–5.1.54	6.9.2017	63.9–63.8
6.1.54–5.2.54	6.11.2017	63.10–63.9
6.2.54–5.3.54	6.1.2018	63.11–63.10
6.3.54–5.4.54	6.3.2018	64.0–63.11
6.4.54–5.5.54	6.2.2018	64.1–64.0
6.5.54–5.6.54	6.7.2018	64.2–64.1
6.6.54–5.7.54	6.9.2018	64.3–64.2
6.7.54–5.8.54	6.11.2018	64.4–64.3
6.8.54–5.9.54	6.1.2019	64.5–64.4

Date of birth	Pension age date	Pension age in years and months
6.9.54–5.10.54	6.3.2019	64.6–64.5
6.10.54–5.11.54	6.5.2019	64.7–64.6
6.11.54–5.12.54	6.7.2019	64.8–64.7
6.12.54–5.1.55	6.9.2019	64.9–64.8
6.1.55–5.2.55	6.11.2019	64.10–64.9
6.2.55–5.3.55	6.1.2020	64.11–64.10
6.3.55–5.4.55	6.3.2020	65.0–64.11
6.4.55	6.4.2020	65

You can find out more about the increasing of the state pension age from leaflet EQP1a *Equality in State Pension Age* which is available by calling the Pensions Info-Line on 0845 7 31 32 33. Alternatively visit the pensions service website at www.thepensionservice.gov.uk.

✎ TIP

It is possible to increase the amount of pension paid by postponing taking it for up to five years. You can request details of how this will increase your pension when you ask for a pension forecast.

What choices do I have to make?

You cannot opt out of the basic state retirement pension. However, you can ensure that you maximize the amount you will be paid on retirement by paying in an additional sum:

This will be the case if you have:

- worked too few years (do not have enough qualifying years)
- had earnings below the National Insurance Contribution limit during some of your working life

What action do I need to take?

Get a pension forecast to check how much you will receive on retirement. It will tell you in today's money, how much state pension you have already earned and what you can expect to have earned by state pension age. It will also include details of any additional state pension.

Application forms (BR19) can be downloaded from the Pensions Service website at www.thepensionservice.gov.uk or requested by calling the Retirement Pension Forecasting Team on 0845 3000 168 (they can fill in the form over the phone). Lines are open from 9 a.m. to 5 p.m. from Monday to Friday and calls are charged at local rates. You can also write to the Retirement Pension Forecasting Team, Room TB001, Tyneview Park, Whitley Road, Newcastle upon Tyne, NE98 1BA – ask for a forecast application and a return envelope to be sent to you. You can also get form BR19 from your local social security office.

Note: You will need to have your National Insurance number.

Once you have received your forecast you can use it to calculate how much extra you need to save for your retirement. You can make additional contributions if you will receive less than the full basic state pension. The forms you receive will tell you how to do this.

Note: The forecast is based on your current circumstances. These can change.

Note: You will automatically be sent details of your state pension entitlement four months before you reach state pension age along with an invitation to claim the state pension. However, you will only receive this information if the Department of Work and Pensions is aware of your up-to-date address.

What if I stop work before retirement?

As you will no longer be making NICs you may have a shortfall in the number of contributions needed to qualify for the full basic state pension. You may therefore need to pay extra contributions. When you receive your pensions forecast you will be told how to do this.

However, if you are a man aged 60 or over you will usually get national insurance credits until state pension age. These start from the tax year including your 60th birthday. You may also be able to get Jobseeker's Allowance which will give you an entitlement to a credit.

What if I want to work past state retirement age?

You will get an enhanced basic rate pension if you defer taking it by up to five years. From 2010, people will gain at least 10 per cent for each year they delay drawing their pension – compared to 7.5 per cent now – to encourage more people to consider later retirement. The government is also looking at the possibility, where people defer taking their pension, of offering a choice of either an increased regular state pension or a taxable lump-sum.

People who defer taking their state pension for five years or longer could see a 50 per cent increase in their weekly payment.

What if I die before retirement?

No rebates of your NICs are given. However, your widow or widower may be able to inherit some of your pension. For example, if your spouse is not entitled to the full basic state retirement pension because he or she has not made enough NICs but you were, when you die he or she may be able to claim the full pension based on your contribution record.

If you die before retirement age, bereavement benefits may be paid to your spouse if they are under state pension age.

What if I move abroad before state pension age.

You will probably not build up an entitlement to the basic state retirement pension for the years you live and work abroad unless you work for a UK company who makes/deducts NICs (in other words if you are taxed as a UK employee).

What if I retire abroad after I retire?

You will still get your state pension if you are over state pension age. However, you will NOT get yearly increases in the state pension unless you live in:

- a European Economic Area (EEA) country

- a country the UK has an agreement with that allows for upratings

See the section on retiring abroad on page 294 in Chapter 13: Planning Your Retirement for further information.

Where do I find out more?

The Department of Work and Pensions has several useful guides including *State Pensions – Your guide (PM2)*, available by calling 0845 731 3233. The line is open 24 hours a day and calls are charged at local rates. Alternatively visit www.thepensionservice.gov.uk.

THE SECOND OR ADDITIONAL STATE PENSION

What is it?

The additional state pension is a top-up pension paid in addition to the basic state retirement pension.

Over the years this additional state pension has changed and the value of it has been eroded – although not for everyone.

People who do not work because they are too ill or disabled to do so or who are caring for others will gain from the new state second pension (S2P) introduced in April 2002. The campaign group Carers UK estimates that by 2050 carers who have spent a lifetime looking after other people could receive nearly £50 per week extra on top of the basic state pension.

Everyone else will eventually be worse off. While those people retiring on the state earnings-related pension scheme (SERPS) benefits today receive a maximum of £131 a week from the state top-up scheme, the twenty-something of today will find the new state second pension (S2P) worth little. Jane Falkingham, of the London School of Economics, says that by 2050 the basic state pension and S2P may be worth just £1 a week more than pensioners without National Insurance entitlements would receive.

How has the state second pension changed?

Between April 1961 and April 1975 it was known as graduated retirement benefit. For every £7.50 (man) or £9 (woman) of graduated contribution paid you got 9.21 pence as a pension per week. From April 1978 to April 2002 the additional pension became known as the state earnings-related pension scheme (SERPS), and in April 2002 SERPS was replaced by the state second pension (S2P).

Do I qualify for an additional pension?

If you are an employee paying NICs you will be paying into the state second pension and would have contributed to SERPS before April 2002 unless:

- you have been a member of a company or an occupational pension scheme or

- have a personal or stakeholder pension

- AND these pensions were opted out of the state second pension scheme and SERPS before that. This is known as 'contracting out' and you would not have paid into SERPS.

However, you may still be able to build up an entitlement to the new S2P. Unlike under SERPS even people who are members of these contracted-out occupational pension schemes can now still benefit from the additional state pension provided they earn less than a certain amount. From 6 April 2002, a member of a contracted-out occupational pension scheme earning £24,600 or less (in 2002/2003 terms) in a tax year will get a S2P top-up for that year. Employees contributing to a contracted-out personal or stakeholder pension who earn less than £10,800 (again in 2002/2003 terms) will also get a top-up for that year.

Note: The self-employed and unemployed do not qualify for S2P and did not qualify for SERPS either.

Why was SERPS replaced?

SERPS was based on Class 1 NICs paid by those employees who were not contracted out of this scheme through their employer's pension scheme. The more paid in, the bigger the SERPS pension. It therefore benefited higher earners. Low earners, those caring for relatives or children and the long-term disabled all lost out.

However, the benefits of SERPS were gradually chipped away. The maximum SERPS pension was 25 per cent of the individual's best 20 years of earnings. It was then cut to 20 per cent of earnings throughout a person's working life – halving its future value. A further reform halved its worth again by reducing the value of lifetime earnings used in the final calculation. Then, from October 2002 only half the pension could be inherited by a spouse as opposed to the previous 100 per cent.

Even so, SERPS was still generous. It was also cheap and cost the equivalent of just 1.6 per cent of earnings subject to NICs.

The state second pension (S2P) introduced on 6 April 2002 reformed SERPS to provide a more generous additional state pension for low and moderate earners, certain carers and people with long-term illness or disability. The benefits will be broadly the same although lower-paid people, the disabled, carers and mothers of young children will all get higher payments.

However, from April 2006 this too will be cut back.

So what happened to my SERPS pension?

Although no new SERPS entitlement can be built up, any existing SERPS entitlements are unaffected by the changes. They are protected both for people who have already retired and for people who have not yet reached state pension age.

Will I be better or worse off following the changes?

You will be better off only if you are a low earner. S2P gives employees earning up to £24,600 (in 2002/2003 terms) a better pension than SERPS, whether or not they are contracted out. Most help goes to people on the lowest earnings (up to around £10,800 at 2002/2003 levels), because anyone who earns less than £10,800 a year is treated as though they *had* earned £10,800 a year. The proportion of their salary up to this limit earns twice the entitlement it would have under SERPS. Earnings that fall into the next band – between £10,801 and £24,600, however, get only half the SERPS entitlement. Any salary over £24,601 is treated as it was under SERPS. This averages out so employees earning £24,600 or more are no better or worse off. Lower earners, however, benefit and so do carers who may not have earned any pension under SERPS but could now receive as much as £57 a week.

So is it worth my while building up a state second pension?

As with SERPS, individuals can contract out of S2P. If they are members of a contracted-out occupational (company) pension scheme they will pay lower NICs. If they are members of a personal or stakeholder pension, rebates – equivalent to the amount they would have paid into S2P – will be invested into their pension. These rebated NICs must be used to fund a pension.

You *may* be better off investing these rebates in an occupational or private scheme. If they are invested wisely, they could – and the emphasis is on could – provide a bigger pension. There are no guarantees. Generally, the chances of you being better off through contracting out are higher if you are younger. The decision depends on your age, what entitlements you have already built up, what other provisions you have made for retirement, when you plan to retire, your attitude to risk and a number of other factors. So there are no hard and fast rules.

However, until a year or so ago, as a general guide, pension providers were informing their customers that they may be better off contracting out if they were under 50 and should contract back in if they were a man aged 54 or over and a woman aged 49 or over. These age limits were then reduced and today some pension providers say there are unlikely to be any benefits from being contracted out.

How big are the rebates?

Contracting-out rebates for personal and stakeholder pensions

Age on 5 April 2002	% rebate 2002/2003
20	4.4
30	4.8
40	5.4
50	9.9
52+	10.5

These rebates are higher than they were for SERPS in 2001/2002 because the government Actuary's Department, in calculating the rebate, has assumed a real (above earnings) rate of return of 2 per cent and has taken into account falling returns on investments (particularly index-linked gilt yields).

So, despite the more generous rebates, the chances of beating the pension from S2P by contracting out are lower.

When I retire, how much will I get?

This depends on several things:

- How many years you are employed and earning over £3,900 (in 2002/2003 terms).

- How much you earn – the more you earn over your working life (up to an upper limit) the more entitlement you build up.

- Whether or not you contract out – if you contract out you have the opportunity to build up a larger pension if the rebated money is invested well.

Currently, the maximum pension you could get from the SERPS is roughly £130 a week on top of the basic state pension. By 2050 some predict the maximum from S2P will be just £44 a week (assuming 44 years membership of S2P). Take this more realistic assumption when calculating your retirement income.

How do I find out how much I will get?

There are two things to check:

Your SERPS Entitlement: From 1978 to 2002 the additional state pension was called SERPS. You would have built up a SERPS pension if you were an employee paying NICs and not contracted out of SERPS through a company pension scheme or a personal pension. Any SERPS entitlement built up in these years is protected.

One recent report put the market value of an accumulated SERPS pension in the example below at £160,000 – that is how much you would need from a private pension to fund an equal income in retirement.

Someone retiring in 2002 who had consistently earned around one and a half times the average male earnings and contributed to SERPS since its launch in 1978 would have received a total state pension of £10,922 a year – including £6,996 of SERPS. In addition, this is increased each year in line with inflation and is guaranteed by the state. The pensioner's widow or widower would also be able to inherit 100 per cent of the SERPS pension (provided they retired before October 2002 when this limit was cut) on the death of their spouse.

You may also have built up a reduced SERPS entitlement if between April 1978 and April 1997 you were a member of:

- a contracted-out company pension scheme

- a contracted-out personal pension called an appropriate personal pension

After April 1997 you would no longer have built up any SERPS entitlement because this benefit had been scrapped.

Any entitlement earned after April 1978 (when SERPS was introduced) and before joining a company pension or starting a personal pension is protected and unaffected by changes to the additional state pension.

Your S2P Entitlement: You will build this up if you are:

- an employee paying NICs and not contracted out of S2P

- an employee earning less than the lower NIC threshold, but more than £3,900 in 2002/2003 terms

- a member of a contracted-out occupational pension scheme earning £24,600 or less (in 2002/2003 terms) in a tax year

- an employee contributing to a contracted-out personal or stakeholder pension earning less than £10,800 (again in 2002/2003 terms)

- if you receive certain state benefits or are a carer

You can find out this information by asking for a retirement pension forecast (form BR19) available from your social security office or by ringing 0845 3000 168. To receive a forecast you will need to know your National Insurance number.

What could this mean in hard cash?

A man who earned £6,000 a year starting work at 16 and retiring at 65 will get an S2P of £59 a week according to the Department for Work and Pensions. This is £46 a week more than under SERPS. A man who earned £20,000 a year through a working life of 40 years would get an S2P of £77 (this would have been £61 under SERPS).

The pension is accrued as follows: Every year you earn £10,800 a year (the minimum level assumed) you qualify for an extra £1 a week in retirement.

Higher earners, currently build up a higher pension.

What if I am a low earner – I won't get much of a second pension, will I?

Under the new system you will, provided you earn more than the lower earnings limit for NICs (£3,900 in 2002/2003). In fact, you will be treated as if you had earned £10,800, so the rate at which S2P builds up (known as the accrual rate) is higher than it would have been under SERPS.

What if I earn less than £3,900 a year?

If you do not pay any NICs, if you earn less than the lower earnings limit of £3,900 for the 2002/2003 tax year, then you will not build up an S2P unless you are not in paid employment, are working part-time or are on very low wages because you are:

- looking after a child under the age of six

- a person with a long-term illness or disability

In this case you should get Home Responsibilities Protection, and if you qualify you will build up about £1 a week S2P for each year you are a carer. So if you were a carer for eight years, on retirement (when you reach state pension age) you will qualify for an extra £8 a week or £416 a year.

People credited as being carers for their entire working life will be entitled to an extra pension worth, in today's money, £57 a week when they retire. Under SERPS they would have got nothing.

Can I build up a second pension without working?

Yes. Unlike under the SERPS system certain carers (see above) and people with long-term illnesses or disabilities whose working lives have been interrupted or shortened will be able to build up an additional state pension for periods when they cannot work.

What if I receive state benefits?

If you are not in paid employment because you are disabled or too ill to work, you will still be able to build up an S2P for each tax year you are entitled to:

- long-term incapacity benefit

- severe disablement allowance (for a full tax year)

Once again, if you qualify, you will build up about £1 a week S2P for each year you are ill or disabled which is paid when you reach state pension age.

However, when you reach state pension age, you must have worked and paid Class 1 NICs for at least one tenth of your working life since 1978.

What if I die before or during retirement?

Your pension dies with you unless you leave a surviving husband or wife who can inherit a maximum of 50 per cent of the pension. The amount of your SERPS pension that can be inherited may be slightly higher.

See *Inheritance of SERPS – Important Information for Married People* available on the Pension Service website at www.thepensionservice. gov.uk.

What are the rules for SERPs?

The amount of SERPS pension that could be inherited was 100 per cent – although when SERPS was reformed the rules changed. The government altered the law so that the maximum a person widowed after April 2000 could inherit from their late spouse was 50 per cent. However, as people were given incorrect or misleading information about this change the government postponed it until October 2002 and altered the rules for the maximum percentage of SERPS that can be passed on to a widow or widower when someone who has paid into the scheme dies.

These percentages are as follows:

Date of birth of contributor		Date when contributor reaches state pension age	Maximum % for surviving spouse
Men	Women		
5.10.1937 or earlier	5.10.1942 or earlier	5.10.2002 or earlier	100%
6.10.1937 to 5.10.1939	6.10.1942 to 5.10.1944	6.10.2002 to 5.10.2004	90%

Date of birth of contributor		Date when contributor reaches state pension age	Maximum % for surviving spouse
Men	Women		
6.10.1939 to 4.10.1941	6.10.1944 to 5.10.1946	6.10.2004 to 5.10.2006	80%
6.10.1941 to 5.10.1943	6.10.1946 to 5.10.1948	6.10.2006 to 5.10.2008	70%
6.10 1943 to 5.10.1945	6.10.1948 to 5.07.1950	6.10.2008 to 5.10.2010	60%
6.10.1945 or later	6.07.1950 or later	6.10.2010 or later	50%

In addition, the maximum amount of SERPS that any person can receive, including both their own and any inherited SERPS pension, is £134.54 a week from April 2002.

The amount that can be inherited also depends on a number of factors:

If you are a woman: The maximum you can inherit depends on:

- when your husband reaches state pension age (or would have)

- the date you are widowed

Women inherit their husband's SERPS pension when they reach state pension age. They can also inherit the SERPS pension before they reach state pension age, but only if they have a child who depends on them financially and they get the Widowed Parent's Allowance. This applies even if your husband dies before reaching state pension age.

In addition, women can inherit a maximum of 100 per cent of their husband's SERPS pension if they were widowed on or before 5 October 2002 or their husband reached state pension age on or before 5 October 2002.

From 6 October 2010 the maximum that can be inherited falls to 50 per cent but those widows whose husbands were due to reach (or did reach) state retirement age between 6 October 2002 and

6 October 2020 will receive between 60 per cent and 90 per cent of their late husband's SERPS pension. Once again the figures depend on the date:

- your husband reaches or would have reached state pension age

- whether you are over or under state pension age at the time of your husband's death

- if you are under state pension age, whether you have children who depend on you financially

If you are a man: The maximum you can inherit from your wife depends on:

- when your wife reaches state pension age

- the date you are widowed

Men inherit when they reach state pension age. However, if they have a child who depends on them financially and they get the Widowed Parent's Allowance they may be able to inherit the SERPS pension before retirement and even if their wife dies before reaching state pension age.

What if I divorce before retirement?

The value of your additional state pension can be taken into account when arriving at a divorce settlement along with any pension built up in an occupational, stakeholder or personal pension scheme. While pension sharing on divorce does not apply to the basic state retirement pension it does apply to S2P.

What action do I need to take?

- Make sure you register for credits if you are a carer or cannot work through disability or illness.

- If you are self-employed, you need to make your own pension provision – S2P will not cover you.

- If you qualify for S2P, review whether or not you will be better off staying with the scheme or contracting out (see below).

Note: Although S2P has only just been introduced there will be a second change likely to start in 2006 or 2007. The link with earnings is likely to drop and the pension will become a flat-rate scheme. This will benefit lower earners but higher earners will find their pension restricted.

Contracting Out

We have discussed what you are likely to get as a pension from S2P or from SERPS. However, you may be entitled to a replacement second state pension as well if you contracted out (opted out) of SERPS or S2P, and had rebates equivalent to the NIC that would have been used to provide a state second pension invested into your pension scheme.

What action do I need to take?

Unless you are a member of a contracted-out employer scheme (in which case the decision has been made for you) you must choose whether or not to remain in the additional S2P scheme. If you choose to opt out, you must join a private scheme instead and have rebates equivalent to what you would have paid towards S2P paid into this personal or stakeholder pension. Although you can pay in – and probably should pay in – additional contributions, you can set up a rebate-only pension plan. These are known as 'appropriate' personal pensions.

Note: You cannot contract out of S2P if you are already a member of a contracted-out scheme, are self-employed or are an employee earning less than the National Insurance threshold.

In addition to deciding to contract out of S2P you may also need to consider opting back in.

So the answer to the above question is probably nothing. Take no action if you want to remain contracted in.

Why contract out?

You have the opportunity (but there are no guarantees) to be better off. By investing the money that would otherwise have gone to pay for S2P, you could end up with a larger amount on retirement. However, as recent poor stock market performance has shown, this is by no means a certainty and you could lose some of this money.

- For final salary occupational schemes there is a 'reference scheme test' to ensure rebates are protected. Schemes must provide broadly similar – if not better – benefits than S2P.

- For money purchase schemes the employer must pay in a sum equal to the total National Insurance Contribution rebates plus an age-related rebate as a percentage of earnings between the lower and upper earnings limits (£3,900 and £30,420 for the 2002/2003 tax year). The value of the pension then depends on how well the money is invested.

- For personal and stakeholder pensions the rebates are invested. Once again the value of the pension paid on retirement depends on stock market performance.

Warning: Actuary William Mercer calculates that many people who contract out will need their pensions to generate average returns of 7 per cent to better the S2P deal. Investment returns are expected to stay lower than this for the foreseeable future. Legal & General has written to personal pension customers saying it is a cost-neutral situation. As a result millions of people are expected to contract back into S2P rather than contract out.

What happens to the contributions I have already made before I contract out?

Any SERPS entitlement you have already built up before you contract out and any S2P contributions will be protected and will provide an extra pension when you retire.

If you rejoin S2P at a later date, these additional contributions will boost S2P on retirement.

When should I contract out?

As discussed already, perhaps you should not. However, if you are prepared to chance getting a bigger pension by investing your rebates the decision will depend on:

- your age

- when you plan to retire

- your earnings

- your other pension provision

- your attitude to risk

As a rough guide, older employees (over 50) should remain in S2P. Younger employees should consider contracting out. Lower earners may be better off in the state pension and higher earners better off opting out.

These rules are just rough guides and it is vital to seek professional independent financial advice before making a decision.

So maybe contracting out is not such a good idea?

Falls in the stock markets in the recent past mean that investing the rebates is less of a sound financial proposition. Many employees may feel it is not worth taking the risk that the pension will grow on the stock market to provide an income in retirement at least as good as the state can provide. It is a case of whom do you trust – the government or an insurance company?

Bear this in mind. The value of the SERPS pension was cut several times between its launch in 1978 and its final abolition. The same could happen for S2P. As from 2006 or 2007 S2P is likely to be reformed and no longer linked to earnings. Higher earners (earning £25,000 or more) are likely to be encouraged to contract out at this point. It may, therefore, be worth contracting out now.

However, less generous rebates for contracting out and falls in stock markets mean that contracting out is also less appealing. Industry experts predict that some three million employees are likely to rejoin the state system, many of them members of con-tracted-out company schemes, as the scheme managers are likely to find the costs of administering smaller rebates and meeting the strict rules are prohibitive.

Having said that, higher earners in particular will be potentially worse off under S2P because it will in future become a flat-rate pension instead of one that favours those who contribute more.

Even so, these higher earners need to be sure that their contribu-tions are invested wisely, must still take a risk that the stock market will perform well and will have to pay charges to a pension provider for managing and investing their money. When the stock market is rising, a 1 per cent charge simply eats into returns; when it is falling, it eats into your pension fund when its value is already being hit by falling share values.

So how do I make my decision?

You need to consider the following:

- The state will make a 'guaranteed' payment whereas money invested in a stock-market linked pension can rise as well as fall in value, so it is a risky option.

- Lower earners will be better off under S2P, because they are treated as though they earn at least £10,800 a year, whereas higher earners will be no better off.

- People with no other pension provision will at least have the certainty that the state will give them a second pension. The wealthy, who usually do not have to rely on the state, will need less certainty and can often afford to take a greater risk.

The decision also depends on where you are going to invest your contracted-out rebates. Investing them in a high-charging, poor-performing pension will wipe out any potential advantage, leave you worse off and benefit only the pension company who will still make its money. Stakeholder pensions, which have a maximum annual charge of 1 per cent, should provide the cheapest option. If your rebates are low (and you are young or a low earner), the charges may eat into these rebates – so check if there are any minimum charges.

The general advice is that older people and the lower-paid should contract back into or remain in S2P.

What rebates will I receive?

These depend on your age. The percentages are based on your pensionable earnings between the lower earnings limit (£3,900 a year for 2002/2003) and the higher earnings limit (£30,420 a year for 2002/2003). A 20-year-old gets 4.4 per cent but those aged 52 or over get 10.2 per cent.

However, this situation is probably going to change. The government is likely to offer a flat rebate – possibly on the lowest level of £10,800 a year – to everyone contracting out regardless of earnings.

Contracting-out Rebates

Age on 5 April 2002	% rebate 2002/2003
20	4.4%
30	4.8%
40	5.4%
50	9.9%
52+	10.5%

How do I contract out?

If you are a member of an occupational scheme the decision will generally be made for you. If the scheme is not contracted out, you may be able to contract out using a stakeholder pension.

If you are not a member of an occupational scheme you can take out a stakeholder or personal pension and have the rebates paid into this scheme. Simply ask your scheme provider for the relevant forms and they will arrange for the rebates to be paid directly into your scheme.

I contracted out under SERPS, should I remain contracted out of S2P?

Millions of people were advised to contract out of SERPS and many have failed to review whether they should remain contracted out or not. Most pension providers inform their customers on a regular basis if they should reconsider. Some write to all investors with general advice, for example, advising women and men over a certain age to now consider contracting back into S2P.

Was contracting out of SERPS such a good idea?

No. One recent report by actuaries William M. Mercer found that 12 million people who opted out of SERPS are being short-changed by £1 billion a year.

It also seems that most people who opted out of SERPS, since we were first encouraged to do so by the Conservative government in 1987, should now contract back into the state scheme. The reason is that the rebates are no longer sufficient to compensate for giving up your right to receive S2P, and because of the investment risks involved.

You cannot, however, reverse your decision. You can only elect to be in or out of S2P on a year-by-year basis. So you cannot decide that you would prefer a SERPS pension and transfer your rebates back into the state scheme.

You also have to take a political risk and bank on the fact that future governments will not cut back on the benefits of S2P – something they have done in the past. The maximum SERPS pension was gradually eroded and this government already plans to cut back on S2P. It will mean anyone born after April 1961 will only earn an extra £1 a week on their pension for each year they pay into S2P. After 44 years, they will get £44 a week. This is a lot less than the £131 maximum paid out by SERPS – but possibly more than they could earn by contracting back in.

So should I contract back in?

This is as complex a decision as contracting out. As a rough guide, men over 50 and women over 45 should ask for their situation to be reviewed by their financial adviser (the exact age when they contract back in may be slightly higher), and so should lower earners. Younger workers may want to take the gamble that their rebates – when invested over 20 years or more – will produce a higher pension than from S2P.

However, some actuaries warn that even for these younger workers the rebates do not compensate fully for the full value of the state pension that will be forgone.

So the answer is yes – for many people.

How do I contract back in?

You may not be able to contract back in if you are in a contracted-out employer scheme. However, if you earn £24,600 or less (in 2002/2003 terms) and are in a contracted-out scheme you WILL still get an S2P top-up. So you can be both contracted out of and a member of S2P.

If you are contributing to a stakeholder or personal pension you can continue making contributions, but ask that your pension no longer be used to contract out of S2P. Contact your plan manager or insurance company.

If your pension is rebate only (you make no additional contributions) what is invested in your pension will simply continue to grow. Check what the charges will be. Older-style personal pensions had higher charges and were less flexible than the new-style stakeholder schemes and you may need to consider where you invest your accumulated fund.

Any contracted-out rebates invested in your pension will continue to grow. However, as explained above, you may not have to contract back into S2P because anyone contributing to a contracted-out personal pension who earns less than £10,800 (in 2002/2003 terms) in a tax year will also get a S2P top-up for that year.

What happens if my work scheme contracts back in?

Most schemes make the decision for you – so there is little you can do. Some may allow personal choice, but generally the safest decision is to contract back in.

If the scheme has yet to review the situation, it is likely to do so in the next year or two – if only for simplicity.

Where can I find out more?

The Department of Work and Pensions publishes the following guides:

Contracted-out Pensions – Your Guide (PM7).
Occupational Pensions – Your Guide (PM3)
Personal Pensions – Your Guide (PM4)
Stakeholder Pensions – Your Guide (PM8)
State Pensions – Your Guide (PM2)

Call 0845 7 31 32 33 – calls are charged at local rates and the line is open 24 hours a day.

S2P Changes – Plan Ahead

Although S2P is not that different to SERPS, other than for lower earners, in that it is an earnings-related pension, this will change. The exact details have not yet been finalized, but in 2007/2008 the second phase of S2P will start changing it into a flat-rate scheme for those under a certain age at that time (possibly 45). For older workers it will remain earnings-related.

Eventually, it is expected that everyone will be on a flat-rate scheme. Currently the rate for earnings up to £10,800 is twice the SERPS rate and thereafter drops to half the limit on earnings up to £24,600 and is then at the SERPS rate thereafter. The flat rate could work out lower.

OTHER STATE SUPPORT

State pensions and benefits are now very complex. Instead of paying a higher basic state retirement pension the government has opted for a mixture of pensions and benefits as a means of ensuring pensioners have a minimum level of income.

Unfortunately, these benefits have to be claimed so not every pensioner who is entitled to help gets it. It is estimated that some 770,000 pensioners miss out on £1.9 billion of benefits to which they are entitled because they fail to claim them.

Even people who do not feel they will need to rely on state benefits in retirement should be aware of what is on offer. If their private pensions perform poorly they may find that their income in retirement is little more than the minimum set by the government and they will have saved to provide themselves with a private pension when they could have received roughly the same income without having to invest a penny.

The Minimum Income Guarantee (MIG)

This benefit, paid as income support, tops up pensioners' incomes to a minimum level. However, it has to be claimed – so although it is called a 'guarantee', there is no guarantee that all pensioners will get it and many do not claim.

If you are 60 or over you can apply for the MIG by calling freephone 0800 028 11 11 from 7 a.m. to 7 p.m., Monday to Friday.

The MIG tops up what you receive from:

- the basic state retirement pension

- SERPS or S2P

- any private or occupational pension

- any other income source such as investments

Every pensioner in 2003/2004 is guaranteed a minimum income of £102.01 a week for a single person aged 60 or more (nearly £25 on top of the basic state pension) or £155.80 (£32 a week more than the total state pension they would get) for a couple. If the income is less than the minimum it will be topped up to the guaranteed minimum.

The drawback of the MIG is that it is a deterrent to saving for retirement because pensioners simply save to replace state benefits – providing little incentive to have a private pension. A man of 65 would need a pension fund of almost £31,000 to equal the extra means-tested income (buying an annuity that rises at 5 per cent a year) and a woman aged 60 a pension fund of just under £44,000. Yet the recent government Green Paper on pensions found that the average size of a pension pot is just £25,000 – so the average retiree has been saving for nothing and getting no benefit at all.

For couples, the joint weekly income from the MIG will be topped up to £155.80 – £32 a week more than the total basic state pension they would get. To buy an annuity equal to that amount (rising by 5 per cent a year with a widow's pension) the husband would need to retire with a pension fund worth just under £51,800. Again, anything less than this amount would give him no more than state benefits provide.

The MIG will rise each year in line with average earnings for the rest of this Parliament.

The MIG will form part of the pension credit (see below).

Other Benefits

Pensioners can also get help paying for:

- housing costs
- Council Tax
- care and help if they are disabled

Once again, it is important to be aware of these additional benefits as well as how to qualify. A modest private or occupational pension can mean you do not receive state support.

The Pension Credit

Why scrimp and save to provide yourself with a private pension when you are penalized for being thrifty and could be better off relying on the state instead? This has been a problem in the past, which is why the government will be introducing the pension credit in October 2003 to give help to pensioners with modest savings who have worked hard to provide for themselves.

Who will qualify?

Around half of all pension householders – about 5.4 million people – will benefit from the MIG or the pension credit, with the average pensioner household gaining £400 a year. Single pensioners with incomes of less than £138.38 a week and a couple with incomes of less than £203.55 a week are eligible. You must be aged 65 or over to apply. Women pensioners age 60 to 64 have been excluded.

How does it work?

The MIG will become part of the pension tax credit and will be called the guarantee credit. It will ensure that no single person over 60 will have a weekly income of less than £102.10, and for a couple £155.80 between them.

As explained above, pensioners who have saved for their retirement often lose out due to the fact that they receive less help from the state because they have saved. When the credit is introduced, pensioners will also receive a second credit known as the savings credit which will give extra money to people who have up to £61 more income than the basic state pension and up to £79 a week for a couple

The total pension credit will start at £24.65 a week for someone with no income above the state pension and taper off as income rises until it disappears when total weekly income exceeds £138.38 or £7,219 a year – couples can add a maximum of £32 a week to the state pension and their benefit tapers off to nothing when total income exceeds £203.55 a week or £10,584 a year.

Those people with savings will receive a savings credit of 60p for every £1 of income they receive (so they keep 60 per cent of their personal pension) up to £102.10 a week (£155.80 for a couple). After this limit the credit is gradually scaled back.

However, they will be better off than under the old system under which those with an extra pension income of up to £25 a week effectively lost it (because it was replace by state benefits). When the pension credit is introduced pensioners will only lose 40 per cent of any extra pension up to £61 a week.

This sounds very complicated, how does it work in practice?

A pensioner with the basic state pension of £77.45 (the anticipated pension from April 2003) and £20 from their own private pension will have his or her income topped up to £102.10 a week (from £97) under MIG. In addition, he or she will receive 60p for every £1 of income from his or her own savings from the pension credit: 60p × 20 = £12. This brings the total income up to £112.

Someone with a slightly higher income – for example, a pensioner getting £40 a week from a private pension as well as £77.45 from the state – will see no benefit from the MIG as their income (£117.45) is already above the £102.10 threshold. However, from October 2003, they will benefit from the savings element of the pension credit.

What counts as savings income?

In the examples above we used private pension income. However, any income other than the basic state pension is taken into account including:

- SERPS

- S2P

- the graduated pension

- personal pensions

- building society or bank savings

- shares

- property

It sounds like there is a lot of paperwork involved?

Yes. However, the process is not completed every year. Your income is assessed at retirement and then once every five years unless you have a major change of circumstances. The old system of weekly means testing used for the MIG will be abolished. If you received MIG you will automatically qualify for the new pension credit.

How is my income assessed?

The first £6,000 of savings is ignored and then it is assumed you earn 10 per cent interest on everything above this threshold – a bit steep considering the low level of interest rates.

This figure may change as the government has come under fire for setting such a high rate when it is impossible to achieve such returns from any bank or building society. Assuming pensioners will be far better off than they are will severely hit the amount of pension credit given.

This assumed income is added to:

- state pensions

- private and occupational pensions

- other income

And then your entitlement is calculated.

How do I find out more?

Visit the Pension Service at www.thepensionservice.gov.uk/mig/ for information and examples of how much different people could receive from the MIG at different levels of income. Or call the Minimum Income Guarantee Claim line on 0800 028 1111.

5 Employer Pensions

Also called occupational, company or superannuation schemes these are pensions provided by your employer. They still account for the bulk of private pensions.

Some ten million employees are in public- and private-sector pension schemes – just under half of all employees – and a further 7.5 million are receiving at least one pension from an occupational scheme. A further seven million have preserved pensions with former employers.

There are two main pension choices: join an employer's occupational scheme or make private provision using a stakeholder or a personal pension or through some other savings or investment scheme.

The benefits of an employer's scheme are that:

- The employer usually makes contributions. Employer contributions are not taxed so employees are effectively getting extra pay, tax free. The only drawback is that this money has to be invested in their pension fund and cannot be withdrawn until they retire.

- The employer usually pays the costs of setting up the pension fund – with a personal or a stakeholder pension these costs fall on the individual (and can be expensive, particularly with older types of plans).

- Life insurance is usually provided as part of the scheme.

Employer schemes are generally the best means of securing a private pension in retirement. However, changing work patterns, the rising costs of providing these schemes and a reduction in the benefits offered by many employers, means that employees should not become complacent. They need to consider what happens if they:

- leave their job

- are made redundant

- are forced to retire early due to ill health

- want to retire early

In addition, their pension entitlements could change if their employer goes bust, is taken over or simply finds the cost of providing the current level of pension entitlements for staff too expensive. Contrary to popular belief your pension benefits are not necessarily protected or safe.

A new technical accounting-rule change – FRS17 – requires companies to highlight pension shortfalls based on current stock market values, and makes firms look financially weaker than previously and many are now reconsidering the types of benefits they offer in order to reduce costs.

The pensions employers offer include:

- Final salary schemes which pay a pension based on your salary at retirement and how long you have worked for the company. The higher your earnings and the longer your service, the bigger the pension.

- Money purchase schemes which pay a pension based on what is paid into the pension (by both the employer and employee), stock market performance, charges and annuity rates on retirement. (Annuities are purchased to provide you with an income for life.)

- Group personal or stakeholder pensions. These also pay a pension based on what is paid into the pension (by both the employer and employee), stock market performance, charges and annuity rates on retirement. However, instead of money being invested in one large pension fund, each individual has his or her own plan.

Historically, the bulk of employees, almost nine million, were members of defined benefit or final salary schemes and just over one million were members of defined-contribution or money purchase schemes. However, the costs of the former type of scheme means that increasingly employees are members of the money purchase variety.

One in ten schemes are now hybrid arrangements – a mixture of the two.

Nine out of ten people in occupational schemes are contracted out of the state second pension (S2P). However, this too could change because of the costs involved and the fact that there is less of an advantage to contracting out in the current stock market environment.

What are the tax breaks?

As with all pensions they are substantial.

- Contributions attract tax relief at the highest rate you pay.

- Money invested grows free of tax.

- On retirement you can take some of your pension fund as a tax-free lump sum.

However, the income paid by the scheme on retirement is taxable.

How much does my employer pension cost me?

Employees usually contribute an average of 3 to 6 per cent of their salary. If the scheme does not require an employee contribution it is known as a non-contributory scheme, and they therefore build up a pension without it costing them a penny. Newer-style stakeholder and money purchase schemes cost the employer less and the employee usually contributes more than under the old-style final salary schemes. (These terms are explained later in this chapter.)

Do I have to join the scheme?

No. Employer schemes are no longer compulsory although the new pensions Green Paper proposes that from April 2004, compulsory membership will be allowed – but people with stakeholder pensions may be able to opt out. However, in most cases (unless you plan to move jobs in the near future and have your own pension to which your employer will contribute) you are generally advised to join the scheme.

Do I have to pay into the scheme?

Yes. If you join the scheme and the scheme rules require you to do so. The level is generally quite low, around 6 per cent of salary.

How much can I pay in?

No more than 15 per cent of your salary (which includes basic pay, bonuses, overtime and some other extra remuneration). This is subject to an earnings cap – you can only pay in a maximum of 15 per cent of the first £97,200 of earnings for the 2002/2003 tax year.

However, the pensions Green Paper proposes ending of income-related investment limits for pensions and instead impose a cap for all savers – regardless of age or salary – of £200,000 a year with a total limit of £1.4 million on the individual's pension fund.

How much will I get when I retire?

Barely 1 per cent of employees retire on the maximum pension. This is because very few contribute the maximum allowed into their pension – £14,580 for the 2002/2003 tax year is a sizeable sum – and do not have 40 years of continuous service with the same employer to qualify for the maximum two thirds of final salary pension.

The amount of pension you receive depends on the type of scheme and how it is boosted. See Chapter 10: Maximizing Your Pension On Retirement.

Note: About one in ten pensions are hybrid schemes – a mixture of both final salary and occupational pensions. A hybrid scheme will provide a mix of benefits and evaluates the member's pension fund on both a money purchase and final salary pension basis. The rules vary from scheme to scheme, and you are advised to read both the final salary and money purchase sections. With some hybrid schemes, employees join the money purchase scheme until they have completed enough service to qualify for final salary benefits.

FINAL SALARY SCHEMES

What is a final salary scheme?

These pay a pension based on a proportion of earnings at or near to retirement and the number of years of service. It is usually paid at the rate of one sixtieth of final salary multiplied by the number of years of scheme membership. So someone who has been a scheme member for 40 years would retire on two thirds of final salary.

When you contribute to a final salary scheme your money goes into a pension fund with that of other members. You have no control over your funds or where they are invested, but if disaster strikes the stock markets just as you retire you will be protected because your company must make up any shortfall. As the pension on retirement depends on final salary, it is not dependent on investment performance – so there is less risk. That is why these schemes are often known as defined-benefit schemes.

Although the majority of employees are members of this type of scheme, the costs of running them mean that increasingly employers are closing final salary schemes to new members.

How is the pension calculated?

Employees receive a fraction of their salary – usually one sixtieth of final pay – for each year they have been members of the scheme. So, after 20 years they will receive 20/60 or one third of their final pay.

The maximum pension they can receive is two thirds or 40/60 of their final salary, which is defined as either:

- Remuneration in any of the five years preceding retirement (leaving service or death) together with the average of any fluctuating payments such as bonuses and commissions, averaged over at least three consecutive years ending with the year of retirement.
  or

- The highest average of the total pay, bonuses, commissions, etc., from the employer of any period of three consecutive years ending within ten years before retirement, leaving service or death.

The maximum rate at which pension benefits can accrue is one thirtieth of final salary for each year of service giving the maximum two thirds of final salary after just 20 years of complete service. These more generous schemes are usually only offered to attract high-flying executives to senior management positions.

When calculating final salary the maximum amount that may be taken into account is subject to the same earnings cap as contributions to other pension schemes, which is £97,200 for the 2002/2003 tax year. So the maximum that can be paid as a pension is two thirds of £97,200 or £64,800.

It has been proposed that this cap be abolished from April 2004 and replaced with a fund limit of £1.4 million.

Employees earning in excess of the earnings cap can still receive benefits on earnings in excess of this cap if their employer offers an 'unapproved' scheme. These schemes can also be used to provide benefits in excess of two thirds of final salary or to provide greater benefits for those with less than 20 years' service (including for those earning less than the earnings cap). See EXECUTIVE SCHEMES on page 110 for details of these.

However, employees who joined schemes before 1990 may not be subject to this earnings cap because when it was introduced in the 1989 Budget, existing schemes could continue to benefit from the old rules. It is important that scheme members check with their pension trustees as to which rules apply.

TIP

High-earning members of schemes that are not subject to the earnings cap (introduced in the 1989 Budget) should think twice before moving jobs or schemes as they could potentially miss out on the chance to receive a far higher pension (if they earn in excess of the earnings cap) as a result.

 TIP

Boosting pay at or near retirement will boost the pension of employees who are members of final salary schemes. While commissions and bonuses can help boost the final pay figure, any income or gains from shares and options acquired through share option, share incentive or profit-sharing schemes cannot be included and neither can golden handshakes – payments on termination of employment.

What income can I expect?

Nothing like the maximum pension given above. However, as the income is worked out on a set formula it is easy to calculate.

The company might pay you, say, one sixtieth of your final pay for every year you have worked there. For example, if you have worked for 25 years and your final salary is £25,000, you will receive 25/60 of £25,000, which is £10,417 a year.

Where is my money invested?

In a pension fund which in turn invests in a broad spread of investments including gilts (government bonds) and shares.

Are final salary schemes better than other types of employer pensions?

Yes – particularly at the moment. This is because of a number of factors:

- employers tend to pay in more into these schemes

- many have surpluses to fund benefits

- the pension paid out is not dependent on stock market performance

- if the stock market falls near retirement you are protected

- the employer pays the cost of running the scheme

- there are usually extra benefits such as life insurance and widow/widower's pensions

Does my employer have to let me join?

No. Although all employers with five or more employees must offer a pension (which can be access to a stakeholder pension), they do not have to give all employees access to existing pension schemes.

The generous nature of final salary pension schemes means they are costly to run. Increasingly, employers are closing their doors to these schemes for new employees

Why have they become so expensive?

We are all living longer, inflation is low, stock markets have fallen, the tax-credit system has changed and there is an increasing regulatory burden on employers. In 1997 a minimum funding requirement was introduced forcing pension-fund managers to invest in safer gilts, which have historically produced lower returns on average than shares (although not in recent years). The actuaries who calculate the funding needed to ensure there will be sufficient to pay pensions have therefore had to revise their forecasts and request more funding.

But my employers have been taking contribution holidays.

Some schemes have had massive surpluses (in the late 1990s, these totalled more than £11 billion) and in the past strong stock market performance has enabled employers to stop paying into the company pension. This is known as a contribution holiday. However, this situation has changed following falls in stock markets. One recent report found that Britain's top 100 stock market quoted companies were sitting on a pension-fund black hole of over £100 billion.

Employers have had to reappraise the situation. Many are now finding that instead of taking contribution holidays (or trying to raid the surpluses) they are being forced to dip into company profits to fund pension deficits. Others are simply abandoning their final salary schemes because they are too expensive and closing them to new employees or accepting no further contributions.

How big is the threat to my final salary scheme?

Half of all the remaining final salary based company pension schemes are expected to close to new staff in the next few years according to a survey of 2,950 companies by the Association of Consulting Actuaries (ACA).

The ageing population, combined with falling stock markets, means huge shortfalls are now opening up and companies are pulling the plug rather than plugging the gap.

Nearly seven million people are currently covered by final salary schemes, but the ACA survey found that 47 per cent of companies are contemplating shutting their final salary scheme, with new employees being offered instead a money purchase scheme. These are widely regarded as second class, in part because the amounts that employers pay into the schemes fall rapidly when they switch over.

Instead of a pension funded by total contributions worth around 20 per cent of salary, the new-style schemes typically see their contributions fall to around 9 per cent, said the ACA.

Already Sainsbury's, Marks & Spencer and the big four banks have shut their final salary schemes to new members and, at some companies, such as Ernst & Young and Iceland, all employees have been switched to money purchase arrangements.

The ACA's chairman, Gordon Pollock, said, 'We are extremely worried that the impact of the changes that are taking place is being underestimated by the government and there has been an inadequate policy response.'

If my employer closes the final salary scheme, what happens to my pension?

Any final salary pension that has already been built up (accrued) is protected as long as the company is liquid. When you read about companies closing final salary schemes, it usually means they are closing them to new members. Existing members can usually continue to receive the same final salary benefits while they work at the company. Some companies, however, could wind up the final salary scheme altogether, meaning any more pension accrued after a certain date will be on a less generous money purchase basis.

What should I do if my company is winding up the final salary scheme?

If you can stay with the final salary scheme, do so. However, if it is being closed entirely and you have to transfer all your benefits out of the scheme, find out as much as you can about the money purchase scheme. How much will the company contribute? Will this leave you with a significant shortfall? If so, seek financial advice as you should consider investing extra money to make up for this shortfall.

Research by consultancy firm KPMG found that employees in money purchase schemes are likely to end up with a retirement income of just 70 per cent of that of someone in a final salary scheme. Nearly half of companies running money purchase schemes put in 5 per cent or less of staff's salaries. In a typical final salary scheme companies contribute 10 per cent or more.

If this is the case you will probably have to top up your contributions to make up for the shortfall. You may need to consider additional saving, through additional voluntary contributions (AVCs), a separate stakeholder pension, or a tax-free individual savings account (ISA). An independent financial adviser will be able to advise you on the differences between old and new schemes and the best way of saving more.

So there is nothing I can do?

Find out whether the change hits existing or just new staff. If you are affected, ask if employer contributions are likely to be lower under the new scheme. Consider whether the change represents a change to the original terms and conditions of your employment. Was membership of a particular pension scheme written into your original contract? If so, it may be worth consulting a solicitor or trade-union official to see if further action can be taken.

Note: From 2004, scheme members may have to be consulted about changes to their scheme.

Would switching to a money purchase scheme be such a bad idea?

Generally, yes. However, some employees may be better off despite the fact that they are in a higher-risk option and employers tend to contribute less.

In most final salary schemes staff pay in 5 per cent of salary while employers pay the equivalent of 10 per cent of salary. In most money purchase schemes employees and employers pay in about 5 per cent. However, employees in money purchase schemes have greater control over the investment of their pension fund; they are also easier to understand and are more transparent, employees can see where their money is invested and check out the charges. They are also more flexible and more easily portable. With many employees changing jobs every five to seven years, money purchase schemes may provide a better bet. Although the scheme manager will deduct administration costs if employees want to take their pension elsewhere (a transfer) they will not make the large (and complex) deduction allowed when transferring a final salary pension.

Whether or not an employee will be better or worse off depends on:

- how much is invested in the money purchase scheme

- how well this money is invested

- the annuity rates when he or she retires

As an indication of the amount employers will need to contribute so that employees are no worse off, financial advisers Bestinvest calculated that the minimum level of contributions should be between 13–28 per cent depending on the age profile of the company's workforce and whether they are replacing a final salary that gave one eightieth of final pay for each year of service or one sixtieth.

Looking at these numbers it seems the calls by UNISON for combined employer/employee contributions of 12 per cent are inadequate, even though they may seem high bearing in mind that employers currently contribute about half that amount. Mind you, this percentage seems small compared to the contribution Members of Parliament have voted themselves – a 20 per cent contribution rate.

These are the approximate money purchase contribution limits required to match a final salary or defined-benefit scheme:

% Gross Salary Contribution Levels Necessary to Retire at 65 with a Pension Equivalent to a Final Salary Scheme

Age now	80ths scheme funding target	Money purchase contributions needed to replace this % of pay	60ths scheme funding target	Money purchase contributions needed to replace this % of pay
20	45/80	13%	45/60	exceeds cap
25	40/80	15%	40/60	20.5%
30	35/80	16%	35/60	21.5%
35	30/80	17%	30/60	22.5%
40	25/80	18%	25/60	23.5%
45	20/80	19%	20/60	25%
50	15/80	20%	15/60	26.5%
55	10/80	21.5%	10/60	28%
Average Level = 17.5%			Average Level = 23.9%	

Source: Best invest. Assumptions in above tables: based on the current national trend (source: Office of National Statistics) we have assumed annual salary increases of 2% p.a. over inflation. The assumed annual real rate of return on investments over inflation is 4% p.a. In our model, annuity terms are for a joint life annuity (50 per cent pension for spouse), with a five-year guarantee and a pension escalating by 3% a year.

But my company says there are benefits to switching to a money purchase scheme?

Yes there are – in theory. However, in practice these benefits often fail to materialize. The theory is this: money purchase schemes are more flexible and therefore job-hoppers – most of us have between five and nine jobs in our working lives – gain. This is because they will not suffer a penalty every time they transfer their pension or leave it behind as a deferred pension.

However, one recent calculation for the career history of a 25-year-old who moves jobs five times in his working life, starting with a salary of £19,600 and retiring at 65 when earning £35,000, found that even this job-hopper would be better off with a final salary scheme than any other alternative.

Even if he was a member of a final salary scheme with a one eightieth accrual rate (many have one sixtieth – which means one sixtieth of pay for each year of service) he would be better off compared to a money purchase scheme in which the employer paid 8 per cent and the employee 6 per cent. These contributions are higher than many employers make.

So while employers claim that money purchase schemes are better for younger employees and are more portable, you need to ask some searching questions:

- What will the employer contribute?

- How could this affect the value of your pension on retirement, i.e. how much worse off will you be?

Accountants KPMG recently discovered that companies making the switch to final salary schemes cut their pension contributions on average by a third. This cost-cutting is bound to affect the pensions paid on retirement.

In addition you should ask about:

- death benefits

- ill-health/early retirement pensions

These are often far lower with money purchase schemes. The trade union Amicus recently calculated that the average money purchase scheme provides benefits which are worth a third less than final salary pensions.

Of course, not all employers pay in low amounts; there are a few exceptions. Marks & Spencer, for example, will pay in 12 per cent to its new money purchase scheme if employees pay in the maximum contribution of 6 per cent. However, this is still less than the 22 per cent contribution rate for the final salary scheme it closed to new members.

My company still has a final salary scheme. But I am worried they will close it.

Some industry pundits predict that in ten years time almost all private sector final salary schemes will have either been wound up or closed to new members.

Even public sector schemes may have to switch to a money purchase basis or face potentially crippling liabilities.

If final salary schemes are so expensive, is there a risk my employer will not be able to pay the pension benefits promised?

Your employer may be forced to change the rules – particularly if there are a large number of older employees and pensioners and few younger employees have been paying into the scheme.

If the scheme is wound up and your employer goes under leaving a deficit, you may get as little as half the pension entitlement you have built up.

Public Sector Pensions

These employer schemes are considered the best of the best. Often, low pay in the public sector is compensated by a good pension on retirement. As with all final salary schemes they are not directly affected by falls in the stock market or poor annuity rates. These pensions generally accumulate at the rate of one eightieth of final salary for each year's service and the pensions are index-linked on retirement. Civil servants come out best of all. One recent report in the *Daily Telegraph* found that it would cost about £300,000 in the private sector to buy the same pension that the average civil servant can expect.

However, the high costs of these schemes (the civil service pension scheme costs around £2.9 billion a year, equivalent to 1p on the basic rate of income tax) has led the government to review public sector pensions. Teachers, nurses and policemen are among the 6.5 million employees in the public sector who could be affected.

Some schemes require very small contributions from employees (although they can pay in extra should they wish) while generous payments are made by the employer.

However, local authorities generally require employees to contribute 6 per cent of their salary and these pensions usually accrue at a rate of one eightieth of final salary for each year of service compared to one sixtieth in the private sector. As these pensions are often for an entire working life (you usually stay in the same profession – teaching, for example) it is possible to build up the maximum 40 years service before retiring. The remaining years of service do not boost the employee's pension and these employees cannot take their pension after 40 years of service unless they retire.

Even so, a public sector employee earning the average of around £22,500 a year with 40 years' service can expect a pension pot on retirement of almost £300,000. To fund the same pension in the private sector would require that employee to save about 15 per cent of his earnings for the entire 40 years – something most employees cannot afford to do. On the flip side, most public sector employees do earn less – as much as 20 per cent less – than in the private sector and this is the downside of their great pensions.

There is talk that the cost of providing these pensions will force reform. One option could be to switch final salary schemes into money purchase schemes taking away the guarantees and leaving scheme members at the mercy of the stock markets and annuity rates. Other options include:

- changing a final salary scheme's accrual rate for future benefits

- modifying some of the additional benefits available to pension scheme members, such as sickness or health benefits, or discretionary early retirement terms

- negotiating an increase in employees' contributions to the scheme

- switching from a scheme based on final salary to one based on career average salary

However, trade unions are unlikely to accept this without a fight and have already threatened industrial action.

Part of the problem is longer life expectancy. When the civil service scheme was set up in the mid 1800s only 5 per cent of people were living over 65. Today, retirement can last for ten to 20 years.

Public sector pensions are not only generous, they also tend to have better terms when it comes to early retirement and ill-health benefits. Nor are workers usually penalized if they move jobs. Switch from one employer to another in the private sector and your pension will usually be hit. If, however, you are a teacher, for example, and you move from one job to another within the public sector you simply carry on being a member of the same scheme. There are usually no penalties for transfers and you do not have to leave your pension behind. Public sector schemes are therefore much more flexible than most final salary schemes.

Members of public sector pension schemes – whether they have past pension entitlements or are current members of a scheme – should not be seduced into switching to a personal or a stakeholder pension. This is unlikely today, but during the pensions mis-selling scandal of the late 1980s and early 1990s, thousands of people were wrongly advised to do just this.

However, a word of caution, public sector schemes may not be as generous in future, so do not bank on the pension entitlements remaining the same. All but seven of the 35 local government pension funds, for example, are now in deficit and councils will either have to up the council tax for millions of homes or take action.

Of every £7 allocated by the government to the police, £1 is now used to fund pension payments, so the police scheme may also have to change. Having said that, policemen and women do already contribute a significant percentage of pay – 11 per cent – not far from the maximum allowed while the police authority invests a further 21 per cent. However, the benefits are also generous – a maximum pension of two thirds of salary after 30 years' service instead of the usual 40 with other schemes.

Teachers contribute much less – 6 per cent of salary – and can only get a maximum 50 per cent of salary (not the usual two thirds). But the scheme does allow voluntary retirement at 55.

While all these public sector schemes are generous, employees are advised to contribute more, if possible, as additional voluntary contributions (AVC), which can buy added years of service to boost the pension or an annuity on retirement.

Note: New members joining service schemes from April 2004, will be able to receive an unreduced pension from age 65 in future, instead of the current age of 60.

Contracted-out Final Salary Schemes

The majority of schemes are contracted into the second state pension (S2P). They must meet a Reference Scheme Test (RST) – a minimum benchmark. This means benefits are significantly more generous than the state benefit given up.

However, the Green Paper is proposing to allow employers, from April 2004, to offer a lower pension, although this will be broadly equivalent to S2P. Employers will also be able to calculate the pension on a career average rather than on a final salary basis.

MONEY PURCHASE SCHEMES

What is a money purchase scheme?

An individual pot of money is saved on your behalf and on retirement, the money is used to purchase an annuity that pays you an income until you die.

The pension paid depends on:

- how much you and your employer contribute

- the investment performance of the funds

- the cost of running the fund

- annuities rates when the individual retires (an annuity, which is a policy that provides an income/pension for life, must be purchased with the bulk of the proceeds of the pension fund. See ANNUITIES on page 241)

With final salary schemes, companies take all the investment risk. With money purchase schemes the risk is shifted onto the employee. If the stock market performs badly or the annuity rate is poor, you suffer. With a final salary scheme you are guaranteed a set pension regardless.

It is therefore difficult for employees to know what level of pension they will receive on retirement. If the stock market slumps for the last few years before retirement or annuity rates fall, they could be worse off than colleagues who retire a few years earlier or later

While final salary schemes are often referred to as defined-benefit schemes, money purchase schemes are often called defined-contribution schemes, because it is the contributions that are fixed not the pension.

What will my employer contribute?

The average is around 5 per cent of your earnings – half the level of many final salary schemes. You have to make up the rest.

What will I have to contribute?

On average, most employees pay in 5 per cent – the same as the employer. However, if you want to match the level of pension you could have expected from a final salary scheme you will have to pay in up to 10 per cent of earnings. The maximum allowed is 15 per cent, although this limit is due to be abolished from April 2004. (For information on the tax rules of contributions see Chapter 3: Tax and Pensions.)

Where is my money invested?

Your contributions usually buy units in one or more investment fund. These form part of your individual pension pot and you can find out how much this is worth and where it is invested by asking the scheme trustees.

Are there different types of money purchase scheme?

Yes. The one you are likely to be a member of is a COMP – a contracted-out money purchase scheme. This means the scheme is contracted out of the state second pension (S2P and SERPS before that). In exchange for forgoing some or all of S2P, the employer pays an amount equivalent to the National Insurance Contributions that would have been paid to fund S2P into the pension fund. Most schemes are contracted out – but not all.

For more information on S2P and contracting out see Chapter 4: State Pensions and Benefits.

What pension can I expect?

As the contributions to money purchase schemes tend to be far lower than for final salary schemes, the pensions paid are lower, and much depends on stock market performance. However, the following is a guide:

Approximate fund values for net contributions of £200 a month*

After 5 years	£15,000
After 10 years	£39,000
After 15 years	£69,000
After 20 years	£111,000
After 25 years	£166,000
After 30 years	£239,000

* Assumptions made in calculating these fund values:

- These figures are for a net contribution and are net of charges.
- The gross contribution is £256 p.m. including basic-rate tax relief at 22%.
- Investment return of 7% p.a.
- These figures are only examples and not guaranteed.
- What is payable depends on how your investment grows and the interest rates at the time you retire.
- You could get more or less than the figures shown.
- The figures are based on a 1% annual management charge.

Source: IFA Promotion

This is your fund size on retirement not the lump sum or income you receive, which will depend on annuity rates. With £100,000 to invest (assuming you do not take a tax-free lump sum) you could expect to receive £6,000 a year but this depends on annuity rates at the time you retire and the sort of annuity you buy. See Chapter 10: Maximizing Your Pension On Retirement.

Warning: The new Statutory Money Purchase Illustrations (SMPIs) introduced in April 2003, now estimate your pension in today's prices – after the effects of inflation. This may give you a shock by showing a dramatic fall in your pension since your last statement. A 40-year-old saving £50 a month could see his pension fall from £240 a month to just £85.

Although stock markets have hit pension values, these falls are due to the more realistic projections. They should be a wake-up call to invest more for retirement.

Group Personal Pensions

These are not occupational or superannuation schemes run by your employer. Instead, they are pensions offered by life insurance companies to which your employer gives you access. They were the main option for smaller employers who did not have an occupational scheme but wanted to offer an employer pension to staff – that was, until the stakeholder scheme was launched (see page 109.

The benefit of a group personal pension (compared to an individual employee investing in his own personal pension) is that the employer usually makes a contribution. As the employer may collect the contributions from all employees (deducting them directly from pay – you will be less tempted to spend the money on something else), lower charges can usually be negotiated. However, charges are still usually higher than for the new stakeholder pension and the employee has no choice of pension provider.

Group personal pension plans must:

- have an employer contribution equal to at least 3 per cent of the employee's basic pay

- have contributions deducted directly from pay and sent to the personal pension provider – if the employee asks the employer to do so.

In all other respects, group personal pensions have the same investment limits and tax benefits as individual personal pensions.

Should I take up my employer's offer of a personal pension rather than arranging my own?

The main benefit of a group personal pension over an individual personal pension is that the employer makes a contribution. It will usually be worth sacrificing choice of pension provider in return for this extra contribution. However, if employees want to set up their own pension they will usually be better off with a stakeholder pension (see page 109).

Stakeholder Schemes Run By Employers

As from October 2001, all employers with five or more employees must offer access to a stakeholder pension scheme unless:

- The employer already has an occupational pension scheme (that all staff can join within a year of starting work with that employer).

- The employer already offers a group personal pension scheme.

Note: Most employers – but not all – have complied with this requirement.

Just over half of all stakeholder pensions bought in the first year were bought through the workplace with the average monthly contribution being just over £80.

Company or group stakeholder pension schemes work in the same way as group personal pension schemes, except that there is no requirement on the employer to contribute. In addition to the fact that there may be no employer contributions, employees get no choice – the employer is only obliged to offer access to one stakeholder pension.

Some employees do not have to be offered a stakeholder pension, including those:

- who have worked for the employer for less than three months in a row

- who are members of the employer's occupational pension scheme

- who cannot join the occupational pension scheme because its rules do not admit employees aged under 18

- who cannot join the occupational pension scheme because its rules do not admit employees within five years of the scheme's normal retirement/pension age

- who could have joined the employer's occupational scheme but chose not to

- whose earnings have not reached the National Insurance lower earnings limit (£77 a week for the 2003/2004 tax year) for at least three months in a row

- who cannot join a stakeholder pension scheme because they live abroad or fail to meet another Inland Revenue requirement for membership of a stakeholder pension

I have heard a lot of good things about stakeholder pensions, should I take up the one offered by my employer?

Employees who are given the choice of joining an occupational scheme or a group stakeholder scheme, will generally be better off with the first type of scheme. This is because employers tend to make larger contributions to occupational schemes (there is no requirement for contributions to group stakeholder schemes) and employees who could have joined an employer's occupational scheme but chose not to do so, do not have to be offered access to the group stakeholder scheme.

Stakeholder pensions are flexible, have low charges and offer better value than most personal pensions. For details on stakeholder pensions, how much can be invested and where they are invested see Chapter 6: Individual Pensions.

Executive Schemes

These are known as unapproved schemes and enable companies to provided additional benefits to employees who:

- have earnings in excess of the salary cap (£97,200 for the 2002/2003 tax year)

- want to have a pension in excess of the normal maximum of two thirds of final pay

- have less than 20 years' service, so cannot build up the maximum pension

Schemes can either be:

- funded (with contributions paid in to fund the benefits) and known as FURBS or

- unfunded, with the benefits paid out of company funds when the executive retires (not out of an investment fund)

There is no limit on contributions by the employer (unless they are excessive) and, as with other pensions the employer gets tax relief on all contributions. This makes these schemes attractive for companies who can offer tempting pension packages to attract highflyers.

However, the same tax breaks do not apply to the employee, who is taxed on contributions paid by the employer as if they were salary. Employee contributions are not usually made because the employee receives no tax relief. The pension scheme does not grow tax free; tax is payable at 20 or 22 per cent depending on the type of income. In addition, capital gains tax of 34 per cent (the rate for trusts) has to be paid. Finally, pensions paid are subject to income tax – as are other pensions.

So if there are no tax breaks, why should I bother having one of these pensions?

Although unapproved schemes do not have the same tax breaks as other pensions and the employee is taxed on both the contributions made by the employer and the pension paid out, they may still be worth having because the costs are borne by the employer and if the contributions were paid as salary instead, they would be subject to the same amount of tax. Funded schemes can pay a lump sum on retirement which will be tax free if it does not exceed the amount of contributions on which the employee was taxed.

More than £5 billion was paid into executive pensions in 2002, a

70 per cent rise since 1997, with most of this money coming from company funds.

INFORMATION YOUR EMPLOYER MUST GIVE YOU

Members of pension schemes, whether company schemes, personal pension plans or stakeholder schemes, have basic rights to a wide variety of information. If you have not been given any of this information, ask – it may not be given to scheme members automatically. The following information was supplied by the Financial Services Authority.

Scheme Booklet

Within two months of starting work or within 13 weeks of joining the scheme you should get a scheme booklet telling you:

- what members of the scheme have to pay

- what benefits members can expect

- how the scheme works

- whom to contact for more information

Full Rules of the Scheme

You will not usually be sent the full rules of the scheme; however, you will be allowed to view them on request. The full rules will tell you exactly how the scheme works. They will be written in precise legal terms.

Annual Report and Accounts of the Scheme

You will probably get a copy sent to you. If not, the trustees must provide a copy of the annual report, free of charge, within two months of the request being made. It should tell you:

• how much was paid into the scheme

• how the pension fund is invested

• what was paid out in benefits

The trustees of many schemes provide members with an easy-to-read summary of the annual report covering all the main items to help you understand how your scheme is being managed.

Benefit Statement

You should usually receive this once a year. If you have left the scheme you should still receive this once every three years.

The benefit statement will give forecasts on the pension and benefits you personally can expect based on your membership and contributions so far. In future, you will also get a 'combined benefit statement' that also shows the state pension you might get based on your National Insurance record.

From April 2003, a statutory money purchase illustration must be issued for money purchase schemes, showing the pension that might be payable from retirement at today's prices.

Transfer Value

You can request details of how much your pension fund will be worth if you want to transfer it to another pension scheme (provided it is 12 months since you last requested this information). You can also request this information if you are leaving the pension scheme. It will include:

- the pension and other benefits you can expect if you leave the funds with this pension scheme

- the cash sum which will be paid over to another pension scheme that you have chosen to join.

Basic Scheme Information

The following are the main items of basic information to be supplied to members of occupational schemes according to the Office of the Pensions Advisory Service (OPAS):

- The categories of people who are eligible for membership.

- Whether membership is by application or whether entry is automatic, unless the person elects not to join, or is subject to the employer's consent.

- The eligibility conditions.

- The period of notice required (if any) if a member wants to end their pensionable service.

- Whether a member whose pensionable service has ended before normal pension age (NPA) may re-enter the scheme and, if so, any conditions that apply.

- How members' normal contributions (if any) and employers' contributions are calculated.

- What arrangements exist for members to pay additional voluntary contributions (AVCs) (this could include the investment funds available and levels of contributions that may be paid).

- Whether the scheme has tax approval or, if not, whether the Inland Revenue is considering an application for tax approval.

- Which employments covered by the scheme are, and which are not, contracted out and the basis for contracting out.

- The scheme normal pensionable age (NPA).

- What benefits are payable and how they are calculated, including the definition of pensionable earnings and the scheme accrual rate.

- Whether the scheme rules contain a power to increase pensions in payment (other than on a statutory basis) and if so, what it is, who may exercise it and whether, and to what extent, it is discretionary.

- Whether survivors' benefits are payable and, if so, the conditions (if any) attached to them.

- For benefits other than survivors' benefits, the conditions for paying the benefits.

- Which benefits, if any, are discretionary.

- The name of the legislation (if any) which sets up the scheme and determines its benefits (this would apply to some public service schemes).

- For members whose pensionable service ends before NPA, the arrangements made, and in what circumstances, for:

  - *estimates of case equivalents*

  - *statements of entitlement to a guaranteed cash equivalent*

  - *preserved benefits or transfers*

  - *refunds of contributions*

- Whether, and in what circumstances, the trustees will accept cash equivalents and provide transfer credits and whether acceptance is at the trustees' discretion.

- Where the trustees have directed that cash equivalents will not take account of discretionary benefits, a statement to this effect.

- A summary of how transfer values are calculated.

- A statement that the scheme annual report is available on request (not required for certain public service schemes).

- Whether information about the scheme has been given to the Registrar of Occupational and Personal Pension Schemes.

- Details of the scheme's internal dispute resolution procedure (unless the scheme is exempted from having a procedure) and the address and job title of the person to be contacted to use the procedure.

- A statement that OPAS is available at any time to assist members and beneficiaries with any pension scheme query they may have.

- A statement that the Pensions Ombudsman may investigate and determine any complaint or dispute of fact or law in relation to an occupational pension scheme, giving a contact address.

- A statement that OPAS is able to intervene in the running of schemes where trustees, employers or professional advisers have failed in their duties, giving a contact address.

- The address where people should send enquiries about the scheme generally or about an individual's benefit entitlement.

Examples of basic information that should be provided automatically to members of personal and stakeholder schemes include the following:

- The address to which enquiries about the scheme should be sent.

- The names and addresses of the scheme's trustees or managers.

- Membership conditions.

- Contracting-out status.

- Effect of tax relief.

- A summary of the scheme's investment policy.

- Illustrative estimates of the transfer value of protected rights at the end of each of the first 5 years of membership.

- A description of how charges have been applied.

- A statement that OPAS is available at any time to assist members and beneficiaries of the scheme.

An Annual Statement

When Will I Get One?

An annual statement should be provided automatically to members of money purchase occupational schemes within 12 months of the end of the scheme year. Members of a final salary occupational scheme usually have to request such a statement. Once requested, a statement should be provided within two months. Members of personal and stakeholder pension schemes should automatically receive an annual statement. For personal pensions this means once in every 12-month period since joining, and for stakeholder schemes, within three months of the end of the scheme year.

What Information Will I Receive?

- The value of your fund on the day before the first day of the statement year.

- The value of your fund on the last day of the statement year and the amount of any investment gain/loss arising from that year.

- Details of member contributions.

- Details of employer contributions.

- Payment of tax relief by the Inland Revenue.

- Payment of any contracted-out rebate made on your behalf (this is a rebate due to being contracted out of SERPS).

- Date of birth and any age-related rebate details.

- The value of any benefits transferred from a previous scheme, including the date it was received and the name of the scheme.

- The amount deducted from contributions towards payment of the scheme charge.

- Any other deductions.

As from April 2003 all members of money purchase schemes will get a single statutory money purchase illustration (SMPI). This must be a real projection – which means in today's prices – and must be given every year. It will show you in today's terms what you can expect to receive on retirement and it may provide a projection assuming that you continue in employment until retirement, which may not be a realistic assumption.

Other Documents

Scheme Annual Report

Schemes that are established under trust (please note most personal and stakeholder schemes will not be) must produce an annual report within seven months of the end of the scheme year. This should be provided on request to members, prospective members, their spouses, beneficiaries and any trade union within two months of being requested.

The annual report should contain the following information:

- Miscellaneous information – for example, the address to which enquiries about the scheme generally or about an individual's entitlement to benefits should be sent.

- Financial information – for example, a copy of the audited accounts and the auditor's statement.

- Investment information – for example, an investment report giving a review of the investment performance of the fund during the year and also for a longer period of between three and five years.

Statement of Investment Principles

The trustees or scheme manager must put in writing a statement of the principles governing decisions about scheme investments. This statement must be provided to scheme members, prospective members, their spouses, beneficiaries and any trade union within two months of being requested.

This statement must cover among other things:

- the policy relating to diversification

- the policy for ensuring the suitability of investments

- the arrangements for obtaining advice on the suitability of investments

- the kinds of investment to be held

- the balance between different types of investment

- risk attitude

- the expected rate of return on investments

- policy for the realization of investments

- the extent to which social, environmental or ethical considerations are taken into consideration in the selection, retention and realization of investments

- the exercise of the rights attaching to investments

Please note that you can only request this statement once in any 12-month period.

Actuarial Valuation

Occupational final salary scheme members, their prospective members, spouses, beneficiaries and any trade union are entitled to receive a copy of the scheme's last actuarial valuation within two months of requesting one. Members are also entitled to receive a copy of the minimum funding requirement failure report should this occur.

Schedule of Contributions

This document must show the total employee and employer contributions over a specified period of time (commonly on an annual basis). This must be provided on request to members, prospective members, their spouses, beneficiaries and any trade union within two months of the request being made.

Future Changes

The pensions Green Paper proposes:

- total benefit statements – one annual statement giving the value of salary pension and other pay and benefits

- information about employer pension contributions to be included on pay slips

- pensions information to be included in recruitment material

- a pension information pack.

YOUR RIGHTS WHEN LEAVING YOUR EMPLOYER'S SCHEME

Have you been with your employer for two years or more?

If you leave your employer's occupational pension scheme without completing two years service you may get a refund of any contributions you have made. This is subject to the rules of the scheme. You will not, however, get any of your employer's contributions and your own contributions will be taxed. As from April 2004, this is set to change and 'immediate vesting' will be allowed, giving you an entitlement to a deferred pension or pension transfer with no minimum period of service. If you are a member of a personal or a stakeholder pension you should be able to take this pension with you when you move job.

If you have more than two years service, the law does not allow you to have a refund of your contributions. Instead, the scheme trustees must give you the choice of a:

- preserved pension payable from the scheme's normal retirement age

- transfer to a new employer's pension scheme

- transfer to a personal pension or a stakeholder pension scheme

- transfer to a Section 32 Buy-out plan (S32B) (if you are leaving a final salary scheme), see page 124.

The information you should receive when you leave your job

If your pensionable service ends, i.e. you leave your job, before the scheme's normal retirement date you should get a document explaining your pension rights and options within two months of the trustees being told your service has ended.

If you are made redundant, examine the possibility of using some of your pay-off to boost your pension if you have been a member of a good final salary scheme. If you are paid more than £30,000 as a redundancy payment any amount over this is taxed – so by paying this element of your redundancy money into your pension, you will avoid this tax. The extra contribution should be made before you

accept your final redundancy payment because after you have been
made redundant you cannot contribute to the scheme.

Section 32 Buy-out plans (S32B) were introduced on 27 February
1981 and for the first time enabled transfers of this type. The
maximum tax-free cash sum from a S32B depends on the length of
service and final year's earnings with your old employer. Although
the retirement ages from the original company scheme are applied
to the S32B plan, you can take benefits earlier by transferring to a
personal pension plan. For more information on S32B plans see
page 124.

THE RULES PROTECTING PENSIONS LEFT WITH FORMER EMPLOYERS

What happened to the pension?

If you left a job and the scheme before 6 April 1975 any pension
you had built up before then was often lost because there was no
legal requirement to provide a preserved pension.

If you left an employer's scheme on or after 6 April 1975 your
pension would have been preserved to give you a pension when
you reached the scheme's retirement age provided you had at least
five years of service. (This was reduced to two years from 6 April
1988.) If you had completed less than five years of service you
would have had your own contributions refunded.

What are your rights to transfer these pensions?

You have the right to transfer any pensions left with former
employer schemes unless the scheme was a contracted-out final
salary scheme which protects the value of preserved pensions. You
may be unaware of this right if you left a scheme before 1 January

1986 because the trustees did not have to offer you a transfer value. It was not until the Pensions Act of 1995 that the right was extended to people who left pensionable service before 1 January 1986.

Where can you transfer them to?

You can transfer any of this money to a new pension scheme – either an employer, personal or stakeholder pension. However, while you have the right to transfer your money, a new employer's scheme is not obliged to accept this transfer.

PENSION TRANSFERS

Before deciding to take a transfer you should take independent advice. To give advice on pension transfers from occupational pension schemes independent financial advisers (IFAs) must be authorized by the Financial Services Authority and hold a recognized qualification such as G60 Pensions.

Final Salary Schemes

You will usually be better off leaving your money where it is even if you are joining a company with its own occupational pension scheme because:

- You may not be able to transfer the money to a new employer's scheme – almost definitely not if it is a final salary scheme ... many schemes no longer accept transfers.

- The benefits are unlikely to be as generous elsewhere as final salary schemes are closing to new members – so your option will usually be a money purchase scheme which could leave you worse off.

- The transfer value will be lower than the value of your deferred pension.

The only benefit of a stakeholder or a personal pension is flexibility: you can take your pension from age 50 (55 from 2010) instead of having to wait until the scheme's retirement age (usually 65); or you can keep your money invested until you are 75, so that it has longer to grow.

When the stock markets were soaring, the fact that your deferred pension would only grow by a maximum of 5 per cent a year made a final salary scheme look poor value on the assumption that you could get double-figure returns by investing in a personal pension. Today, 5 per cent or inflation (whichever is the lower) looks generous compared to seeing the value of your personal pension fall by up to 40 per cent in two years.

Public Sector Pensions

If you are a member of a public sector scheme that operates a transfer club arrangement, you will be able to transfer to another final salary scheme. However, check how your transfer is treated, as additional years, or, with changes on the cards, might you have to transfer into a money purchase scheme? The number of added years is usually less than the number of years service actually accrued in the old scheme. This loss of benefit, in theory, could be made up by salary increases in the new scheme. As with all final salary schemes, benefits are guaranteed.

Section 32 Buy-out Plans (S32B)

These are money purchase arrangements offered by most life offices and they are specifically designed to accept transfers from final salary occupational schemes. Any guaranteed minimum pension (GMP) element must be retained in the same format as in the ceding scheme (the one you are leaving). When benefits are taken, they continue to come under occupational pension scheme legislation, so you can get a pension based on final salary even though you are no longer a member of a final salary scheme. If investment returns are very high, S32Bs can become over-funded. Any excess goes to the employer or the life office. It cannot go to the member. Death benefits before retirement are usually superior to those from a personal pension. Benefits can be taken between age 50 and 75 provided the GMP element remains guaranteed.

Some 500,000 people who have changed jobs have taken out S32B plans.

The main benefits were seen as: retaining life insurance benefits in the form of a tax-free lump sum for your widow even after leaving the final salary scheme, whereas with a deferred pension in a final salary scheme your widow may not receive a tax-free lump sum – or one that is significantly lower. However:

- The lump sum – while being tax free – is subject to inheritance tax.

- With a personal, stakeholder or occupational pension any lump sum escapes inheritance tax.

If you took out a S32B plan, reconsider your financial situation. You can transfer to a personal or a stakeholder pension, benefit from more tax-free cash on retirement (25 per cent of the fund) and on death. There is also more flexibility about how benefits are taken. Also bear in mind that the S32B may have higher costs. However, you will be giving up the right to take your pension based on your final salary.

Money Purchase Schemes

The choice is mainly down to costs, but also investment perform-ance to a lesser extent, and flexibility. Much depends on whether your new employer's scheme accepts transfers.

Pension transfers is a specialist area and independent financial advisers need advanced qualifications to do this work. You are recommended to opt for fee-based advice to ensure there is no potential for bias (after all, recommending you stay where you are will not result in a commission). For a transfer to take place the Financial Services Authority will require a transfer analysis to be done and a good case made (in writing) for a transfer to a personal or a stakeholder pension.

The question you need to have answered is: can my benefits be improved by switching my pension elsewhere? This needs to take into account the risks involved.

These are the other issues to bear in mind when considering a transfer from a money purchase scheme:

- With a stakeholder or personal pension you can take your pension from age 50 (55 from 2010) instead of having to wait until the scheme's retirement age (usually 65).

- You can keep your money invested until you are 75 so that it has longer to grow, instead of having to take your pension when you retire.

Information You Need

Final salary schemes: You should ask for your transfer value which will give a 'guaranteed date'. This gives you the right to the amount stated if you want to transfer your pension to another occupational scheme or a personal or a stakeholder plan. You must write to tell the trustees within three months of the guaranteed date that you do want to transfer your pension. The trustees have up to six months from the guaranteed date to pay the transfer value. If they take longer, they should increase the amount either by adding interest or recalculating the value.

Money purchase schemes: Members of a money purchase occupational scheme should receive an estimate of their transfer value or the cash equivalent within three months of requesting one. The trustees have six months from the date of you writing to request a transfer in which to make that transfer.

Personal and stakeholder pensions: The provider has up to six months in which to pay the transfer value.

PRESERVED PENSIONS

You no longer suffer when you move jobs because any pension left behind will continue to grow. This was not always the case. In the past, pensions were frozen which meant the amount of pension remained the same from the date you left your job until you retired.

From 1978, any pension built up in a final salary scheme contracted out of SERPS has to pay a guaranteed minimum pension (GMP), which must be increased for each complete tax year between the date of leaving the scheme and state retirement age. These increases can be either:

- in line with annual rises in average earnings

- at a set rate of interest set by the government (for the 2002/2003 tax year it was 4.5 per cent)

- a more complex calculation by which it will rise by 5 per cent a year compound, but if the increase in average earnings is higher, the state scheme pays the balance

However, these increases only apply to the GMP element and not to the rest of the preserved pension.

Employees leaving schemes after 31 December 1985 get a better deal, which applies to pension service earned after 31 December 1984.

Any pension in excess of the GMP must increase from the date of leaving employment to the date of retirement by inflation (the rate of increase in the retail price index) subject to a maximum of 5 per cent compound.

Employees leaving schemes after 31 December 1990 have even more rights. All their pension in excess of the GMP – not just any earned after 31 December 1984 – has to be increased by inflation or 5 per cent, whichever is the lower.

Employees leaving schemes on or before 31 December 1985 have no rights to any inflation increases (apart from the rules applying to the GMP). However, many schemes have given discretionary increases to these preserved pensions.

WILL I BE BETTER OFF LEAVING MY PENSION OR TRANSFERRING IT?

A guarantee that your preserved pension will rise by inflation or 5 per cent may not appear very generous. When the stock markets were booming you could get a far better return by investing the money. However, falls of 40 per cent or more in share values now makes this guarantee look very generous.

Remember, if you transfer your pension you will generally lose out. With final salary schemes a large deduction is usually made from the preserved value and with money purchase schemes a deduction for administration is made (although this is far lower than the penalties suffered by employees with final salary pensions). So you have to make up for this shortfall by increased investment performance. In addition, you may have to pay charges for investing your money. This will be the case if you opt for a stakeholder or personal pension. Your existing scheme may be far better than your new one although the generous benefits of final salary schemes are being restricted. You may therefore only have the option of swapping the guarantees of a final salary scheme with the risks of a money purchase scheme, which is dependent on the stock market and annuity rates when you retire.

Once you have a transfer value, ask the adviser to give you a critical yield figure which shows how much annual growth the private plan will need to match the pension promised by the existing scheme. Then it is down to risk. If the growth needed is only 4 per cent, there is a chance you could do better. However, if your private pension needs to grow by 10 per cent or more, the prospect of a better pension are slim.

Employees (unless they are very young) are often advised to leave final salary pensions behind as a preserved pension. Unless the firm is in serious financial trouble scheme members should stay put, particularly if the company is still making contributions.

If, however, the scheme is closed with no further contributions being paid or you have rights preserved in a scheme with a previous employer, you should ask for advice about switching out. Remember, private pensions are more risky but this fact needs to be balanced against the risk that the company may not pay out in future.

Schemes are required to balance their books to within 90 per cent of their liabilities every three years – known as the minimum funding requirement. If this was done some time ago, the transfer will be based on that higher valuation before share values plummeted.

You should consider switching from a money purchase scheme, but only if:

- the new scheme's charges are no higher

- investment performance is comparable or better

Pensions You Have Left Behind

Making an informed decision to leave a pension 'preserved' is one thing. Leaving a pension behind with a former employer because you do not know what else to do is another. Sadly, the latter is often the case. Employees leave a job, leave their pension behind and forget about it. Keeping their pension in a good final salary scheme may be the best option, but only if they are actually paid this pension.

Some £6 billion of pensions is 'lost' – left behind in former employer's schemes by employees who have moved on, married, changed address and forgotten they have built up an entitlement. If the employer cannot track you down, you cannot be paid your pension. Those employees who realize as they approach retirement that they have a missing pension entitlement can find it difficult to track down. Companies merge, are taken over, go bust, relocate and are often difficult to trace. Thankfully, there is a pensions tracing service to help which is run by the Occupational Pensions Advisory Service.

The first thing you must determine is if you were after all a member of a pension scheme.

Look through any old paperwork or payslips to check. Often employees did not have to make any contributions to the scheme (these were made only by the employer) so this may not be easy to confirm. Then you must find out if you were entitled to a preserved pension. Until April 1988 scheme members with less than five years service were not entitled to a preserved pension. However, they could take a refund of their contributions. Do you remember receiving a refund? Try to find out if your scheme was contracted out of the state second pension at that time known as SERPS. If so, a benefit would be secured in the scheme even if you had less than five years service.

After April 1988 you would have been entitled to a preserved pension after just two years of service.

HOW SAFE IS MY PENSION?

Not as safe as you might think. Following the Maxwell scandal pension regulation was tightened up but pension scheme members can still lose out.

For example, when steel firm Allied Steel and Wire ceased production in 2002 it was revealed there was a £12 billion deficit in its pension fund which would increase further as share values continued to fall. This black hole meant a loss of more than £3,000 a year on retirement for some workers.

When companies go bust, employees often lose out. So although employer pensions are considered the best, they can still be risky. Some 30,000 pensions schemes are currently in wind-up according to the Occupational Pensions Regulatory Authority. Although most of these are small schemes with just one or two members, some are larger and thousands of workers are affected.

How can I find out if the scheme is in trouble?

A new technical accounting rule change – FRS17 – requires companies to highlight pension shortfalls based on current stock-market values – so serious holes are now easier to spot. However, a deficit is only a problem if the company is no longer making contributions, or there is a risk the firm may go under.

Apart from that, you need to ask questions or examine your scheme's accounts. These show the current assets and expenditure as well as membership of the fund. If, for example, there are a large number of pensioners and deferred pensions but only a comparatively few current members of the scheme there may not be enough money going into the fund to meet future liabilities. However, your employer could simply contribute more – it does not necessarily mean the scheme is in trouble. Note that while the scheme's accounts may appear to show that the scheme is healthy the figures will be out of date and not take account of recent stock market falls.

Your scheme may appear to have run into difficulties because of FRS17. Many actuaries used assumptions that were a long way from this ruling, so the schemes appeared to be healthy before, but are now showing a deficit.

If a company falls on hard times it can close the final salary scheme and distribute the benefits, even if there is a deficit. Provided the schemes meets an actuarial formula, known as the minimum funding requirement (MFR), the employer is under no obligation to make good any shortfall – in practice the MFR has been found to cover only about 65 per cent of members' benefits on winding up – not 100 per cent as might be expected.

New rules on the winding up of schemes are unlikely to be in place before April 2004 so, in the meantime, expect companies thinking about winding up their scheme to do so.

The good news is that if you have a money purchase pension, the only requirement is that the cash contributions are up to date. This is because these pension schemes do not have to guarantee a pension based on salary and simply rely on investment performance.

So it is only final salary schemes that have problems?

Generally, yes.

What happens if my employer goes bust?

Any pension scheme is automatically wound up when a company goes into receivership. The assets are divided as follows:

- Existing pensioners get priority. Their pensions are guaranteed including any further discretionary and inflation-linked increases.

- Employees who have yet to retire (including current or past employees with deferred pensions) get what is left. Those closest to retirement lose most. The new pensions Green Paper proposes that members with the longest service are given priority along with those within 10 years of retirement and that a new class of creditor is introduced – placing pension scheme debt above any other unsecured creditors but below secured and preferential creditors such as the Inland Revenue and the banks.

- There are also proposals to introduce an insurace scheme to protect the pensions of members whose employer becomes insolvent.

Aren't the assets kept separately?

Yes. The pension fund is a trust with a legal identity and assets, which are separate from the company. If the fund is in deficit or there is a shortfall the company does not have to make up this deficit.

What happens if the scheme is wound up?

If it is being wound up because the company is insolvent, an independent trustee (a company rather than an individual) will usually be appointed. The trustee will realize the pension scheme's assets and put them on deposit. Then each member's pension entitlement will be calculated along with a transfer value for those who have yet to retire. Once total costs are known, any shortfall can be identified (known as a deficiency). If there is a surplus – the assets are worth more than the liabilities – this is usually paid back to the employer and not given to pension scheme members although enough should be set aside to cover statutory pension increases.

In the case of a deficiency, the shortfall can be claimed from the company or the liquidator or receiver – although there is no guarantee there will be sufficient funds to make this up. Basically, the employees become just another creditor (although this should change from 2004).

Only if there are outstanding contributions that the company has not paid over can a claim be made to the state. If the shortfall is due to fraud or theft the Pensions Compensation Board may provide compensation.

The government has proposed a new insurance scheme to protect members whose scheme winds up following their employer's insolvency – but this is open to consultation. There are currently restrictions on the amount of compensation that can be paid in cases of dishonesty. For defined benefit schemes, it is restricted to the amount needed to bring the value of the scheme's assets up to 100 per cent of its liabilities for pensioners and members within 10 years of retirement, and 90 per cent of its liabilities for other members or, if lower, the amount of the actual loss. For defined contribution schemes, compensation is limited to 90 per cent of the loss.

The government is proposing to remove these restrictions so that employees are compensated for the full amount of loss as a result of acts of dishonesty.

I contracted out of the state second pension (SERPS), isn't that protected?

Yes. If the members were contracted out of SERPS, then there may be a guaranteed minimum pension (GMP) to pay. If the available money is not enough to cover even the GMP, the state will meet the cost of any difference so that scheme members get at least their GMP.

So generally there is little protection of my pension?

Not as the current legislation stands, although an actuary must monitor the fund's finances and check that it can meet its current liabilities, this only happens every three years. In the meantime, circumstances can change and stock markets can fall. However, there is pressure for change from the Institute of Actuaries, the Faculty of Actuaries, the National Association of Pension Funds (NAPF), the Pensions Ombudsman and the Pickering Report on pension reform.

Under current legislation companies must fund their pension schemes up to a level called the minimum funding requirement (MFR). However, this is not a guarantee that the scheme is solvent or that members will be able to secure all their accrued benefits if the scheme is wound down.

Even if the scheme is fully funded on an MFR basis, the benefits payable if the scheme were wound up would cover only between 60–80 per cent of the members' accrued benefits.

The minimum funding requirements of occupational schemes will be replaced from 2004 with scheme-specific regulation to allow schemes greater flexibility. It will also make the funding position more transparent for scheme members. The changes will save companies £80 million a year and allow them to invest more appropriately given the characteristics of their own particular membership.

Aren't the trustees supposed to help?

Yes. The pension fund has a board of trustees usually made up of equal numbers of elected member representatives and company appointees. However, while they represent your interests they may be unaware of how serious problems are and be in no position to force an employer to contribute more to a scheme or to retain the same level of benefits.

So what protection can I expect in future?

The MFR will be scrapped and replaced with a scheme-specific funding requirement.

In addition, a new kind of regulator will focus on protecting scheme members. It should be more proactive and take a harder line with employers who wind up their schemes when there appears to be little justification for such actions.

In addition:

• Employees will be given the right to be consulted on changes to an employer's pension scheme to prevent firms changing closing schemes without dialogue with employees.

• Better investment by occupational pension schemes will be encouraged.

PART-TIMERS – YOUR RIGHTS

Employer or occupational pensions fall within the definition of pay and there must be equal pay for women and men performing work of equal value. This means equal access to pensions and equal benefits from these pensions for both men and women.

This has not always applied to part-time workers. It took a judgement from the European Court of Justice in 2000 and a House of Lords ruling on 8 February 2001 to extend equal rights to part-time workers, who must now be treated the same as comparable full-time workers.

In the past many part-timers were excluded from joining their employer's scheme.

What happens if I did not have equal rights?

- Part-timers must lodge their claim for backdated pension rights with an Employment Tribunal before they leave the employment to which their claim relates, or within six months of leaving, or within six months of their company being taken over by a new employer.

- If the case is accepted, the Tribunal may consider backdating the pension rights to 8 April 1976, or the date the claimant began the relevant employment, whichever is the later.

- If the claim is accepted, any member contributions which would have been paid, must be paid for the period of scheme membership granted.

- Part-timers who benefit from the House of Lords ruling giving them backdated pension rights have since found out that they will not get any tax relief on their backdated contributions if they have already retired or moved to another employer.

MATERNITY LEAVE – YOUR RIGHTS

If you take paid maternity leave, you are entitled to have your pension rights maintained as though you were working normally. This applies to both full-time and part-time employees.

However, mothers can still lose out. Contributions to final salary schemes will usually be based on what the woman is actually being paid and not on what her normal salary would be. As final salary schemes depend on earnings, this could lead to a drop in her final pension.

With occupational money purchase schemes, personal pensions and stakeholder schemes the company is required to maintain its contribution on the basis of the remuneration the mother was likely to earn had she worked normally. Any pay increases must also be factored in if they would have led to an increase in pension contributions. However, the mother does not have to keep up the same amount of contributions. She will pay a reduced amount – the same percentage of earnings, but based on the amount of pay and maternity pay actually paid.

In schemes where the rules state that the employer will match the employee's contribution, the view is held that the employer must still contribute at the level the employee would normally pay and not what she is actually paying during her maternity leave. Any death benefits payable under the scheme must be based on the same benefits as would have been paid had the employee been working normally.

Rights When a Business is Taken Over

The government is consulting about pension rights when private sector companies are taken over. These will require the new employer to continue making pension contributions if the old employer died.

THE RETIREMENT RULES

Equal opportunities mean equal retirement rules. Most schemes have equalized their retirement ages at 65 for both men and women, although women can still take their pension at an earlier age (usually 60) if they built up a pension with an employer before the retirement rules changed.

Although 65 is the normal retirement age, the Inland Revenue allows pensions to be paid from your 50th birthday if the trustees allow (this is usually in the case of ill health). This will rise to 55 from 2010.

With a company scheme you have to retire from that employment to receive your pension early.

For personal and stakeholder pensions the earliest possible retirement date (except in the event of ill health or special occupations) is your 50th birthday (55 from 2010) and the latest is your 75th birthday. If you have contracted out of the state second pension (formerly SERPS now S2P), the earliest you can claim the contracted-out part of the fund (known as protected rights) is on your 60th birthday. The government plans to unify these retirement dates allowing contracted-out pensions to be paid at the same time as the scheme pension.

With a personal or stakeholder pension you do not have to retire to take your benefits. You can carry on working if you wish.

The government is introducing more flexible retirement from April 2004. Older workers are increasingly expected to phase in retirement downshifting, job-sharing or working part-time.

You will be able to stay working part-time for the same firm, drawing part of your company pension at the same time under the new proposals.

Some companies are already adopting more flexible work prac-tices to encourage staff to stay longer. BT, for example, had an average retirement age of 52 which was thought 'unsustainable'. Its flexible retirement policy has now increased this age to nearer 60.

If you are planning to continue working, check:

- What death-in-service benefits are available to those who have passed normal retirement age.

- How the scheme deals with late retirement. Final salary schemes may award extra accruals for each year of service or increase the pension by a set percentage.

Lump Sums

On retirement you can take part of your pension as a tax-free lump sum. This will reduce the amount of pension you receive but gives you the option to invest the money. It could even provide a better income than you would get if you left this amount in your employer's scheme.

The amount you can take as a lump sum depends on the scheme.

Final salary schemes: The maximum is usually 1.5 times final salary although this will only apply if you have built up the maximum pension which usually requires 40 years of service. Or, you can take 2.25 times the pension available before you take out the lump sum (and including any additional voluntary contributions (AVCs)) if this is greater. From April 2004, tax rules will be harmonized and final salary scheme members will also be able to take 25 per cent of their pensions as a tax-free lump sum.

Money purchase schemes: You can take up to 25 per cent of the fund as a tax-free lump sum.

Personal/stakeholder pensions: You can take up to 25 per cent of the fund as a tax-free lump sum.

Warning: If you retire, take a tax-free lump sum and then decide you wish to return to work and work for the same employer, you could find that your tax-free lump sum is taxed. If you work for someone else or you transfer your benefits to a personal pension plan before taking the lump sum, you will get round this rule. Bear in mind that transferring your pension will cost you, and you will give up generous final salary benefits. A very few final salary schemes may not be covered by this rule, but only if the scheme was approved before 27 July 1989 and the scheme member did not opt to be subject to 1989 changes in the Finance Act.

From 2004, if legislation is passed, you will be able to include your contracted-out pension as part of your lump sum.

Pensions

Final Salary Schemes: The maximum pension payable is two thirds of final pay (that is final remuneration at or near retirement). Few employees receive this maximum.

Money Purchase Schemes: The pension depends on how much was contributed, how well it was invested and the annuity rates on retirement (annuities must be purchased to provide an income for life).

EARLY RETIREMENT

Your Rights

The rules for employer occupational schemes are different for those applying to personal or stakeholder schemes (even if these are arranged by your employer).

Employer Final Salary and Money Purchase Schemes

Each scheme sets its own rules within the framework of what is permitted by the Inland Revenue. Early retirement is allowed any time after age 50 (this will rise to 55 from 2010), but the scheme can adopt any age it wishes provided it is not before age 50. For benefits to be paid early under an occupational scheme you have to actually leave the employment to which the pension scheme relates. With a personal or stakeholder pension this is not the case.

With all pensions, if you take your pension before the scheme/state retirement age, you will receive a REDUCED pension. You cannot retire early and live on the same pension you would have received if you retired a few years later. The reduction takes into account the fact that:

- the pension is paid earlier

- the pension will have to be paid for longer

- no contributions are made for the years after early retirement and before the scheme's retirement age

If a scheme was contracted out of the earnings-related part of the state second pension (SERPS) prior to April 1997, the scheme must pay – from state retirement age, not the early retirement age – a pension similar to what SERPS would have paid. This is known as the guaranteed minimum pension (GMP). Early retirement can mean you initially receive less than this GMP and often schemes refuse to grant early retirement until the reduced pension is at least equal to the GMP.

Scheme rules usually require the employer's consent and they often refuse to grant early retirement unless it is on the grounds of ill-health.

One way to retire early without suffering from a large reduction in your pension is to accept redundancy with an enhanced early retirement deal. As an incentive to encourage older employees to accept redundancy, employers can offer to pay either:

- the pension in full (with no reduction for early retirement)

- a lower reduction in the pension than they would have received if they had retired early rather than accepted redundancy

- an augmented pension – increasing the pension benefits that have been earned to the date of redundancy

Public Service Schemes

Starting from April 2004, an unreduced pension will be payable from age 65 rather than age 60 for new members of schemes.

Top-up Contributions, Additional Voluntary Contributions (AVCs)

Few employees retire on the maximum pension allowed because they do not have the 40 years of service required by many schemes to qualify for a pension of two thirds of their final salary. However, they can make up for some of this shortfall if they have moved jobs or taken career breaks by paying into a top-up pension known as an AVC. These are explained in greater detail in Chapter 9: How To Boost Your Pension.

Although the extra contributions you pay to your occupational scheme through AVCs are treated as part of that scheme, they can now be treated differently on retirement (but only if the scheme's trustees allow). Under the new rules you can take your AVC pension any time after age 50 (55 from 2010), but before age 75, without having to retire and you no longer have to take your AVC pension at the same time as your occupational pension. The same rules apply to free-standing AVCs (top-up AVCs offered by a life insurance company rather than through your occupational scheme).

Retiring Early Due To Ill Health

Occupational Schemes

While occupational schemes may be reluctant to grant early retirement to everyone who simply wants to give up work at 50, they view the needs of employees who are forced to take early retirement because of incapacity with more generosity.

The definition of incapacity is usually in the scheme rules and requires 'an inability to carry out one's own job due to physical or mental illness'. In some cases such employees must be incapable of carrying out any job at all rather than just their own job. Incapacity must be permanent.

Once again, the pension may be reduced because it is being paid early, although some schemes may be more generous. The maximum pension that can be given is the maximum that would have applied had the member continued in work to the scheme's normal retirement age, but based on final salary at the date of the early retirement.

Ill-health pensions have been the subject of dispute as trustees tighten up procedures, and new case law, following a complaint that went to the Pensions Ombudsman, requires that a refusal to give an early pension can only be challenged if one of the following has been infringed by the decision-making body:

• It must ask the correct questions.

• It must direct itself correctly in law; in particular it must adopt a correct construction of the scheme rules.

• It must take into account all relevant but no irrelevant factors.

- It must not arrive at a perverse decision, i.e. a decision at which no reasonable body could arrive.

Personal and Stakeholder Pension Schemes

Benefits can only be taken from age 50 or earlier if in serious ill health.

Phased Retirement

From 2004, it will be possible to phase your retirement – working part-time for your existing employer while taking some of your pension.

INFORMATION YOU SHOULD BE GIVEN ON RETIREMENT

If you are retiring at the scheme's normal retirement age the following rules apply:

Money Purchase Scheme: Six months before you reach retirement you should receive details of your retirement options. This statement should be issued automatically.

Final Salary Scheme: You should receive details of your retirement options within one month of your retirement (the date the benefit becomes payable).

Personal or Stakeholder Pensions: You should receive details of the options open to you on retirement at least four months before you are expected to retire. Your plan provider should have asked you to nominate your expected retirement date when you first joined the plan. If you want to change this retirement age you should inform your scheme manager within five months of your selected retirement age.

WHAT HAPPENS IF I DIE
BEFORE RETIREMENT?

Many employers' schemes provide what are known as 'death-in-service' benefits. This is a form of life insurance which generally pays three or four times your annual pay as a lump sum to your dependants should you die during service. However, if you are a member of a group personal or stakeholder scheme you may not have any life cover unless you opt for it and pay an extra premium. Note: when you change jobs the death-in-service benefits end so you should consider taking out additional life insurance cover.

The death benefits are paid as a lump sum and are tax free. It is important that you fill out an expression of wish form stating whom you wish to receive the benefits. If you marry, divorce or start a family you may want to change your request so that the right people inherit. Although any payments are at the discretion of the scheme trustees they usually make payments in accordance with these expression of wish forms.

If you die in service (before your retirement date but while still working for your employer) your beneficiaries will get a lump sum and an amount will be set aside as a pension for your spouse or dependants. Scheme rules do not usually have any provision for co-habitees or same-sex partners, so they will lose out. The death benefits are generous – usually four times annual salary.

If you die after leaving the employer's service or after leaving the pension fund (but before retirement date) only a lump sum is paid out less the cost of providing any guaranteed minimum pension (if the scheme was contracted out) that is required to provide for your spouse. The death benefit is far less generous – usually the value of the fund, which may be as little as a few thousand pounds.

Warning: Although 90 per cent of people live until retirement age, dying before retirement can cost your family dearly if you are no longer a member of a company pension scheme. Die in service and you could get £100,000 from your employer's scheme. Die after leaving service and this amount may be only £15,000. You have therefore lost out significantly. However, as transfers to other final salary schemes are now almost out of the question, you have to weigh up this potential loss against the almost guaranteed loss from leaving a final salary scheme for a money purchase one. Section 32 Buy-out plans (S32B) enable more generous life-insurance terms; however, these too have their risks. See the section on TRANSFERS on page 128.

WHAT HAPPENS IF I DIE AFTER RETIREMENT?

Employer pension schemes usually provide for widow/widowers pensions and in some cases pensions for dependants. However, there is no provision for co-habitees and if you have no spouse or dependants your pension will die with you.

The pension paid to the spouse is usually half the rate given to the retired employee. If you die shortly after retirement (say before 60 monthly payments have been paid) an additional lump sum may be paid by the fund to reflect the fact that the fund has paid out so little.

The pensions Green Paper proposes limited lump sums (taxable at 35 per cent) for those dying after retirement, so there is likely to be more flexibility in future.

WHAT HAPPENS TO MY PENSION AFTER RETIREMENT?

Employer schemes usually pay an inflation-linked pension up to a maximum of 5 per cent. However, the government is consulting on whether compulsory indexation for the contracted-out portion of pensions should be limited to pensions up to £30,000 a year.

Inflation may be at an historical low, but that does not mean it doesn't erode the value of your savings and income. If you retire on £100 a week today, it could be worth only £80 in terms of spending power in a few years time. Most retirees are advised to opt for an escalating pension. These normally increase each year in line with inflation or by a pre-agreed percentage.

While employees who have to purchase an annuity to provide their pension income – this is the case if you have a stakeholder or a personal pension – initially suffer a reduced income to pay for this escalation and therefore may think twice about paying for it, employees with occupational schemes are required to have their pension inflation-proofed. They have no choice.

The 1995 Pension Act requires occupational pensions to provide increases in line with inflation (the retail price index) subject to a maximum of 5 per cent (known as limited price indexation). This applies to both final salary and money purchase schemes but not to the top-up pensions, additional voluntary contributions (AVCs) or free-standing AVCs (these are similar but are run by pension providers and are not offered by your occupational pension scheme). This increase applies to part of the pension earned after 6 April 1997. Some schemes are more generous, increasing all the pension, although they are not required to by law.

However, separate rules apply if the scheme was contracted out of SERPS. The guaranteed minimum pension (GMP) which replaces the SERPS pension must be increased as follows:

- No increase on any GMP accrued before 6 April 1988.

- On the GMP accrued between 6 April 1988 and 5 April 1998 the rate of increase is inflation (the retail price index) up to a maximum of 3 per cent.

- After that the 5 per cent maximum applies.

The contracted-out element of money purchase schemes is known as protected rights not the GMP. However, similar rules apply. Prior to April 1997 the protected rights must increase in line with inflation subject to the 3 per cent maximum. After 6 April 1997 the protected rights payments must increase in line with the limited price index (inflation or 5 per cent whichever is the lower).

WHERE CAN I GET FURTHER HELP AND ADVICE?

Your first contact should be the human resources (or personnel) department, who should be able to put you in touch with the scheme's trustees. All schemes must offer an internal formal complaints procedure.

If you are still not satisfied with the response to any questions you can contact:

The Office of the Pensions Advisory Service (OPAS) gives help and advice to people who have problems with their pension and has volunteer advisers throughout the UK. You can contact your local OPAS volunteer (a pension expert) through the OPAS office or through your nearest Citizens Advice Bureau. OPAS: 11 Belgrave Road, London sw1v 1RB. The OPAS helpline number is: 0845 60 129 23.

The Pension Schemes Registry helps people to trace pension schemes they have lost touch with usually because they have changed jobs or their former employer has changed its name. Every year it helps more than 10,000 people get in contact with pension schemes they have belonged to.

The Pensions Ombudsman has the power to make a final decision about complaints that cannot be settled through the pension scheme's own complaints procedures or by OPAS. Usually, OPAS will try to sort out the problem before the Pensions Ombudsman gets involved.

The Occupational Pensions Regulatory Authority (OPRA) helps to make sure that occupational pension schemes are safe and run properly. OPRA will investigate – and take action if necessary – if an occupational pension scheme puts its members at risk. Its power includes banning, fining and taking people to court if they do not run pension schemes properly. Their phone number is: 01273 627 600.

6 Individual Pensions

Employees who do not have the option of joining an occupational scheme or who do not want to join one as they are planning to move jobs in the near future, need to make their own pension provision as do the self-employed. The basic state pension is not called basic for nothing and additional savings will be required.

The main options for individuals are personal pensions and stakeholder pensions (these terms are explained later in this chapter starting on page 150). Both benefit from generous tax breaks – tax relief at the individual's highest rate on any contributions, a fund which grows free of tax and the ability to take a tax-free lump sum on retirement.

Should I opt for an individual pension rather than a company scheme?

Given the choice, most employees will be better off joining an occupational scheme because the employer usually makes a generous contribution to the scheme and pays for the costs of running the scheme.

Only if you are planning to leave the scheme within two years should you look at alternatives. This is because if you leave within two years your contributions will be refunded (less tax), your employer's contributions will be lost and you will not build up a pension. If you have a group stakeholder or a personal pension (one arranged by your employer) this will not be a problem – you can simply take this with you when you move jobs.

Is an individual pension better than savings and investments?

Usually. The tax breaks are good, but you have to buy a pension income (using an annuity) with the bulk of your money – so you cannot spend it how you like. Some people think this restricts their freedom, but at least you are guaranteed an income for life – something you may not get if you spend your savings or your investments perform badly.

However, if you are near to retirement – by a few years – or are already retired think twice before investing in a pension. Although you can invest in safe funds and do not have to risk your money on the stock market, and you will receive tax relief, you may not have sufficient time to build up a sizeable pension. More flexible options that have higher contribution limits may be a better bet – with an ISA, for example, you can invest £7,000 but many people can only invest a maximum of £3,600 in a stakeholder pension. Some annuity companies require minimum fund sizes of £10,000, so you may not have enough time to build up a sufficient fund on retirement (or before age 75) to purchase an annuity on the open market and give yourself a better return. With less than £10,000 you will have to accept the annuity rate offered by your pension provider, which may not be the best rate available.

I am worried about investing in a pension, look what has happened to Equitable Life.

The near collapse of pensions company Equitable Life knocked confidence in the pensions industry at a time when stakeholder pensions were being launched and the pensions mis-selling scandal of the late 1980s and early 1990s was finally being resolved.

The problems stemmed from guaranteed pensions or guaranteed annuity rates (GARs). Pensions were sold with generous guarantees at a time when interest rates were high. In today'slow-interest environment they became unaffordable. Policyholders (only those who had with-profits pensions were affected) voted through a so-called compromise scheme to give up their right to sue and some of the generous rights to GARs to keep the company afloat.

However, the GAR issue is not over. Equitable Life has imposed swingeing exit penalties on investors who want to transfer their money and with-profits policyholders remain vulnerable to any continuing problems. In addition, other companies have been affected by the GAR issue – although not so badly.

What the Equitable Life debacle has shown is that even the most established financial names can get into difficulties. Spreading your money between companies and investment types will reduce risks.

Read the section HOW SAFE IS MY PENSION? on page 130.

Note: Personal and stakeholder pensions can be used to opt out of the state second pension – now known as S2P but previously called SERPS – and you can contribute to your pension only your rebated National Insurance Contributions that would have paid for this pension. This is covered in Chapter 4: State Pensions and Benefits. Anyone with an existing individual pension or planning to invest in one should read that chapter.

STAKEHOLDER PENSIONS

Stakeholders became available to almost everybody in April 2001 offering flexible, tax-efficient savings for retirement. They are cheaper than most of their predecessors, personal pensions, more flexible and, for the first time, give tax relief on investing even to non-taxpayers. Designed to encourage everyone to save for retirement – even if they are not working – they have failed to be a success.

While some 637,000 schemes had been set up by the summer of 2002, 80 per cent of these remained empty with neither employees nor employers making any contributions. Why? They feel they cannot afford to. There is also concern that saving too little will simply result in a pension that is roughly the same as the income you would have got from the state under the minimum income guarantee.

Although stakeholder pensions and personal pensions have broadly the same tax regime (the same contribution limits and tax reliefs) there are differences between the two types of pension.

Generally, stakeholder pensions are cheaper and more flexible. To qualify as a stakeholder, the plan must meet certain conditions:

- Charges must be a set percentage of the pension fund to make them easy to compare (that means no separate policy fees or penalties).

- The maximum charge is 1 per cent of the fund a year (personal pension fund charges usually have charges of 1.5 per cent).

- Low charges may mean no advice. If investors want detailed advice, the plan provider can charge extra. Most do, however, offer very good basic guides, so detailed advice may not be needed.

- No charges can be made for transfers in or out of the scheme.

- Transfers should be accepted from other schemes.

- Minimum contributions must be no more than £20.

- There can be no penalties for stopping and starting contributions.

Who can invest in one?

- the self-employed

- employees with no pension provision

- members of occupational (employer schemes) who earn less than £30,000 a year

- members of occupational (employer schemes) who earn more than £30,000 a year and have a source of earnings additional to their main employment

- people with no earnings and income – stay at home mums and even children

- anyone aged under 75 (the benefits of a stakeholder must be taken at this age)

Until they were launched, only people with earnings, rather than income from investments, for example, could take out a pension plan and get tax relief on their contributions. Now you can get tax relief even if you do not pay tax.

Although stakeholders were designed to appeal to people on lower incomes who would otherwise not have any private pension provision, they have proved a valuable tax break for higher earners who are using them to boost their pension contributions by a further £3,600 a year – and receive higher-rate tax relief. It means the extra pension boost only costs them £2,160.

In addition, until stakeholders came along, employees who were members of occupational schemes were generally barred from also having a personal pension. Provided they earn no more than £30,000 (and are not controlling directors) they can now have a stakeholder, pay in up to £3,600 a year and receive tax relief on these contributions as well as having a company scheme.

So stakeholders have a broad appeal – from children to high earners to people who have already retired.

Note: Maximum contribution limits and restrictions on the amount that can be invested in different types of pension are set to be removed from April 2004.

Warning: If you are unlikely to build up a fund of at least £10,000 on retirement, think twice about investing in a stakeholder. You may not have sufficient to shop around when buying an annuity – this is the plan you must buy with the proceeds of your pension (either on retirement or before aged 75) to provide you with an income for life. You will have to take the rate offered by the pension provider. With less than £1,000 you may have too little to buy an annuity at all.

How long do I need to invest for?

The minimum period can be one day.

Basically, you can invest a gross premium of £10,000 of which £4,000 is tax relief (if you are a higher-rate taxpayer) so it has only cost you £6,000 – and you can then take £2,500 out as a tax-free lump sum leaving you with £7,500 invested – which is more than your pension has cost. Although this is a simplistic calculation that does not take into account charges, it illustrates how financially advantageous this option can be. Most stakeholder providers allow you to do this. It is called 'immediate vesting'. Some companies impose qualifying periods ranging from one day to one month or even one year.

How much can I contribute?

Everyone can contribute up to £3,600 a year and receive tax relief on these contributions at their highest rate or at 22 per cent if they are basic-rate or non-taxpayers. So as an absolute minimum the Inland Revenue contributes £792 in tax relief. Tax relief forms part of the £3,600 limit and is not in addition to it.

You can contribute as little as £1 although most schemes have a £20 minimum, and either pay in on a regular basis or as a one-off or series of lump sums.

Basic-rate tax relief is given automatically, so if you invest £50 a month, tax relief will increase your contributions to £64.10. Higher-rate tax relief needs to be claimed. This is paid as a tax rebate or will reduce the total tax liability assessed when you fill in your tax return.

Higher investment limits apply to:

- the self-employed

- employees who are not members of occupational pension schemes

- employees who are members of occupational pensions schemes and earning £30,000 or less a year (or at any time in the last five years from 2001/2002)

- employees who are members of occupational pensions schemes and earning more than £30,000 a year who also have significant additional earnings from either self-employment or another job

Note: You can have more than one stakeholder and/or personal pension. The only limit is on the total contribution.

The current contribution limits depend on a number of factors including age.

Maximum contributions as a % of net relevant earnings
to both stakeholder and personal pensions

Age on 6 April
(start of tax year)

35 or less	17.5%
36–45	20%
46–50	25%
51–55	30%
56–60	35%
61–74	40%

These limits are in turn subject to an earnings cap, which usually rises at the start of each tax year. For 2002/2003 it was £97,200. So higher earners aged 52 can contribute a maximum of:

30% × £97,200 = £29,160 a year.

The net relevant earnings that can be taken into account for employees are: salary and bonuses, less expenses or payroll donations; and for the self-employed the taxable profits of the business.

Note: From April 2004, the earnings cap and maximum contribution limits are set to be replaced with an annual £200,000 investment limit and a restriction of £1.4 million on the value of an individual's pension fund.

When can I retire?

From age 50 to 75. However, if you have a professional career that has a short life – you are a professional jockey or footballer, for example – the Inland Revenue allows you to retire earlier than aged 50. Everyone – even professional footballers and others who have benefited from early retirement – will have to retire from age 55 from 2010. Only those turning 50 in or before 2009 will still be able to retire at 50.

How much will I get when I retire?

This depends on a number of factors:

- how much you invest

- how well your investments grow

- how long you invest for – generally the longer you invest the more chance your money has to grow

- the charges taken from your stakeholder pension

- the annuity rates given at the time you retire

What could that mean in cash terms?

There are two things to assess:

- your fund on retirement

- the annuity (pension for life) that this will buy

Your fund on retirement

Let us assume that you are using a stakeholder to boost your pension near to retirement. You will probably be investing a regular amount each month (not every investor has hundreds or thousands of pounds to set aside). If you invest £50 a month (including any tax relief) for five years and the fund grows by 7 per cent a year, even with a low charging fund you will be lucky to receive £3,500 back after five years. So you would get back just £500 more than was invested. However, the pension would only have cost you £2,640 (the rest would have been tax relief) or less if you were a higher-rate taxpayer.

This assumption is based on the industry standard projection rate of 7 per cent growth per annum. There is no guarantee that your pension will perform this well and, if the last few years are to be used as an example, the amount you invest could go down in value not up.

Annuity rates

Compulsory annuities must be purchased with at least 75 per cent of your stakeholder pension fund on retirement, which can be from aged 50 (55 from 2010) and must be purchased before you reach 75. You generally need at least £10,000 to buy an annuity on the open market – enabling you to shop around for the best rate. So even investing £50 a month for ten years is going to leave you well short of the minimum required – giving you just over £8,100 assuming a 7 per cent growth rate.

However, as 4 in 10 annuities are for £10,000 or less, the government is proposing that people with small annuities can take these as a lump sum – so they will not be forced to buy an annuity in future.

Annuity rates depend on a number of factors:

- your age – the older you are, the shorter your life expectancy and therefore the higher the income you will receive

- sex – women tend to live longer than men so get a lower rate

- health – those in poor health have a shorter life expectancy and as such receive a higher income

- if you smoke – smokers get higher rates

- the annuity rates at the time you retire

Annuities are discussed in greater detail in Chapter 10: Maximizing Your Pension On Retirement.

An example of how age can affect what you may receive if you have £10,000 on retirement is as follows:

Age on retirement	Annual income
Man aged 55	£600
Man aged 60	£670
Man aged 65	£800
Man aged 70	£900

So with £10,000 on retirement you will be lucky to get an extra income of £15 a week.

To get a significant income you will need £50,000 or more.

Wouldn't I be better off with savings instead of a stakeholder?

If you are unlikely to build up a fund of £1,000 or more – yes.
The other advantages of not being tied to a pension are that you:

- don't have to buy an annuity when you retire, or by the age of 75

- you can do what you want with the money

- you can retire when you like

- you will not pay charges

- there are no risks involved

However, you will forgo up to £792 in tax relief each year – a nice handout from the government for no work whatsoever.

You can, however, let your money grow free of tax by investing in tax-free schemes such as individual savings accounts (ISAs). See Chapter 12: The Pension Alternatives for further tips. And if you have money saved rather than invested you will not be hit by stock market falls.

So stakeholders can go down in value as well as up?

Yes. All financial institutions are required to give the warning, 'The value of your investments can go down as well as up'. However, in the past, few investors heeded this advice.

Historically, the stock market has outperformed other forms of investment. It is only when the markets fall significantly that investors are reminded that shares do not rise in a straight line. If they fall before you retire – when you may not have time to sit and wait for them to recover – you can see your pension drop dramatically. Over the last few years someone with a £100,000 pension could have seen this fall to just £60,000 or less, reducing their income from £6,000 a year to £3,600.

The only option is to hold off retirement (if you can afford to) and hope that the markets recover. Of course, you do not have to invest in the stock market. As retirement approaches you are generally advised to switch to safer funds based on bond and gilt (government bond) income rather than risking your retirement savings in the stock market.

So what are the risks?

These depend on the pension fund or funds in which you invest. There are several types of investment – some are safer than others. See Choosing a Stakeholder Pension on page 161.

Following stock market falls should I stop paying into my stakeholder?

The advantage of stakeholder pensions is that you can stop and start and vary your contributions at any time without penalty. This is not the case with personal pensions. However, if you do not keep up payments – or retire earlier than expected – your pension will probably be worth less than you were expecting at retirement.

How much can I take as a lump sum?

Up to 25 per cent of the fund can be taken as a lump sum on retirement. This is known as commutation, and is tax free. The advantages are:

- You can do what you want with this money – spend it, or invest it.

- It does not have to buy you an income for life (an annuity).

- If you invest it wisely you may get a better return than from an annuity.

The rest buys a pension – how does that work?

As has already been explained you must buy a compulsory purchase annuity with at last 75 per cent of your fund.

You can take your fund from age 50 (55 from 2010) regardless of whether or not you retire, or you can delay taking it until age 75. You do not, however, have to purchase your annuity immediately.

You can delay doing so and invest the money instead. This can produce a higher return – but there are risks and no guarantees. In the meantime, you can take an income equivalent to that which you would have received had you purchased an annuity. You must then purchase an annuity when you reach 75.

There are risks with this option and it is only open to people with larger amounts to invest (£100,000). See Chapter 10: Boosting Your Pension On Retirement, for further information on annuities.

Can I boost my pension by opting out of the state second pension (S2P)?

Yes. This is known as contracting out. National Insurance rebates – equivalent to the amount that would have gone to fund your S2P – are paid by the Inland Revenue into your stakeholder pension. However, there is no guarantee that these rebates will provide a pension better than you would have received from S2P. It depends on:

- how well the rebates are invested

- the charges deducted from your stakeholder

- annuity rates when you retire

Generally, older workers will be better off sticking with S2P than younger ones. See Chapter 4: State Pensions and Benefits for further advice.

Note: There is no tax-free lump sum from the contracted-out portion of your policy and the income receive must not be taken before you reach 60 (the rules are 50 for your stakeholder pension) and no later than 75. However, pension reform may change this, allowing the contracted-out part of your pension to be included as part of any lump sum and taken at the same time as your private pension.

The following table is indicative only and shows how much better or worse off you could be by contracting out. The figures for 2002/2003 are based on a male earning an annual salary of £15,000 and assume the stakeholder has a 1 per cent charge.

Age on 5 April	S2P pension on retirement	What a stakeholder could provide if you contract out if growth after inflation is	
		1% pa	3% pa
20	£65	£40	£115
25	£65	£41	£108
30	£65	£43	£102
35	£65	£45	£96
40	£66	£48	£94
45	£74	£56	£99
50	£84	£87	£138
55	£96	£92	£133

Although National Insurance rebates rise as you get older (someone earning £15,000 a year would get a rebate of around £1,700 a year compared to the £750 paid to a 20-year-old), this money does not have so long to grow. If growth rates are low – 1 per cent in real terms – regardless of age you will generally be better off sticking with S2P. Only if you are younger and growth rates average a higher rate will you be much better contracting out.

The figures are based on those for men on below average earnings. They will be different for women who can still retire early – between 60 and 65 – and for higher earners.

So I risk being worse off if I contract out?

Yes. The replacement pension you get depends on the size of your rebate (which in turn depends on your earnings), the charges deducted from your pension, the rate of growth of the investment and annuity rates when you retire.

Can I put the pension I have built up from the state into my stakeholder?

No. You can contract out on a year by year basis only. That means you can only backdate contracting out to the start of the current tax year.

My income varies so how will the tax man know what rebate to pay?

Rebates are not paid in on a month by month basis. In fact, it takes until September or even October to pay in rebates for the previous tax year (ending 5 April). By then the Inland Revenue will have all the information on your earnings it needs.

The state lets your spouse inherit half your S2P. What happens if you contract out?

The contracted-out element will be included as part of your fund. If you die before you retire, the pension (the value of your fund) will be paid to your spouse. If you are not married your estate will receive a lump sum. If you die after retirement your spouse will get 50 per cent of the contracted-out proportion of your pension.

What if I change my mind?

If you think you will, after all, be better off in the state second pension, you can contract back in. The decision is made year by year.

Could I be better off contracting back in?

Yes. As you near retirement you will generally be better off in S2P than contracting out. Once you reach 45 you should get a financial adviser to review your situation. If you earn less than £10,000, you should also move back into the state scheme.

Choosing a Stakeholder Pension

Who Offers Stakeholder Pensions?

Practically every financial institution including banks, building societies, friendly societies and life insurance companies as well as financial advisers sell stakeholders.

A list of registered stakeholder pensions is available from the Occupational Pensions Regulatory Authority (OPAS). Either visit their website www.stakeholder.opra.gov or call the helpdesk on 01273 627 600 (it is open from 9 a.m. to 5 p.m. Monday to Friday).

What Should I Take Into Account?

Charges

There will be no initial charge and an annual charge of no more than 1 per cent. Buy through a discount broker (one that will give you no advice) and you could pay even less – as little as 0.3 per cent. Although this may seem like very little it can make a large difference to your fund on retirement. According to one recent survey, a man aged 40 investing £100 a month to retire at age 65 could pay anything between £9,540 and £14,656 in charges. This may seem high, but with a personal pension he could be charged as much as £22,500. A second survey found stakeholder charges for a man aged 30 investing £100 a month until retirement at 65 could vary from £29,000 with Legal & General to £46,000 with AXA.

The golden rule is to shop around. To check out the best deals and the effect of charges on each stakeholder visit the Financial Services Comparative tables at www.fsa.gov.uk/tables.

To illustrate the importance of comparing charges consider this: on a stakeholder plan with a premium of £200 over 30 years, investing in a pension with a 0.7 per cent charge instead of the 1 per cent charge could mean a difference of £14,000 on retirement and around £1,000 a year to your pension.

Investment fund choice

You will usually be given a choice of funds although this can be very limited, for example either keeping your money in a cash fund (like a savings account) or putting it in a managed fund.

The main fund types are as follows:

With-profit funds: These funds smooth out rises and falls in the stock market by investing in a wide range of investments – not just shares but also property, cash and fixed-income investments. Investors earn their money through bonuses (known as reversionary bonuses), which are usually added to the fund each year. In good years the fund holds back some of the returns so that there will be sufficient to pay bonuses in bad years. This irons out the fluctuations in the markets. Once added, these reversionary bonuses cannot be taken away. This smoothing prevents large swings in the levels of bonuses from year to year. The level of future bonuses is not normally guaranteed: they can be lower than previous ones or in some years they may not be paid at all. In addition, investors earn a final or terminal bonus when their pension matures (they take their pension). Bonus rates have been cut in recent years, but with-profits have remained true to their aim and have suffered less from stock market falls than the other main investment choice, unit-linked funds. Stakeholder pension investors, however, rarely get access to these funds as only a few providers give this as an option.

Unit-linked Funds: These invest directly in the stock market and rise and fall as it does. The fund is divided into units of equal value and investors purchase units with their contributions. The value of these units is assessed daily and depends on the underlying value of the investments held by the fund divided by the number of units. When the stock markets were booming these were considered a better bet because of the superior performance of some funds. Even so, some perform badly and there is a much greater variation in performance than among with-profits funds, so it is vital to make your choice carefully.

The main types of unit-linked fund offered by stakeholder pensions are:

- Cash funds – these are basically deposit accounts and are offered so that people approaching retirement or waiting to make an investment choice can keep their money in a safe fund. Other safe funds include retirement protection, and low-risk include protected or safety funds.

- Passive funds – these are mainly tracker funds which track a stock-market index, usually the FTSE All Share or sometimes the

FTSE 100. They are not actively managed – instead a computer ensures that the fund mirrors the performance of the index. There will often be some underperformance compared to this index to take account of charges. Some passive funds do not track and index but instead invest in a balanced portfolio.

• Actively managed – the investment choices are made by fund managers who aim (but often fail) to beat the performance of the stock market or a particular sector. They split into (with the lowest risk first):

  • *Fixed-interest – these invest in government and corporate bonds and tend to have a low-risk approach.*

  • *Managed – general funds with a wide spread of investments. Can also be called balanced managed or cautious managed.*

  • *Growth – these have different degrees of risk but most UK growth funds are broadly invested. The larger the number of shares held, the lower the risk. However, if the fund invests in one market (the UK for example) and that is hit, the wide number of holdings are no protection, although a well-managed fund should suffer less.*

  • *Geographical sectors such as North American, European or Japan funds.*

  • *Investment sectors – these are more specialist and therefore more risky and include technology and property.*

Unitized With-profits: These are similar to the above. Investors buy units in a fund but also benefit from bonuses. Depending on the stakeholder pension, you can invest in anything from one to 19 different funds at any one time.

Note: Tracker funds are one of the predominant investment choices for stakeholder pension funds. However, these are exposed to stock-market risk because they do not invest in any safer investments such as bonds.

Minimum contributions

These can be as low as £1 a month but generally the minimum is £20. As has already been explained you should be looking to invest far more than this. You can make monthly as well as lump sum contributions.

Flexibility

You can expect to be able to reduce contributions (to the minimum) and take contribution holidays without penalty.

Large investment bonus

Known as a loyalty bonus this really is a bonus for investment of more than a minimum amount – for example, £10,000. This usually takes a few years to build up although some investors may invest this amount in lump sums. They also benefit people who are transferring a lump sum into a stakeholder from an existing pension, and usually lead to a lower annual management charge.

Investment performance

Remember past performance is no guarantee of future performance. Investment choice is not everything – a provider with one or two low-charging, high-performing funds may be a better bet than a stakeholder with half a dozen investment choices. However, choice *is* important – if one sector or type of fund is hit, if you have choice you can switch to a safer bet such as a cash fund.

Although you cannot predict future performance, you can check:

• Consistency – that past performance is consistently good. It avoid funds that do spectacularly well one moment but have performed badly before that.

- The fund manager – how long he/she has been in the job, the back-up and support team and past performance.

- Investment goals – does the fund aim to have a broad spread of investments or adopt a higher-risk approach?

- Fads and fashions – is the fund the latest investment fad? Look what happened to technology funds. If you are investing for 20 years you want a fund manager that looks for long-term not for short-term profits.

Unit-linked v. With-profits

Until the recent stock-market falls unit-linked pensions were viewed as a better bet than with-profits for younger investors (although older investors were advised to opt for the safety of a with-profits fund). However, this has now changed. The following past-performance figures (for personal pensions because stakeholders have not been around for long enough) show how much investors would have received from the two types of fund.

PAST PERFORMANCE

	With-profits			Unit-linked		
Term	Average	lowest performance	highest	Average	lowest performance	highest
15 years	£36,222	£29,858	£46,828	£19,746	£16,924	£22,965
20 years	£83,687	£63,010	£116,386	£39,745	£34,123	£60,271

Source: Life & Pensions Moneyfacts, January 2003

These figures assume a man retiring at the age of 65 years having contributed a gross annual premium of £1,000. The figures show the accumulated cash fund after the charges have been deducted.

With-profits funds have far outperformed unit-linked funds. Even over the shorter term when more with-profits funds have turned into unitized with-profits funds, the unit-linked personal pensions underperform.

A man retiring at the start of 2003 aged 65 after contributing £200 a month for 10 years into an average with-profits pension would receive a £33,727 payout, producing an income of around £2,530 a year. The average balanced managed fund, however, would pay £23,433, providing an annual income of just £1,757. Yet unit-linked pensions have outsold with-profits plans since 1988.

Payouts on with-profits personal pension plans have plunged by 28 per cent since 1997, when Gordon Brown imposed taxes of £5 billion a year on pension funds, according to *Money Management* magazine. Where investments of £200 a month over 10 years would have produced an average fund of £42,650 in 1997, by 2003 this had dropped to £30,615.

Maturity values on unit-linked personal pensions have slumped by 38 per cent over the same period with a £200 a month investment producing £38,315 in 1997 but only £23,540 six years later – £460 LESS than the amount paid in. At the same time, the retirement income these pensions could buy has fallen by a third over the same period. In 1997, a £100,000 pension pot would have bought a man aged 65 a fixed annual income of £10,800 – by early 2003 this had dropped to £7,400.

Note: Some with-profits funds are under pressure. Falling stock markets have led to sharp cuts in bonus rates and there are concerns about the solvency of a very few funds. As a result, the with-profits performance is unlikely to be repeated. The strong performance is mainly down to the fact that with-profits funds smooth out rises and falls in the markets – however, they still suffer when share prices plummet.

The average with-profits pension has fallen by almost 18 per cent over the last five years (to the start of 2003). Terminal bonuses used to account for as much as 70 per cent of the final payout – that has now shrunk to under 20 per cent and some companies no longer pay final bonuses on 10-year pension plans.

Who Offers With-profits Pensions?

Sadly, very few providers. Of the 28 stakeholder pensions reviewed for a survey published in September 2002, only three offered a with-profits option – Norwich Union, Standard Life and CIS.

If you do not want to invest with one of these companies or believe that a different company has a better with-profits fund you will have to invest in a personal pension. Most personal pensions sold today have similar charges to stakeholders, but not all – you have been warned.

Lifestyle Pensions

Many stakeholder pensions offer a 'lifestyle' choice. This is a fund that changes its investment remit depending on your age.

Because one third of all people taking out personal pensions stopped paying into them within the first three years, pension providers have tried to overcome this problem by offering a pension that is flexible enough to cope with lifestyle changes. When you are young and adventurous, and have the luxury of time, you can take a higher degree of risk. As you move through your working life to the prospect of retirement, you can start to move your money into more stable, less volatile funds. Lifestyle pensions tend to offer three basic investment options: cautious, balanced and adventurous. But the aim is the same: to offer various levels of risk/return.

Making an Informed Choice

What information should I be given to make my choice?

A projection of what you will receive on retirement which is likely to be one of the biggest factors affecting your decision. As from April 2003 all pension forecasts must be in today's terms instead of the telephone number projections given previously. This statutory money purchase illustration (SMPI) must be given every year.

So you should be told in cash terms what you would get to spend when you retire at today's prices. However, the forecast will still make certain assumptions.

- If you do not keep up your contributions, you will get less.

- If the stock market continues to fall, you will also get less.

- If you retire earlier than the date given, your pension will be reduced.

In addition, projections *can* assume a rate of investment growth. This is under review and at present is 7 per cent. This may not be realistic in the current market. An annuity rate is also assumed which may or may not be the rate you could achieve on retirement. The current assumed rate is 2.4 per cent a year in excess of inflation. The projection may also assume that your pension increases in line with inflation each year (it may not) and may or may not make correct assumptions about widow/widower's pensions.

So all projections assume the same growth rate even though performance varies widely.

However, the projection will take into account the actual charges of the fund. This shows that charges can vary by hundreds of pounds over the term of a 25-year pension plan; although they eat into returns, poor performance also has an impact but no account is taken of this in the forecasts.

Warning: The new SMP1 illustrations may not be given to you when you take out your pension. You should ask for one. Someone paying £100 a month gross into their fund over 35 years will have seen a quoted estimated fund of £140,000 (based on 7 per cent per annum investment growth) at age 60. Take into account inflation at 2.5 per cent and the buying power of £140,000 is more than halved to £59,000.

Where can I go for help in making my decision?

You are advised to seek independent financial advice. Before doing so visit the Stakeholder Pension Decision Tree at the Financial Services Authority website www.fsa.gov.uk/comsumer/decision_ trees.

If you have any questions about stakeholder pensions you can also contact the Pensions Advisory Service (OPAS) helpline on 0845 601 2923. It can give you guidance on stakeholder pensions but not individual, professional financial advice, for that you will need to contact a financial adviser. See Chapter 15: Getting Advice for further information.

Should I seek financial advice?

The low charges imposed on stakeholder pensions may mean you find it difficult to get independent financial advice without having to pay a fee. Check that any stakeholders that do NOT pay a commission to the adviser are also considered before he or she decides which one is the best for you.

If you know that a stakeholder is the right decision for you and you simply want to buy the cheapest deal you can forgo advice and buy instead from a discount broker. These pass on the commission that the salesman would have earned from selling you a stakeholder. It may be just 10 per cent off (bringing the costs down to 0.9 per cent a year); however, the savings add up. For example, a 25-year-old paying £100 per month for 35 years would pay £29,064 in charges when buying direct (with no advice) from one provider, and £46,372 if he received advice from another.

However, you should seek advice about contracting out of the state second pension (S2P). If you contract out you will give up your entitlement to this state second pension and will instead receive National Insurance rebates with which you can build up a replacement pension. You will not be able to contract out if you have already done so through your employer's scheme and you are using your stakeholder as a top-up pension instead of an AVC.

See Chapter 4: State Pensions and Benefits for further advice.

Generally, if you are around 50 you have some key decisions to make. As a first step, you can ask the pension provider for a comparison of the S2P you will be giving up and the possible replacement pension you might get from the stakeholder. Remember you are giving up a pension that is certain for one that relies on stock market performance.

You will also need on-going advice. Deciding to contract out today may not be the best idea next year or the year after. You should also reassess your pension contributions regularly to make sure your retirement plans are on track.

What information will I be given after I have made my choice?

After making your choice, but before signing the proposal you should receive:

The 'Key Features' Document: this is the most important piece of paper you should read. It sets out the important details of the stakeholder or personal pension including: your date of birth, your chosen retirement age, commencement date and current annual earnings.

Contributions: How much you will invest, for how long and whether these premiums will increase – for example, in line with inflation or by a set amount – say by 5 per cent. The figure should include tax relief.

Projected Value of the Pension on Retirement: (This is not guaranteed.) All insurance companies use the same rates of growth for illustrations – 5 per cent, 7 per cent and 9 per cent – but their charges vary.

What This Could Mean on Retirement: What you might get as a tax-free lump sum and as a projected income each year. Once again, all companies use the same rates to show how funds may be converted into pension income.

A Warning: If you transfer or take early retirement during the early years, the value of your pension fund could be less than you have paid in.

Charges: How the charges will eat into your investment (known as a reduction in yield). These are given for years 1–5 and years 10, 15, 20 and 25, if the plan lasts that long. For example (the following is based on a personal pension not a stakeholder and on the projections given when 7 per cent growth rates were assumed):

Year	Lump sum paid in including tax relief	Total actual deductions to date	Effect of deductions to date	Projected transfer value
5	£15,000	£2,090	£2,470	£18,500
10	£15,000	£4,330	£6,060	£23,000
15	£15,000	£7,160	£11,700	£29,600
20	£15,000	£10,700	£20,600	£37,300

Investors may be horrified to discover that after 20 years their insurance company has charged them over £10,000 to invest their pension and that if the money had been invested instead of swallowed up in charges this would have been worth over £20,000 extra in their pocket. Worse, after 20 years they could have built up a pension of nearly £60,000 had they not had to pay charges.

A second projection for the same amount invested over the same term but with different charges is as follows:

Year	Lump sum paid in including tax relief	Total actual deductions to date	Effect of deductions to date	Projected transfer value
5	£15,000	£791	£985	£2,000
10	£15,000	£1,430	£4,060	£27,300
15	£15,000	£2,300	£4,060	£37,300
20	£15,000	£3,490	£7,120	£50,900

This shows just how charges affect what you get when you retire.

Warning: You will not get these sorts of comparisons when you buy your pension. You will only be given an illustration of the effect of charges for the pension you are being recommended. So you may never know just how much worse or better off you could be by opting for a different pension.

The pension provider will then show how the charges reduce the investment growth. For example, if the pension fund grows by 7 per cent a year, charges will bring this down to 4.6 per cent a year.

If the stock market falls – as it has done – the charges will simply compound these losses.

Charges should be specified and are likely to include:

- An annual management charge (up to 1 per cent per annum for stakeholders – and that should be the only charge). This could increase in future.

- An initial charge which can be up to 5 per cent for personal pensions.

- A fund-based fee (for example, 0.5 per cent of the value of the fund).

Some plans pay a loyalty bonus, for example, 1 per cent of the value of units every five years.

As part of the new government's statutory money purchase illustration (SMPI) rules introduced in 2003, pension firms will be required to give individuals a yearly illustration of their money purchase pension benefits in real terms – in today's prices, assuming inflation of 2.5 per cent a year. It is likely that this projection will be included in the key features document. This is currently optional, but under review.

Commission: How much the adviser will earn for spending an hour or so (if you are lucky) flogging you the pension. It will be shown in cash terms for the amount at the commencement of your pension plus what they get each year – a percentage of the encashment value of the pension and a fund-based fee (for example 0.5 per cent of the encashment value of your pension).

If some or all of the commission is rebated the total paid may be very low – £50 or £100 a year.

Investments: Where your money is invested and the investment remit of each fund.

A Your Right To Change Your Mind Notice: once you have signed the proposal and invested your first premium you will receive this notice. You will usually have a minimum of 14 days within which to cancel the agreement, although most pension providers give you 30 days.

However, if you bought the product on an 'execution only' basis – direct and with no advice – you do not automatically have this right.

If you cancel, there should be no charges, but a deduction may be made from the repayment in respect of any market fall in investments between the date you paid the money into the pension and the date on which notice of cancellation is received.

What if I cannot decide on a particular fund?

All stakeholders have a default fund where contributions are invested automatically unless you choose a particular investment fund. This default fund will either be a safe option – a managed fund or a lifestyle option – but could be a tracker, which is open to the full volatility of the stock market. Safety first may be fine if you are an older investor but not if you are younger when a tracker may be more suitable. The only snag is that only one default fund can be offered per stakeholder so this has to appeal to old and young and those wary of risk as well as those prepared to take some risk in the hope of a higher return.

After You've Taken Out Your Stakeholder

What information should I receive after that?

Every year you should receive an annual statement showing:

- how much has been invested

- the tax relief given

- how your fund is growing

It will also include a forecast of how much you might receive as a pension. This is the statutory money purchase illustration (SMPI) which will be sent to policyholders once a year. Projections in the past have not taken inflation into account, even though this impacts on the buying power of the pension you will receive when you retire.

The SMPI will:

- Give customers an estimate of how much their pension might be in today's prices at their selected retirement date.

- Show the pension income (annuity) figure on an index-linked basis (so that it rises in line with increases in the retail price index – the standard inflation index). It will also allow for the cost of providing a continuing pension payable to the widow or widower of one half of the policyholder's own pension.

- Change the annuity rates used – these must take into account changes in interest rates (on which annuity rates depend) every year. This will give a more accurate picture.

It is calculated by projecting forward the current fund value plus any additional contributions that are expected with an assumed rate of growth of 7 per cent per annum less any management charges until the selected retirement date. Inflation – of 2.5 per cent each year (the Bank of England's long-term inflation target) is then taken into account discounting the growth figure back to the date the projection is given. This gives a fund's buying power in real terms.

What if I am not happy with my stakeholder pension?

You can transfer your investments to a different fund with the same stakeholder provider at no extra cost, although some limit the switches that can be made within a year free of charge.

Alternatively, you can transfer your accumulated pension to:

- another stakeholder provider

- an occupational pension scheme

- a personal pension

Stakeholder pensions cannot charge for transfers out of the scheme (unlike other types of pension).

Warning: Recent stock market falls mean that if you switch from a with-profits fund the company can impose a market value adjuster (MVA), or surrender value reduction (SVR), which can knock as much as 20 per cent off the value of your fund.

What should I do if I already have a personal pension?

You can continue to contribute to your existing personal pension. However, compare the charges with the stakeholder. Many personal pension providers have brought their charges into line with stakeholder schemes but some still charge more.

If the stakeholder is cheaper you may consider switching your accumulated pension into the stakeholder. However, check if there will be any penalties and what the charges are for switching because these can wipe out much of the gains you will make from moving to a low-charging stakeholder.

Some older-style personal pensions had front-end charges, which meant the bulk of the charges were taken in the first few years. After that, charges drop significantly. If this is the case, you may be no better off switching, because you have already paid these charges and the on-going annual charges are 1 per cent or less.

If you cannot afford to contribute to both the personal pension and the stakeholder you can leave your personal pension paid up. The money will continue to grow, but charges will eat into this return. Be sure to check if there is a penalty for doing this.

Can I make transfers into a stakeholder pension?

Yes. You may find that transferring pensions from a former employer or a personal pension into a low-cost and flexible stakeholder leaves you better off. However, as you will usually pay charges or penalties for transferring out of another pension, you could find these losses outweigh any potential benefits.

What happens if I change jobs?

You can simply keep the stakeholder pension going. If you have the chance to join a good occupational scheme you may consider doing so and either:

- leave your stakeholder where it is

- transfer it to the occupational scheme (if it accepts transfers – not all do)

- keep it going (you can be a member of an occupational scheme and contribute up to £3,600 a year to a stakeholder provided you earn less than £30,000 a year)

Alternatively, you can keep your stakeholder going and ask your employer to contribute to the stakeholder – an option if you are unlikely to remain with your employer for very long or if the scheme is a money-purchase one with few additional benefits.

What happens if I need my money before retirement?

You cannot take money out of your pension until you are aged 50. So once you have invested, your money is tied up until that age. However, you do not have to retire to take your pension.

What happens when I retire?

You can take your pension – although you do not have to. You can delay until you are 75 and even continue contributing to your stakeholder should you wish.

Once you take your pension you must decide on the tax-free lump sum. You can take up to 25 per cent out of the fund, but it will eat into the pension you receive. The remainder must be used to purchase an annuity to provide you with an income for the rest of your life. You must do this by the age of 75. See Chapter 10: Maximizing Your Pension On Retirement for further tips and advice.

You will generally have to nominate a retirement age when you take out your stakeholder. Check there are no penalties if you want to change this date.

Self-invested Schemes: the individual manages his or her own investment and can invest in either insurance company funds, individual shares, gilts or bonds.

How can I boost my stakeholder pension?

The simple answer is 'invest more'. But what if you have already reached the investment limits – either £3,600 a year or the maximum allowable percentage of your net relevant earnings? (These limits may be removed from April 2004.)

Carry Back: This enables you to use up unused tax relief from the previous tax year. Not only does it help boost your pension but you also get more tax benefits. You can only carry back a contribution if you did not invest the maximum allowed in the previous tax year. You can make your contribution by 31 January (the current tax year) and elect for it to be treated as being paid in the previous tax year (up to 5 April) to use up your unused pension allowance.

You need to complete Inland Revenue form PP43 when you make your carry-back application. Basic-rate taxpayers should send in the original, but only a copy is required for higher-rate taxpayers who should send the original to the Inland Revenue with your self-assessment tax return.

The following rules apply in electing to carry back.

- Contributions cannot be carried back more than one year.

- Election must be made by 31 January in the current tax year, i.e. carry back is not available between 1 February and 5 April.

- The election to carry back must be made before or at the time the contributions are paid.

- It is not possible to carry back an employer's contribution.

- Contribution limits are as per the previous tax year.

The Basis Year Rules: You can also boost the amount you invest in your stakeholder by using a different year's earnings as your basis year. Because you can only pay in a maximum percentage of your earnings (if you want to contribute over £3,600) you will be able to contribute more if you elect a year with the highest earnings. You can use the best year's earnings from the last five years under the rules.

The rules mean that if you suffer a dramatic drop in salary or even have no earnings at all you can continue to make contributions over £3,600 for up to five years.

If you are contributing to a stakeholder at the same time as being a member of an occupational pension scheme (known as concurrency) you can still elect for a different basis year to the current tax year.

It may sometimes pay to elect a year with lower earnings. If your earnings increase to over £30,000, you can no longer have a stakeholder and be a member of an occupational pension scheme. By electing for a basis year with earnings of £30,000 or less you can continue to contribute to the stakeholder for up to five years.

Note: if contribution limits (up to a maximum of £200,000 a year) are scrapped, you will simply be able to pay in what you want.

Personal Pension Plans

So far, this chapter has concentrated on stakeholder pensions, which offer a good choice of investments, are flexible and have low costs. They were introduced by the government in April 2001 because personal pensions – the existing type of individual pension – were often high-charging, inflexible, poor performing, had high minimum investments, usually £50 or even £100 per month, and were widely mis-sold. But fewer than 1 per cent of the 4.5 million personal-pension investors bothered to switch their high-charging plans for low-cost stakeholders in the first year. As a result, it is estimated that they are being overcharged by £2 billion. However, personal pensions were not withdrawn from sale.

You may be wondering who would want to buy a personal pension when they appear to offer worse value for money than stakeholders. Well, they can still be worthwhile because:

- The investment choice is often greater. Strong performance can easily cover any extra charges – although there is no guarantee that a higher-charging pension will perform any better than one with low charges.

- Personal pension charges have come down. Many providers have cut their charges to nearer or equal those they levy on their stakeholder pensions.

- Only three out of the main 28 stakeholder providers offer with-profits funds as an investment choice. See the section on Investment Performance on page 165 earlier in this chapter.

Until 2002/2003 you could not carry back a pension contribution to a previous tax year with a stakeholder pension. Carry back enables you to maximize the overall contribution as well as your tax relief if you did not pay in the maximum contribution allowed in the previous tax year.

However, the biggest difference between stakeholder and personal pensions is the amount you pay in charges and the confusing way these charges are levied. This tends to work to the advantage of financial advisers who often have an incentive to recommend personal pensions rather than stakeholder pensions because the commission they earn is higher. The charges that can be deducted from a £100, 25-year personal pension taken out by a man aged 40 (and assuming 7 per cent per annum growth) can be as much as £22,500 for a personal pension. With a stakeholder you can expect to pay as little as £9,500 – still a sizeable amount.

So why such a difference in costs?

Investors are paying for not only investment performance but also for marketing and promotions and – of course – the lucrative commission of often £2,500 or more up-front plus an ongoing kick-back paid to the salesman.

Is this why personal pensions have such a bad name?

The real problem stemmed from when personal pension plans were introduced in 1988 offering generous incentives to contract out of the then state second pension, SERPS. Personal pensions were widely mis-sold to millions of employees who would have been better off joining or remaining in their employer's schemes and to people who would have been better off if they did not contract out. Over three million people were affected. Compensation reaching £11 billion has so far been paid for mis-selling and pension providers have been named, shamed and fined.

The selling of these schemes has since been more stringently regulated. However, a second wave of pensions mis-selling could occur if individuals are recommended to take out a personal pension plan rather than a stakeholder scheme, because personal pension plans are usually far less flexible and have higher charges than the new stakeholder pensions.

What should I do if I have an existing personal pension?

People who invest in personal pension plans should not automatically switch to the new stakeholder schemes. Some personal pension plans impose penalties on planholders who wish to transfer their pension plan to a different provider, which can mean that even though the value of the pension plan may be several thousand pounds, only a few hundred may be given as a transfer value.

Investors unhappy with the performance or charges of their personal pension plan have several options:

- Leave their pension paid up (make no additional contributions) and start up a stakeholder pension, but check first what penalties will be charged. They can then take their pension from this personal pension when they reach 50.

- Continue with the personal pension. If the personal pension provider has reduced charges to bring them into line with stakeholders and performance is good, you should not be worse off unless there are particular features of the stakeholder that are not available.

- Switch to a different investment fund(s). If poor performance is the problem and charges are competitive, ask if you can switch to a different fund offered by the same pension provider. These switches can be done for no or little cost.

- Transfer the accumulated pension to a stakeholder pension. Check first on the size of the penalty charged.

Warning: If you have a personal pension with a guaranteed annuity rate (GAR) do NOT give this up. Most GARs are far, far higher than the annuity rates payable today. By switching to a stakeholder you would lose this valuable benefit. However, several companies have scrapped annual and terminal bonuses for with-profits pensions that have guarantees because the guaranteed funds are worth more than the underlying assets. As such, your pension may not be growing.

So personal pensions can be better than stakeholders?

Yes – GARs are no longer offered, so they are worth holding on to. The high rates are what caused problems for Equitable Life which ran into financial difficulties after selling pensions with annuity rates that have proved very costly to the company.

Even if your personal pension does not have a GAR it still may work out better value than a stakeholder, because of the way charges, known as front-end loading, were levied on personal pensions. The bulk of charges are deducted in the first few years (poor value for a large number of investors as many would have ceased paying into their pension within ten years). As a result, if you have had a personal pension for a number of years you would already have paid these charges. Your annual charges could now be 1 per cent or less – comparable to or even lower than those taken out of a stakeholder pension.

So maybe I should stick with my personal pension?

Despite the benefits of a few personal pension plans listed above, they are generally much poorer value than stakeholders.

A recent paper from the Financial Services Authority (FSA), called *To switch or not to switch, that's the question*, discovered that only 1 per cent of the 4.5 million pension policyholders in Britain switch schemes each year. So despite the advent of much cheaper and more flexible pensions, most policyholders have not taken advantage of these changes. The report found that while stakeholder pensions have maximum charges of 1 per cent a year, some personal pensions have charges as high as 3.8 per cent a year.

The majority of personal pensions sold more than ten years ago still have high charges – and many of these have poor performing funds, so the costs are not even covered by improved performance.

So how do I make the decision?

It is not easy.

The FSA paper, entitled *To switch or not to switch that's the question*, which is available from the FSA or at www.fsa.gov.uk under publications, is 35 pages long and includes tables, graphs and some hard to understand terms.

However, the answer comes down to cost.

- Are the annual charges higher on your personal pension than for a stakeholder pension?

- How long will it take you to make up for any penalties or losses on transferring your money from the personal pension out of the savings you make on switching to a lower-charging stakeholder pension? Generally, the younger you are when you switch the longer you have to make up for the losses suffered on exit penalties.

Warning: If you have invested in a with-profits policy you may suffer what is known as a market value adjuster (MVA) or surrender value reductioin (SVR). Following stock market falls, life companies have imposed these extra exit penalties to stop investors switching out of the with-profits fund. These losses could make it very difficult for you to recoup from the savings you make from lower charges.

If my pension provider has a stakeholder can't I just switch to that?

Yes. Some pension providers allow their customers with personal pensions to switch to their new stakeholder scheme at little or no cost. If yours will let you do this, take the offer up.

The golden rule is to talk to your personal pension provider first before taking any action.

How much can I invest?

The investment limits are the same as for stakeholder pensions – up to 40 per cent of your earnings depending on age. These limits are due to be scrapped from April 2004.

What can I invest in?

More funds than are usually available for stakeholder pensions. However, for the definition of the different types of fund and their relatively performance see the section on Investment Fund Choice on page 162.

What are the tax breaks?

The same as for stakeholder pensions – your contributions attract tax relief at your highest rate, the fund grows free of tax and, on retirement, you can take up to 25 per cent as a tax-free lump sum.

What help and advice should I get if I want to invest in a personal pension?

You are unlikely to buy a personal pension. Unlike stakeholders (which can be bought direct very cheaply) personal pensions tend to be sold by financial advisers so you will generally receive advice.

As with a stakeholder pension you should get a key features document once you have been recommended a personal pension which sets out the important details of the stakeholder or personal pension including:

- Personal information – your date of birth, chosen retirement age, commencement date and current annual earnings.

- Contributions – how much you will invest and for how long.

- Projected value of the pension on retirement (this is not
  guaranteed). All insurance companies use the same rates of
  growth for illustrations – 5 per cent, 7 per cent and 9 per cent –
  but their charges vary, so the projection should show what this
  could mean on retirement for the tax-free lump sum and for the
  projected income each year. Once again, all companies use the
  same rates to show how funds may be converted into pension
  income.

- A warning that if you transfer or take early retirement during
  the early years, the value of your pension fund could be less
  than you have paid in.

- Details of charges and how these will eat into your investment
  returns (reducing the rate of growth from 7 per cent to 4.6 per
  cent, for example) and the effect of the deductions on the value
  of your pension over 1–5 years and every five years thereafter.

- Commission – how much the adviser is being paid as an initial
  and an annual commission.

- Investments – where your money is invested and the investment
  remit of each fund.

Warning: Personal pensions tend to be far more expensive than stakeholder
pensions but you may not be informed of this. You will only be given an
illustration of the effect of charges for the pension you are being recommended,
so you may never know just how much worse or better off you could be by
opting for a different pension.

Once you have signed the proposal and invested your first premium
you will receive: a your right to change your mind notice. You
should also be told of your rights to cancel and change your mind.
You will usually have 14 days within which to cancel the agreement
although most providers give you 30 days.

What if I cannot or could not afford to keep up my pension contributions?

This is not a problem with a stakeholder which allows you to stop, start and vary your contributions without penalty, whereas some older-style personal pensions imposed penalties on those who failed to keep up their contributions.

Warning: One in three people sold personal pensions stopped paying into them within the first three years. The charges on the fund will simply erode what little you have invested.

With some policies you could take out a 'waiver of premium' policy, which pays your premiums if you cannot work due to disability or ill-health. The costs could be high – up to 6 per cent of the premium paid and the restrictions onerous, with strict definitions on what constitutes permanent disability and inability to work. In some cases you must be unable to perform any occupation at all and not be able to perform a number of activities of daily living. However, changes in pension legislation mean it is no longer possible to include a waiver of premium option as an integral part of your pension contract.

What should I do with the personal pension I took out years ago and then forgot?

You may have taken out an appropriate personal pension. These were also known as rebate-only personal pensions and were set up purely to accept National Insurance rebates for employees contracting out of the state second pension (SERPS). If you then joined a company scheme, opted back into SERPS or took out a separate pension and left that one behind, you could find your SERPS rebates are being eroded by high charges.

If you have any old personal pensions, you are strongly advised to switch these to stakeholders. The first generation of personal pensions offered very poor value for money.

My financial adviser recommended a personal pension even though I thought he would opt for a stakeholder.

Financial advisers are supposed to give you suitable advice. However, the financial incentive is to recommend a personal pension because the commission paid is usually higher. Salesmen who work for just one life insurance company which may not have a stakeholder, do not have to advise you to go elsewhere and will simply recommend the best product from the range the company they work for (or are tied to) offers. Even independent financial advisers, who should be impartial, can be swayed by commission.

Your best bet is to pay for advice. The charges of stakeholder pensions do not cover much commission, so for a thorough review of your financial needs you may be better off paying a fee. At least you will know the advice you are getting is not then swayed by commission (any of which, incidentally, will be invested in your pension not put into the adviser's pocket). Or you can take advantage of new generic advice.

See Chapter 15: Getting Advice for details of how to find a financial adviser.

Warning: Before switching from a with-profits fund check that the company has not imposed a market value adjuster (MVA) or surrender value reduction (SVR). This takes account of falling share values and can cut 20 per cent off the value of your fund should you want to switch to a different provider.

So who should take out a personal pension?

Mainly people wanting a wider investment choice. Some personal pensions, for example, allow you to choose from a range of investment managers.

Performance is just as – if not more than – important than charges and flexibility. If you believe you can get a better performance with a personal pension you may forgo some of the benefits of a stakeholder. In addition, if you want to make your own investment decisions you should opt for a self-invest personal pension (SIPP). These are discussed later in this chapter on page 191.

What are the charges?

This is where it gets confusing. With a stakeholder there is only one charge – up to 1 per cent of what the pension is worth as an annual charge. With a personal pension there can be:

- Policy fees of as much as £3 per month or £80 for lump sums.

- Initial charges – although most pension providers no longer charge these.

- Annual charges – either a percentage of between 0.2–1.5 per cent.

- Bid/offer spreads – again this is less common, but there can be a difference of up to 5 per cent between the price you pay for units in a fund and the price you are paid when you sell.

- Allocation rates – these are the most confusing of all. You may think that 100 per cent of what you contribute is invested. Not so. It can be as little as 90 per cent. However, it can also be higher – say 102.5 per cent. This means that for every £100 you contribute £102.50 is allocated to the fund. Sounds generous? Well the pension provider makes its money (usually far more than with a stakeholder) in other ways and high allocation rates are usually only given if the financial adviser is prepared to take a cut in commission.

- Switching fees – most providers offer free switches between investment funds (or a limited number of free switches) but some can charge as much as £50 to switch from one fund to another.

- Market value adjusters (MVA) or surrender value reduction (SVR) – these apply to unitized with-profits investments only. Basically, if the stock market falls dramatically, some of the guaranteed bonuses that have been added to your pension are clawed back by adjusting the value of any investments taken out of the fund on retirement or if you are transferring the pension.

On the plus side, investors may also qualify for a loyalty bonus. So many pensions are paid up (contributions are no longer made) within ten years, that bonuses are given by a very few pension providers as an incentive to keep investing. Investors with large lump sums to invest may also get a bonus.

What to do if you think you have been mis-sold a personal pension

Between 1988 and 1994 pension salesmen raked in vast amounts of commission selling personal pensions to some people who should never have been advised to take them out mainly because it involved them leaving an employer's scheme or the state scheme even though they would lose financially.

The selling of some 1.6 million personal pension plans has so far been reviewed and a total of £11.5 billion in compensation has been paid. A few cases are still being looked into but most have now been resolved.

So if I was given bad advice I should have been informed?

Yes. All personal pension providers have had to review past cases to check to see if people were wrongly advised. If this appeared to be the case, they should have contacted you. If they had insufficient information to assess whether or not the advice you were given was bad, they should still have contacted you to ask whether or not you want to claim compensation.

If you missed the review or were not contacted, first complain to the firm that sold you the plan. You may, for example, have moved and have a paid-up personal pension, which you had forgotten about.

However, most cases should have already been resolved, so it is unlikely that you were a victim of pensions mis-selling and remain unaware of it.

Having said that, in the summer of 2002, the Financial Services Authority (FSA), the city regulator, fined Royal & Sun Alliance £1.35 million for failing to uncover up to 13,500 customers whose cases should have been reviewed as part of the mis-selling review. The redress, which may otherwise have been overlooked, exceeds £32 million.

What you can do if your pension has run into problems

The recent stock market falls have left many investors nursing losses including those who have invested in personal pensions. However, you cannot get compensation for this poor performance or for the quality of advice given. So you will have to bear the losses yourself.

Only if the life company goes bust or if the adviser was fraudulent (for example, he ran off with your investment) will you get some compensation and even then that is limited to a maximum of £48,000.

What happens if my life company suffers in the same way as Equitable Life?

If you are an Equitable Life customer, you have probably been bombarded with offers to transfer your pension elsewhere and should, probably, have taken these up (unless you have a guaranteed annuity) even if you had to suffer the huge penalties for doing so. Only with-profits policyholders are affected by these penalties although all policyholders may be worried about the future of their pensions. The unit-linked business was bought by HBoS (formerly Halifax and Bank of Scotland).

For other companies to be affected they would have had to offer guaranteed annuity rates (GAR), but even these companies are not in as difficult a situation as Equitable.

In the case of Equitable Life, policyholders voted to waive their rights to these generous pensions in exchange for policy uplifts of, on average, 17.5 per cent. Those with non-GAR pensions received uplifts of 2.5 per cent. In exchange they agreed not to sue the company. People who had already left Equitable Life before the compromise deal was agreed in January 2002 can still take legal action.

What if I am still with Equitable Life?

If you are a member of the with-profits fund you will suffer heavily if you transfer your pension. This penalty started at 10 per cent and is now 20 per cent of your fund. If you are over 50 you should consider taking your pension. If you have guaranteed annual bonus rates you should consider staying. If you have more than 10 years to go before you can take your benefits you should consider moving to a new provider. There are fears about the solvency of Equitable Life.

Self-invest Personal Pensions

Reluctant to keep your pension with an insurance company following the Equitable Life fiasco but still want the tax relief and tax breaks of a pension? Well, there is an alternative. A SIPP is exactly like a personal pension, except that you have a wider choice of investments (which do not have to include life company funds), greater flexibility on retirement and you can make your own investment decisions – although if you do not want to, you don't have to.

SIPPs have been around for just over a decade, but in the past the high charges meant that only investors with £100,000 or more found them worthwhile. However, greater competition and the advent of online trading means that SIPPs are now available for people with as little as £200 a month to invest, and they can have the same low 1 per cent charges as stakeholder pensions.

Who should consider a SIPP?

In addition to people who want to make their own investment decisions SIPPs also appeal to those approaching retirement who want to take advantage of income draw-down, which allows them to invest their fund on retirement and take an income, instead of having to buy an annuity (a decision they can delay until they reach 75). The flexibility offered by SIPPs enables investors to consolidate existing pensions into one large fund and then invest this how they want.

Online SIPPs, which are bought and run via the internet, have brought down charges to very low levels and are accessible to and affordable by a far wider audience who until now have been stuck with what the life insurance companies have to offer.

What can they invest in?

Although SIPP investors can choose from funds offered by insurance companies, they can also invest in:

- individual shares – including those listed on the alternative investment market (AIM)

- unit trusts

- investment trusts

- open-ended investment companies

- gilts, bonds and other fixed-interest securities

- cash deposits

- commercial property (although the government is likely to stop this)

- debentures and other loan stock

- warrants

- convertible securities

- traded endowment policies

- futures and options

- foreign currency accounts

Should I take out a SIPP or a stakeholder?

When considering a SIPP v. a stakeholder it is a matter of choice v. charges and how much you have to invest (see below).

The maximum charge with a stakeholder is 1 per cent of the fund. With a SIPP charges can be this low, but you have to take into account:

- Dealing charges – each time you buy and sell an investment you will pay a charge. The more often you trade, the higher the charge.

- Fund manager charges – in addition to dealing charges, the unit trusts you invest in can charge up to 1.25 per cent a year as an annual fee, as well as charging an initial fee of up to 5 per cent (although many SIPP providers rebate any commission they would have been paid bringing these charges down to 2 per cent).

- Plan management charges – the costs of setting up a SIPP and running it. The cheapest internet deals are around £100 to set up the SIPP with no annual charges.

However, even with the low-cost SIPPs on offer you will need at least £1,500 to make investing worthwhile and to cover the charges – more if you pick a SIPP that has an annual charge even if you do not deal in any shares.

What is the minimum I can invest?

Generally £200 a month gross (including tax relief) or £3,600 as a lump sum although some providers will accept lower amounts.

Who sells SIPPs?

Stockbrokers, financial advisers, fund managers and pension providers.

What should I consider if I want to buy one?

- Costs – these will eat into returns.

- How often will you deal – if you are dealing regularly you will need to go to a cheap on-line stockbroker. However, you will generally be advised not to use your pension for trading – it is a long-term investment.

- Accessibility – how easy is it for you to check the balance of your fund and to trade? Can you do this on-line or do you have to go to the hassle of talking to your stockbroker or going to see your financial adviser?

- Investment choice – not all SIPP providers offer a wide range of investments.

Can I have a stakeholder and a SIPP?

Yes – you are not restricted on the number of personal pensions and stakeholders you can have. The only limit is that you do not invest more than the allowed percentages of your net relevant earnings – these rise from 17.5 per cent to 40 per cent as you near retirement – and are due to be scrapped and replaced with a fund limit of £1.4 million from 2004.

RETIREMENT ANNUITY CONTRACTS

This was the name for individual pensions before personal pensions were introduced in July 1988. Although no new retirement annuity

How do contribution limits vary compared to personal and stakeholder pensions?

Age at start of tax year	Maximum contribution as % of net relevant earnings for stakeholders and personal pensions	(Limits for retirement annuity contracts taken out before July 1988)
Up to 35	17.5%	(17.5%)
36 to 45	20%	(17.5%)
46 to 50	25%	(17.5%)
51 to 55	30%	(20%)
56 to 60	35%	(22.5%)
61 to 74	40%	(27.5%)
75 and over	nil	nil

These limits are due to be scrapped from 2004.

contracts could be taken out after that date, existing ones, also known as Section 226 contracts, could continue to grow and accept contributions.

Retirement annuity contracts are high charging and inflexible compared to stakeholders; however, they may still be worth holding on to. Although they have lower contribution limits as a percentage of earnings, the maximum lump sum that can be taken tax free on retirement is different – and may be higher.

How much can I take as a tax-free lump sum on retirement?

With retirement annuity contracts the maximum is three times the income from the remaining fund, confusing compared to the maximum of up to 25 per cent of the stakeholder or pension plan fund which can be taken as a tax-free lump sum on retirement.

As a rough example, if the income you would get from the fund (after you take your lump sum) is £10,000 a year, you could take a £30,000 tax-free lump sum. To get an income of £10,000 a year you would probably need a fund of at least £160,000. So with a stakeholder you could take £40,000 as a lump sum but with a retirement annuity contract only £30,000. The maths can work the other way – it depends on the income you get from the fund.

The remainder of the fund must be used to purchase what is known as a compulsory purchase annuity. This is an investment plan, which provides the retiree with an income for life.

So what are the benefits?

Lower contribution limits and the possibility of a lower tax-free lump sum do not sound very appealing. However, there is no earnings cap on the contributions made into a retirement annuity contract. So higher earners – those earning more than the £97,200 earnings cap – can be better off. Once again, the earnings' cap is due to be scrapped from April 2004, and if this legislation is passed as planned, it will create a more level playing field in terms of tax.

HOW SAFE IS MY PENSION?

Not as safe as you might think. All firms selling stakeholder pensions are regulated by the Financial Services Authority (FSA) and by the Occupational Pensions Regulatory Authority (OPR). But this only provides limited protection.

Insurers, battered by dwindling stock market returns, are going cap in hand to the city to raise money, free asset ratios (which indicate the financial strength of a life company) are down and reform could make the situation worse.

The Sandler Report on pension reform published in 2002 says that the process by which annual returns are calculated should be made clearer. Controversially, it says the practice of giving 10 per cent of with-profits returns to providers' shareholders, in return for their willingness to inject cash into the pension fund if necessary, should be scrapped because this makes it even harder for savers to assess their fund's performance. However, analysts believe that this could penalize publicly quoted insurers, whose profit structure often depends heavily on returns from with-profits policies.

How can I check that my money is safe?

If you have a with-profits pension, check the financial strength of your life company. Reports are published regularly. One recent survey on financial strength by KPMG found that Pearl, Equitable Life and Sun Life are all having problems. Pearl had to close its life fund to new business because of problems with solvency margins.

One of the key figures to look for is the free asset ratio. In the case of Pearl these fell to a negative. Part of the problem was that when it was taken over, the orphan funds (funds that were not allocated to any particular policyholder) of over £900 million were released to shareholders along with just over £40 million of future surpluses from the with-profits funds.

So the funds can be raided?

Yes. Just because you may think they belong to policyholders, that is not the case. Orphan funds can be given to shareholders or used to pay for mistakes such as the mis-selling scandal or even to cover losses. However, the city watchdog has now warned that shareholders – not investors – should pay for these mistakes.

Warning: The falls in the stock markets have hit life company reserves, and free-asset ratios – which give an idea of a life company's financial strength – are falling. These free assets are needed to bolster returns and bonuses when markets fall – the ironing out of rises and falls is the aim of with-profits funds. The free assets are the assets in excess of the life company's liabilities including maturity values or death benefits to homebuyers, pension savers and other investors.

However, free-asset ratios do not always give a full picture of the state of a life company's finances. Investors are advised to read the financial press. Assessing the strength of life offices is complex and analysts look at the capital a life company has, its cash flow and the type of business it has been writing to give a fuller indication of its strength.

(Unit-linked funds are ring-fenced and are unaffected.)

INDIVIDUAL PENSIONS – YOUR RIGHTS

What happens to my personal or stakeholder pension if I die before I retire?

Your pension provider will pay out the value of your pension at the date it is told of your death. The whole amount can normally be used to provide a cash sum. If you are contracted out of the state second pension, S2P or SERPS, this element must be used to provide a spouse's pension. You should state whom you wish to receive this money.

Cash sums paid on death are normally free of inheritance tax.

What happens if I die after I retire?

You will have probably purchased an annuity to provide an income for life. What your spouse and dependants receive depends on the annuity. However, they will not get a lump sum unless you have delayed purchasing an annuity. See Chapter 10: Maximizing Your Pension On Retirement.

7 Pensions For Those Running a Business

YOUR BUSINESS – YOUR PENSION

Many people running their own businesses – be they self-employed or owners of limited companies – view their business as their pension. This is a high-risk strategy.

- There are no guarantees that anyone will want to buy your business or business assets when you retire.

- If you do manage to sell, the price may not be right.

- You may be forced to retire earlier or later than expected because you could not find a buyer at the right time or at the right price.

- Your business may fail before you retire – and you will lose your pension as well as your income.

- You may fall ill before you retire and be forced to close your business.

However, if:

- you run a business that is relatively easy to sell as a going concern (a shop, restaurant, manufacturer, etc.)

- you have shares in the company that can be sold (to a business partner, another investor)

- you are self-employed and have business assets that can be sold (machinery, premises, equipment, vehicles)

- you are a partner who can sell his or her share of the business to another partner you should be able to boost what you have to live on in retirement without paying large amounts of tax.

Capital gains tax (CGT) is paid on all gains in any one tax year above the CGT threshold (£7,700 for 2002/2003) and is paid at the highest rate of tax you pay. So a higher-rate taxpayer (40 per cent) with gains (sale proceeds less certain costs including the cost of purchasing the asset) of £50,000 from the sale of a business has a taxable gain of:

£50,000 – £7,700 = £42,300

If this was taxed at 40 per cent the CGT bill would be £16,920. However, the longer the asset was owned the lower this tax liability, thanks to taper relief (taper relief has now replaced retirement relief).

Any gains made on the sale of business assets suffer less CGT than personal assets.

How Taper Relief Reduces the Equivalent CGT Rate on Business Assets

Complete years after 5 April 1998 the asset was held	Percentage of gain chargeable (this is the taper)	Equivalent CGT rate	
		Basic-rate taxpayers	Higher-rate taxpayers
0	100%	20%	40%
1	87.5%	17.5%	35%
2	75%	15%	30%
3	50%	10%	20%
4+	25%	5%	10%

Provided you have owned your business for more than four years the maximum tax you will pay is 10 per cent – not 40 per cent.

This is a specialist area and you should seek advice from your accountant and possibly a solicitor and a business adviser if you are planning to retire and sell your business or its assets in the near future.

USE YOUR BUSINESS TO BOOST YOUR PENSION

Any contributions made towards a pension fund are tax deductible.

If You Are Self-employed

You can deduct the contribution before arriving at your final tax bill when submitting your tax return. You can backdate contributions to the previous year – so you can make a contribution before 31 January 2004 for the 2002/2003 tax year. Ask your pension provider for the forms required to backdate contributions (these must be filled in before or when you pay into your pension).

This backdating is valuable because you will not know your final profits and therefore will not know how much you can invest within Inland Revenue limits until after the tax year has ended.

Warning: It is particularly important for the self-employed to contribute to a personal or stakeholder pension because they do not qualify for any state second pension – SERPS or more recently S2P (although the pensions Green Paper has put forward the idea that they may be able to pay extra to join the scheme in future).

The self-employed can take greater control over their pension investments – and use their business to boost their pension fund and vice versa (by getting the fund to invest in the business premises, for example, although this is likely to be swapped in future) by taking out a self-invested personal pension (SIPP). These are discussed in greater detail on page 201.

If You Own a Company

Contributions paid by the company into pensions are tax free. These contributions are in addition to the 15 per cent you are allowed to contribute as an employee to a pension scheme (the maximum employees are allowed to contribute under Inland Revenue rules for the time being. The limit is likely to rise to £200,000 a year subject to a total fund value cap of £1.4 million). As a result, you can use your business to fund a generous retirement.

You can even set up your own pension fund (instead of contributing to a personal pension or stakeholder). These are known as small self-administered schemes (SSASs) and are discussed in greater detail on page 203.

Employ Your Spouse

If you do not do so already – employ your spouse. You can pay him/her up to the National Insurance threshold without paying any tax or National Insurance – so you can boost your family income tax free. At the same time, pay into your new employee's pension – the contributions are tax deductible.

SELF-INVESTED PERSONAL PENSIONS (SIPP)

These are similar to personal pensions in all respects other than that you – not a life company – control the investment (although you can delegate this responsibility to an investment company, should you wish). The main benefit for people running a business (the self-employed) is they can invest in commercial property. However, this concession is set to end – possibly as early as 2004 – and although companies and investors will be given time to adjust, there could be problems for those needing to purchase a property from their pension fund.

How can I buy my business premises with my pension?

While many new low-cost SIPPs allow you to invest as little as £3,600 gross, if you want a SIPP that is more sophisticated, allowing investments in commercial property, you will generally need at least £100,000 to invest.

In very simple terms the tax concessions worked like this: your pension can buy your shop or office – helping your business to grow – usually buying a long lease or a freehold. In return, your pension fund grows by investing in a sound commercial property which is let to a good tenant – you. Your rent goes into your pension fund. So although you still pay rent, you benefit. When you retire, your pension fund can sell the asset without having to pay capital gains tax. And you can take a quarter of this fund as a tax-free lump sum using the rest to provide yourself with an income for life by purchasing an annuity.

However, as the ability to invest in commercial property is likely to end, this will no longer be an option.

What else can SIPPs invest in?

Although SIPP investors can choose from funds offered by insurance companies, they can also invest in:

- individual shares – including those listed on the alternative investment market (AIM) (direct investment is not allowed with a personal or a stakeholder pension)

- unit trusts

- investment trusts

- open-ended investment companies

- gilts, bonds and other fixed-interest securities

- cash deposits

- debentures and other loan stock

- warrants

- convertible securities

- traded endowment policies

- futures and options

- foreign currency accounts

SMALL SELF-ADMINISTERED SCHEMES (SSAS)

These are defined-benefit schemes – like final salary schemes, so the Inland Revenue does not limit the contributions but instead limits the pension that can be taken on retirement. They are an option for people running companies rather than for the self-employed. They allow greater flexibility of investments and allow the pension fund to make loans to the company or its members.

There are some 30,000 of these pension funds, set up for the benefit of controlling directors. They can decide what to invest and when, and act as their own trustees controlling all investments which, because they are held in a pension, grow tax free with no income or capital gains tax to pay. As with all company contributions they are tax deductible.

In addition to being able to invest in a range of shares or investment schemes the directors can use the SSAS to:

- Buy the company's premises. Investing in commercial property is a key feature of the SSAS, because the property in question is often then rented out to the new tenant, the limited company. There are some restrictions as to suitable properties (i.e. limited use properties such as petrol stations may not be allowed, and residential property is banned unless incidental, such as a flat for the caretaker), but the offices, factories and warehouses can all be purchased. The company then pays a tax-deductible rent to the pension fund. This tax concession is set to be scrapped, and the Inland Revenue is consulting on how firms can adjust their portfolios and find purchasers for the property.

- Borrow money to lend to the company for a specific project – for example, purchasing premises. Some people say that an SSAS is a private bank that always says yes. Your company pays interest at a prescribed rate, but it goes into your own pension rather than to a bank. You cannot lend money for cash flow only for specific projects. The maximum level of loans is 50 per cent of fund value for a trust with over two years history.

- Buy shares in the company or an unlisted company.

As well as the company being able to borrow from the SSAS, the SSAS in turn can borrow money, subject to strict limits, 45 per cent of the loan plus three times annual contributions. Because money is then tied up in the property transaction this is only usually suitable for directors with ten or 15 years to retirement.

In addition an SSAS can provide:

- A generous pension – the company can put in as much as it likes to give you the maximum allowed (two thirds of final salary subject to the earnings cap of £97,200, which is likely to be scrapped from April 2004).

- Protection of your pension against financial problems – the SSAS is protected from creditors (unless you are fraudulent and hide money in the pension fund just before your firm goes under).

- A way to retire rich, get rid of a director you no longer want or to give him or her a bigger pension than he or she is entitled to. This is because the fund is pooled (everyone's pension is in the same pot). If the other members agree, they can use some of their own share of the fund to enhance another member's benefits. So a retiring older member of a family business can pass the business on to the next generation without the company having to buy him or her out at a high price. The pension fund provides enough for him or her to retire on comfortably.

Such generous rules mean that SSASs can be valuable for business, tax and pension planning. However, they can be expensive to set up and run and you will need a specialist pensioneer trustee to oversee the fund.

Rules prevent abuse of the fact that you run your own pension fund.

- Assets must produce income.

- The scheme must prove liquid enough to provide benefits (hence the need to limit investments in property).

- No loans can be made to members.

- No assets can be bought to benefit the members (a house, a boat, etc.).

- The pension cannot buy or sell assets to any of the directors or their families.

Once again this is a specialist area and you are advised to seek advice from a firm specializing in these schemes.

8 How Much Do I Need To Invest?

A decent pension should cost about as much as the family home – yet most people spend far more on mortgage repayments than they ever invest in a pension.

Because few of us start to save for retirement when we are in our 20s and only start to seriously think about old age when we are in our 40s or even 50s, we have to make up for 20 years when we may have had nothing or little invested in a pension. A person in their mid twenties earning the current national average salary of £23,500 a year and aiming for a pension of half their final earnings after taking 25 per cent of their pension fund as a tax-free lump sum will have to invest £337.70 net – or £483.34 gross – each month to draw an £11,750 pension (or the inflation equivalent of £24,000) according to independent financial advisers Hargreaves Lansdown.

The following is a rough guide to how much you will need to invest to get a pension of two thirds of your final salary when you retire *including* pensions from the state.

Age when starting pension	% of earnings that should be invested
20	10%
30	15%
35	17.5%
40	20%
45	22.5%
50	25%

Source: Legal & General

So those who delay, pay. In cash terms, these amounts can be significant. The next table shows how the amount individuals need to invest each month to provide a £10,000 per annum pension rises the longer they delay investing in a pension.

Length of investment	Amount per month
30 years	£132.80
20 years	£285.59
10 years	£797.05
5 years	£1,863.70

These figures assume 6 per cent growth per annum and that to produce a £10,000 pension will require a fund of approximately £129,500.
Source: Chase de Vere

Remember that this pension may have to last for 20 years or more. So a 40-year working life may have to produce enough income for us to live on, buy a home, start a family, pay taxes and all the other expenses that are unavoidable and leave enough to live on for a further 20 years. It is not surprising that many people feel they just do not have enough money to pay for all life's commitments, let alone save for their retirement.

However, it is usually better to do something than do nothing; to have some money saved, rather than planning to rely on the state.

The Financial Services Authority has produced a more detailed table. It looks at what you need to invest as a regular monthly contribution to get a certain amount per month (at today's prices) when you retire. It assumes your contributions will increase each year in line with inflation. The amounts invested are before tax relief – so the figures show what your monthly contributions will be (rather than the gross contributions once tax relief is added). The figures also assume a set rate of investment growth (7 per cent per annum) which is not guaranteed, and that your pension will increase in line with inflation. Remember, nothing is certain, and these figures show what you *could* get, not what you will *actually* receive on retirement which could be higher or lower.

Monthly contribution before tax relief in first year

Age now	£20	£50	£100	£200
	Initial monthly pension if you retire at 65			
20	£133	£333	£667	£1,334
25	£107	£269	£538	£1,076
30	£85	£214	£428	£857
35	£67	£167	£335	£670
40	£51	£127	£255	£511
45	£37	£94	£188	£376
50	£26	£65	£130	£260
55	£16	£40	£80	£160
60	£7	£18	£37	£74

Source: Financial Services Authority

The pension is paid monthly. Investing £100 a month from age 40 will still only result in an extra pension of less than £60 a week – just £8.40 a day. So although the monthly figures may seem high, consider in day to day terms what you could actually buy with this much money.

You also have to bear in mind that these figures for a stakeholder pension show what you will get in addition to any other pensions, including those from the state. No account is taken of other individual circumstances. You will probably not pay into one pension plan all your life and may have periods of unemployment, career breaks or may be a member of an employer's pension scheme for part of your working life. Retire earlier than 65 and your pension will also be hit.

WARNING – A REALITY CHECK

The illustrations so far in this chapter show what you will receive on retirement assuming certain levels of investment performance. As from April 2003, these inflated forecasts are being replaced by 'real money'. So you will be shown in real terms what you will get on retirement both when you purchase a pension and every year.

The old forecasts would show that a 40-year-old man who has just started saving £50 a month in a personal pension would retire on a fund of £36,200 at age 65 and that this could provide a pension of £240 per month before tax. The new forecasts will show that in today's spending terms it would be nearer to £85 a month before tax. Some providers are already encouraging investors to inflation-proof their pensions by offering automatic increases in contributions in line with either inflation, national average earnings or a fixed percentage each year.

This can make a large difference. Paying £100 a month from age 25 until you retire at 60 will give a pension of £59,000 in real terms (assuming 7 pr cent growth less 2.5 per cent inflation). To get a pension of £140,000 you would have to pay in £231 per month. However, index-link your contributions, assuming 4 per cent rises in national average earnings) and you will start with an initial contribution of only £139 per month – far lower than the £231 level premium required and more affordable as your contributions rise with your earnings.

What if I have an existing pension?

If you have an existing money-purchase pension – either an employer's pension or a stakeholder or personal pension – it will be covered by these new rules called the statutory money-purchase illustration or SMPI.

You may be shocked to find, when you get your next annual statement, that the pension you hoped to get has been slashed from £100 a week to nearer £25. This is not just because the stock market has fallen. It is because your pension provider has had to change the way it forecasts what you get on retirement.

It may be shocking. You may feel your pension is poor value, but think of it as a wake-up call to start investing more to secure a comfortable old age.

To find out how much *you* need to invest follow these steps:

Step 1: What Pensions and Savings Do You Already Have?

Before considering how much you need to invest, you need to look at what you already have.

Take into account:

- pensions you will get from the state including any state second pension (S2P or SERPs) entitlement

- pensions with current – and past employers

- any personal pensions

This may take a bit of detective work and some time as you track down pensions and request pension forecasts. Follow these tips.

From the State

Find out how much basic state pension (contrary to popular belief not everyone is entitled to the full amount) and any SERPS or S2P you will be paid by contacting the Retirement Pension Forecasting and Advice Unit. See Useful Contacts on page 347.

From Employer Schemes

Write to the trustees of existing and past occupational schemes to find out what pension will be paid on retirement. Because many employees leave their pensions in their previous employer's scheme (where the money continues to grow by at least 5 per cent a year or inflation whichever is the lower), they may find they have two or even three fairly generous deferred pensions. If your former employer has moved premises, closed, merged or been taken over and you are finding it difficult to trace a missing pension contact the Pension Schemes Registry. See Useful Contacts on page 347.

Note: While 10.5 million people of working age are members of occupational pension schemes, pension funds are looking after 34 million individual pensions – that works out at three pensions each. The chances are that you may have at least one pension entitlement left in a former employer's scheme by the time you retire.

From Individual Schemes

Ask your pension provider(s) or financial adviser for a pension forecast in real terms. Ignore past forecasts that assumed 7 per cent per annum growth – these may not be realistic and made certain assumptions about investment performance (the stock market has failed to match these recently) and annuity rates (an annuity must be purchased with at least 75 per cent of the pension fund either on retirement or by the age of 75 to provide an income for life).

As a rough guide, men retiring at 65 are looking at an 8.5 per cent annuity rate if they want a pension for their widow, so a £100,000 fund will buy £8,500 of income for life. However, if they want this inflation-proofed, the initial amount of income would fall to £6,400. To trace a pension company contact the Association of British Insurers on 020 7600 3333 or email at info@abi.org.uk or visit their website at www.abi.org.uk.

Step 2: What Could This Give Me When I Retire?

Add up all the pensions you will be paid, and look at the income you will get – not the lump sums. Your pension fund from your personal pension may look like a large figure but you must remember that 75 per cent of this must be used to purchase an annuity to give you a pension for life. Also bear in mind that all the forecasts you receive make certain assumptions, that:

- You continue paying National Insurance Contributions in the case of the basic state pension.

- You continue to make contributions (and in some cases increase these contributions in line with inflation) in the case of a personal pension.

- You continue to work for the same employer (in the case of occupational pensions).

- Inflation is 5 per cent (even though it is lower) if you have a pension frozen in a final salary scheme. These make assumptions about inflation which may not be realistic.

- Tax rules do not change.

- You retire at a certain age (you could change your mind or be forced to take early retirement due to ill-health). Those hoping to retire before state pension age need to invest more.

So you will only get a rough idea of the income you could receive, and no account will be taken of investment performance which could leave you far better – or worse – off.

However, you will need a rough idea of what you can expect on retirement to complete the following steps. After adding up your pension income you can do a separate calculation showing how much less you would get if you took any tax-free lump sums allowed. As most people invest far too little for retirement they are usually better off using all of their pension to provide an income rather than taking any lump sum and suffering a fall in their retirement income. However, they can invest the tax-free lump sum instead of using it to purchase an annuity and may be able to achieve a higher income as a result. See Chapter 10: Maximizing Your Pension On Retirement for further advice.

Step 3: What Will I Need As An Income When I Retire?

Most people aim to retire with a pension that is at least half of their salary (calculate this in today's terms), with two thirds being the ideal.

However, you may feel that this is more than you need. Once you have paid off your mortgage, cleared any debts (perhaps with any tax-free lump sum), no longer have to pay the costs associated with going to work and possibly move down the property ladder to release some capital from your home, you may feel you could survive on only a third of your current salary. It is important to be realistic.

If, for example, you earn £26,000, around the national average salary, then a third of this will be £8,666 a year giving you an income of £167 a week. Think carefully. Will this be enough?

Remember this is not just money to live on, it will also have to pay for repairs to your home and your car, new items of furniture or electrical goods, holidays, birthdays and possibly even medical bills. Although you may have additional savings these can quickly run out. Also bear in mind that you will probably not be able to go out and earn money to make up any shortfall. Once you retire that's it – what you retire with must last you.

While certain costs may be lower when you retire, others such as heating bills can be higher. It is vital that you budget carefully.

Consider this, campaigning groups say that the basic state pension needs to be raised to £100 a week to pull pensioners out of poverty. Retiring on £30 or £40 a week more than this minimum required for a very basic existence is hardly going to give you a luxury lifestyle.

Step 4: What Is the Shortfall?

Compare the income you expect to receive on retirement with the amount you feel you need to live on in retirement. The chances are there will be a significant shortfall. Although it may only be £20 or £40 a week, to achieve this you will need to start your retirement with another £20,000 or even £40,000.

Step 5: How Much Will I Need To Bridge This Gap?

As a rough guide, people who expect an annual investment return or an annuity rate of 6 per cent should take the shortfall in annual income – say £6,000 – and multiply it by 100/6 (the investment return) to give the additional capital sum they will need. So £6,000 $\times$ 100/6 = £100,000.

While £100,000 may seem a lot of money, remember it has got to last you a long time.

A more accurate calculation can be done by looking at the sort of annuity rate you can expect based on:

- the age when you plan to retire

- whether or not you need a spouse's pension (it is advisable – if you do not purchase one when you die any money left in your annuity dies with you)

- whether or not you plan to inflation-proof this pension (it is advisable)

- your state of health (people with a poor health history – for example, a past heart attack – can expect a higher annuity rate)

- whether or not you smoke

You generally need to look at annuity rates because these will be the main source of additional income to bridge the gap – they must be purchased with at least 75 per cent of your fund from a money purchase scheme, stakeholder or personal pension.

Step 6: How Much Will I Need To Invest To Build Up This Amount?

A significant amount of your salary, particularly as there are no guarantees that:

- The benefits of any final salary scheme (these are generally the best of the best) will last.

- Stock markets will rise as predicted – in fact they have fallen in recent years.

- The current tax benefits of investing in pensions will continue.

So the amount you are going to have to invest is likely to be far more than you think. The following should concentrate the mind . . .

Financial advisers Bestinvest have built a Retirement Income Calculator to project savings needs. Its key findings are:

25-year-olds on national average earnings will need to find around £500,000 after clearing mortgages and other debts to retire at 65

According to the new earnings survey the gross salary of a full-time UK employee in the 2000/1 tax year was £23,504. Average earnings are increasing by 2 per cent above inflation so, assuming this continues, by age 65 today's average-earning 25-year-old will have a final salary of £51,898 (in today's prices). A sum of £475,374 will be required to fund an annuity equal to half final salary (joint life with a five-year guarantee and 3 per cent per annum escalation).

The current personal and stakeholder contribution limits are not high enough to fund retirement for many workers

The level savings rates required to retire at 65 on half of final salary assuming pay rises of 2 per cent above inflation, are:

Age when investing starts	25	30	35	40	45	50
% gross salary to be saved	15%	19%	23%	29%	38%	52%
Personal pension/ stakeholder allowances	17.5%	17.5%	20%*	20%	25%†	30%‡

* from 36   † from 46   ‡ from 51

Once again, the calculation assumes a joint-life annuity is purchased to give a 50 per cent pension to the spouse and that it has a five-year guarantee and 3 per cent escalation.

Under the existing rules the Inland Revenue will not allow you to invest the amounts needed to fund a comfortable retirement if you leave pension planning until you get older. As from April 2004 these limits will be scrapped, enabling individuals to invest far more. An alternative option is to invest in additional schemes such as tax-free individual savings accounts (ISA). See Chapter 12: The Pension Alternatives.

Starting to save at a young age is no guarantee of a comfortable retirement, your savings must rise in line with your pay

High fliers and career professionals face the greatest challenge. With every promotional pay jump their savings rate must increase broadly in accordance with the table above if they are to retire on half of final salary.

For example, if a graduate earning £25,000 per annum aged 25 saves 15 per cent of pay and then receives a salary rise to £40,000 at age 30, they will need to pay approximately 19 per cent on the £15,000 pay rise as well as continuing the 15 per cent on £25,000.

The goal of early retirement is a pipe-dream – a 25-year-old would need to start saving 41 per cent of gross earnings to retire at age 50

The level savings rates required for a 25-year-old to retire early on half of final salary based on the assumption of pay rises of 2 per cent above inflation are:

Early retirement age	60	55	50
% gross salary to be saved	21%	30%	41%

Once again, the calculation assumes a joint-life annuity is purchased to give a 50 per cent pension to the spouse and that it has a five-year guarantee and 3 per cent escalation.

People ignoring savings until they are aged 40 have virtually no chance of retiring early and in fact face financial crisis and will need to contribute 29 per cent of gross earnings to retire at 65.

The Retirement Income Calculator is at http://www.bestinvest. co.uk. It will enable you to estimate the amount of savings you need to commit each year in order to purchase a range of types of annuity at different retirement dates. The tool can take account of existing savings, changing assumptions of annual wage inflation, rates of return and contribution levels. Assumptions can be changed to provide alternative projections.

Step 7: How Much Can I Afford To Invest?

This is deliberately placed at the end of this chapter after you have calculated and then read the shocking news that you are probably investing far too little and have far too much catching up to do if you want a comfortable retirement. Perhaps reading that your expectations do not match your pocket may make you think twice about saying 'I cannot afford to invest any more'.

You have two choices:

- Lump sums – consider if you have any savings (other than savings you need for a rainy day) that you could put to better use in your pension.

- Regular payments – this is the most common way to invest in a pension, by making a regular monthly contribution. Increasing your contributions by just £10 a month will make a significant difference when you retire. Surely you can find an extra £10, £20 or even £50 a month.

Freeing Up Extra Cash To Invest

Paying in an extra £50 a month to your pension may not actually cost you £50 a month. The average household is wasting as much as £1,000 a year by failing to shop around for the best deals. So you could boost your pension, without having to make any financial sacrifices, all you have to do is shop around:

- The average family could save up to a third off insurance premiums including £120 a year on home insurance and £150 on car cover, according to the AA.

- Mortgage apathy costs millions each year. A few minutes checking what is the best deal on a £100,000 mortgage could save £20,000 over the term of a 25-year mortgage.

- The difference between a low rate and an average rate on a £5,000 loan borrowed over five years can be as much as £1,000 in extra interest over the term of the loan.

Even people struggling to make ends meet who have already trimmed their expenditure to the bone can usually find savings. The areas of finance where waste is most likely to occur are: household insurance, car insurance, life insurance, credit cards, current accounts, mortgages and household bills.

9 How To Boost Your Pension

We have looked at how much you need to live on in retirement and the shortfall you have between your expectations and your existing pension provision, it is time to look at the investment options – how you are going to invest to bridge at least some of this gap. The good news is that most people have plenty of scope to boost their retirement provision and still benefit from the generous tax breaks currently given on pension scheme investments. Your options will depend on:

- What pension provision you already have.

- How long you have until retirement.

- How much you want to invest.

- Whether you have or will exceed the Inland Revenue investment limits or not.

- Your attitude to risk.

- When you want to retire (before age 50 or before the retirement age of your occupational pension fund, for example).

In some cases more than one option may be open to you. For example, you may want to boost your employer pension by paying into a top-up scheme known as an additional voluntary contribution (AVC) but you may want to exceed the investment limits allowed so you could also opt for a stakeholder pension as well.

The first step is to regularly review your pension planning to ensure you are investing enough for retirement and have made the best decisions.

However, few people bother to do so. Research from life company the Prudential reveals that seven out of ten people have not reviewed any aspect of their retirement planning in the last year. Women lag behind men when it comes to financial planning with over a third of men having reviewed their retirement plans in the last year compared to less than a quarter of women.

Although experts recommend at least 10 per cent of your salary is contributed to your pension, 15 per cent is an even better amount. The most important thing is for you to increase your contributions as your earnings increase.

To help you make your choice of the best ways to top up your pension answer the questions below; how to boost your pension if you are a member of an employer scheme, individual scheme or are not currently a member of a scheme is then discussed in greater detail after the question and answer session.

For information on ways to boost your pension from the state read Chapter 4: State Pensions and Benefits.

ARE YOU A MEMBER OF AN EMPLOYER'S PENSION SCHEME?

NO
Skip to the next Q & A section.

YES

Is it a money purchase scheme?

NO
Skip to the next question.

YES
Your options:

- If your scheme allows – increase your contributions to the scheme up to 15 per cent of earnings allowed. From April 2004 this cap will be scrapped and replaced with a £200,000 limit.

- Invest in an AVC – a top-up plan that all schemes must allow you to contribute to (provided you do not exceed the 15 per cent limits before they are scrapped in 2004).

- If you earn £30,000 or less (or have done so at any time in the last five years) and are not a controlling director of your company, you can pay up to £3,600 into a stakeholder pension instead of, or in addition to, the above. This will give you greater flexibility on retirement and, combined with AVCs, will boost the amount you can invest tax free.

Is it a group stakeholder scheme?

NO
Skip to the next question.

YES
You can increase your contributions. Depending on your age you can invest between 17.5 per cent and 40 per cent of your earnings. Again, these limits will be replaced by a single £200,000 cap from 2004.

Is it a group personal pension scheme?

NO
Skip to the next question.

YES
You can increase your contributions. Depending on your age you can invest between 17.5 per cent and 40 per cent of your earnings but, from 2004, up to £200,000.

However, you may be better off taking out a separate stakeholder pension particularly if the personal pension does not have competitive charges, you want to hedge your bets by taking out a separate pension, or you want the flexibility to take some of your pension at a different time to your main pension.

Is it a final salary scheme?

YES

Do you earn £30,000 or less a year? Or have you earned less than this at any time in the last five years from 2001/2002?

NO
Skip to the next question.

YES
Consider a separate stakeholder pension. You can invest up to £3,600 gross a year.

Do you have earnings in addition to your main employment?

NO
Invest in an AVC.

YES
Consider a stakeholder pension.

Do you want to invest in something other than an AVC and/or stakeholder?

YES
Read Chapter 12: The Pension Alternatives.

Advice For Scheme Members

Employees generally need to have 40 years' continuous service with the same employer to build up the maximum pension allowed by the Inland Revenue. However, jobs for life are a thing of the past and most workers have between five and nine jobs in a working life-time. This means they may never build up a decent pension.

Employees can boost their occupational pension – and the amount of tax relief they receive – by investing in AVCs.

They can also:

- Buy 'additional years of service' if they transfer a pension from other schemes into a final salary scheme (not all schemes accept transfers).

- Increase their pension pot (with a money purchase scheme) by transferring another pension into the new employer's scheme.

All occupational pension schemes must offer an AVC facility; however, the benefits paid are not the same as for the main pension scheme:

- AVCs cannot be used to boost the tax-free lump sum taken on retirement.

- They can only be used to increase the amount of pension (and this is taxable).

This rule does not apply to schemes started before 8 April 1987, so members of these older schemes have a significant tax advantage – they can take some of the pension built up by their AVC contributions as a tax-free lump sum instead of having to take it as a taxable pension.

What is the maximum I can contribute?

From April 2004 it is planned that the current limits on pension-fund investment are replaced by a single cap of £200,000 a year subject to a total limit of £1.4 million on the size of an individual's pension fund.

Under current rules, combined contributions to employee schemes and AVCs cannot exceed 15 per cent of the employee's remuneration in any tax year. There is no limit, however, on the amount employers can pay into final salary schemes.

As employee contribution rates are often set at, say, 3 or 5 per cent there is plenty of scope to increase your contributions.

If you are a member of a personal or stakeholder pension scheme the limits are far higher, starting at 17.5 per cent and rising with age to 40 per cent of remuneration up to the earnings cap of £97,200 for 2002/2003.

Should you wish to top up your pension benefits while in an occupational pension scheme you can do so by contributing to an AVC scheme run by your employer or by a stakeholder pension plan. If you earn no more than £30,000 p.a. and are not a controlling director you will be able to make concurrent contributions to a personal pension plan, including a stakeholder pension. Contributions of up to £3,600 p.a. gross will be permissible, in addition to any AVCs. Alternatively, you can look outside the company and go to the provider of your choice for a stakeholder pension or a Free Standing AVC (FSAVC) scheme. But note that an FSAVC will generally be more expensive when it comes to charges.

What is the maximum I can receive on retirement?

Final Salary Schemes: The maximum benefits are usually two thirds of final salary. If, as a result of AVC contributions, these limits are exceeded, the contributions will be refunded with tax deducted at 32 per cent. This refund is treated as being paid net of basic rate tax, so higher-rate taxpayers will have to pay further tax – this is on the equivalent gross amount received, making the total effective rate 47.8 per cent.

Money Purchase Schemes: The limits are on the contributions you can make not the pension you can take.

What is an AVC?

AVCs are top-up pensions that run alongside your main scheme. All schemes must provide access to one of these. They were the best way to boost your pension until stakeholders were launched because:

- Your employer set up the scheme – saving you the hassle.

- The costs were lower than the alternatives – saving you money.

- Your contributions are taken out of your pay – taking away the temptation to spend the money elsewhere.

However, while AVCs were and still are usually good value for money they have certain drawbacks:

- All your money must be used to fund a pension – none of it can be taken as a tax-free lump sum

- Contribution limits are subject to the 15 per cent of salary cap until April 2004.

Another problem with AVCs is that you could only take your pension from your AVC at the time you retire from your main scheme, not before and not after, although this is now less of an issue. The rules have been relaxed by the Inland Revenue, and you can now take your pension from age 50 (55 from 2010) and up to the age of 75 (but it depends on scheme rules) and you no longer have to retire to take your AVC pension. This means you can:

- Retire early – and perhaps work part time or become self-employed or a consultant but not take your main pension until you really need it at 65.

- Wait to top up your pension when you are older when perhaps your living costs are higher.

Should I use the AVC offered by my employer?

You should definitely choose an AVC rather than a FSAVC because the charges will generally be significantly lower. The argument that FSAVCs may be more flexible no longer washes, particularly as rules on retirement for AVCs have been relaxed and stakeholder pensions have been introduced.

What if I have already got an FSAVC?

The widescale selling of FSAVCs by commission-driven salesmen was the second major mis-selling scandal of the personal pensions era. Thousands of employees were advised to invest in FSAVCs offered by life companies even though the charges were much higher and the performance often far worse than the AVC offered by the employer.

If you were sold an FSAVC you should have been contacted by the life company involved to check that you were not mis-sold your policy.

Investors who feel they were wrongly advised to take out an FSAVC can apply for compensation from the Financial Services Authority. Call 0845 6061234 for a factsheet or see www.fsa.gov.uk.

Tax relief on these contributions is given automatically at the basic rate. Higher-rate taxpayers contributing to an FSAVC (rather than an AVC) will have to claim higher-rate relief and will either receive this through their PAYE coding or at the end of the year after filling in the tax return.

What happens on retirement?

Both AVCs and FSAVC can only provide a pension, not a tax-free cash lump sum.

They do not have to be taken at the same time as the pension from the occupational scheme and employees do not have to wait until they retire. AVC pensions can be taken at any time from 50 (55 from 2010) to 75. See the section RETIREMENT RULES on page 137.

Although the pension built up in an AVC/FSAVC cannot be taken as a tax-free lump sum, the amount accumulated can be used when calculating how much can be taken as a tax-free lump sum.

Schemes can only pay a lump sum up to 2.25 times the pension available. AVCs can enhance the tax-free lump sum because they boost the 'pension available' figure. However, check that the rules of the scheme allow this.

Like other occupational pensions, the pension from an AVC or FSAVC is paid net of basic-rate tax under the PAYE system.

The government is proposing a single set of rules on retirement, so it is likely that AVCs will become part of the total 25 per cent limit on tax-free lump sums.

Could a stakeholder be a better option?

Yes. In fact, AVCs and FSAVCs may become largely redundant. From April 2001 it has been possible to invest in a stakeholder instead. Until then, employees could not be members of company schemes and have a personal pension (unless they had additional earnings other than from employment from which to fund these personal pension contributions). However, employees earning less than £30,000 a year who are not controlling directors of their company can, instead of investing in an AVC, pay additional contributions of up to £3,600 a year into a stakeholder.

The advantages are:

- This £3,600 can enable them to exceed the maximum 15 per cent contribution into a company pension scheme (although this will be less of an issue from 2004, when this limit is scrapped).

- They can take part of their stakeholder fund as a tax-free lump sum.

- They can keep their stakeholder for life – so they will not be penalized when they move jobs

- They can get the benefits of an employer scheme and the chance to build up a decent pension.

In addition to a stakeholder giving you the ability to take a lump sum on retirement and to making higher contributions, they are often better value. The charges deducted from a stakeholder pension cannot exceed 1 per cent making them one of the cheapest ways to invest.

Both types of pension – stakeholders and AVCs – currently attract tax relief at your highest rate with the fund growing free of tax.

Which enables me to contribute more?

Until 2004, if you are a member of an occupational pension scheme, consider a separate stakeholder if it enables you to contribute more than the 15 per cent allowed by your scheme. This will depend on your earnings. For example:

Mr X earns £30,000 a year.

His scheme deducts 5% of his pay – £1,500 – as a pension contribution

If he wanted to pay the full 15% allowed he would only be able to pay in up to £3,000 into an AVC.

With a stakeholder he could contribute £3,600.

Mr Y earns £50,000 a year.

His scheme deducts 5% of his pay – £2,500 – as a pension contribution.

As he earns more than £30,000 a year he CANNOT have a stakeholder pension.

He can only therefore pay into an AVC contributing a further 10% of his pay or £5,000. This is greater than the £3,600 allowed by a stakeholder.

 TIP

If, however, Mr Y wanted to pay into a stakeholder he could get round the rules. Employees can only contribute to a stakeholder if they earn less than £30,000 a year. However, if they have any income from self-employment – in addition to being an employee – they can have a stakeholder after all. All Mr Y has to do is do some paid consultancy work as a freelance or set up a self-employed sideline and he could have a stakeholder as well.

He would therefore be able to contribute:

£2,500 – his 5% basic deduction to his company pension

£5,000 – his 10% contribution to an AVC

£3,600 – the maximum allowed as an investment in a stakeholder

TOTAL £11,100 into his pension

This is over a fifth of his pay.

Note, that if he was not a member of an occupational scheme and contributed to a stakeholder or personal pension scheme he could contribute up to 40 per cent of his salary as the £3,600 limit does not apply.

Do you want to contribute more than is allowed?

YES
If you are going to breach the maximum percentage of net relevant earnings limits your options are:

- Carry back a contribution to the previous tax year if you did not pay in the maximum allowed in that year. See Chapter 3: Tax and Pensions for further advice.

- Consider investing in alternative tax-efficient schemes such as ISAs. See Chapter 12: The Pension Alternatives.

- Wait until April 2004, when these limits are increased.

ARE YOU CONTRIBUTING TO A STAKEHOLDER OR PERSONAL PENSION?

NO
Skip to the next Q&A session.

YES
Are you contributing the maximum allowed?

NO
Then you should increase your contributions. You can pay in between 17.5 per cent and 40 per cent of your net relevant earnings depending on age.

Age at start of tax year	Maximum contribution as % of net relevant earnings	(limits for retirement annuity contracts taken out before July 1988)
Up to 35	17.5%	(17.5%)
36 to 45	20%	(17.5%)
46 to 50	25%	(17.5%)
51 to 55	30%	(20%)
56 to 60	35%	(22.5%)
61 to 74	40%	(27.5%)
75 and over	nil	nil

These limits will be scrapped from April 2004 and replaced with a £200,000 a year investment limit.

You can invest these contributions in:

• your existing pension (provided you are happy with the performance and the charges are good value)

• a separate pension

Bearing in mind that some personal pensions offer poor value for money, if you are in one of these schemes consider a stakeholder.

You may be better off hedging your bets with a second pension – preferably a stakeholder because:

• All your eggs are not in one basket, and if the company goes the way of Equitable Life you have some protection.

• You can phase-in your retirement – take out several stakeholders and you can then take your pensions at different times, increasing your pension, for example, as you get older.

• You can phase-in your retirement to make the most of fluctuations in annuity rates. If you retire when annuity rates are at a low, you will suffer for your entire retirement. By having several pension plans you can delay taking some of these until annuity rates improve. If they do not, you will still get a

better annuity rate because you get a higher income the older
you are.

YES
Read Chapter 12: The Pension Alternatives.

IF YOU ARE NOT CURRENTLY IN A PENSION PLAN OR HAVE OLD PENSIONS YOU ARE NO LONGER CONTRIBUTING TO

Can you join an employer's scheme?

NO
Skip to the next question.

YES
Then you should do so unless it is a final salary or money purchase
scheme and you plan to be with your employer for a very short
period. If this is the case and you leave within two years you will
not be able to build up a pension (apart from with a few schemes)
and instead will get your contributions refunded (less tax). As from
2004, it is proposed that the two-year service limit is scrapped and
transfers will be available from day one of employment.

If it is a group stakeholder or personal pension scheme you should
consider taking out the pension, particularly if your employer makes
a contribution and/or has negotiated low charges. Even if this is not
the case, the fact that contributions come directly out of pay – so you
do not miss them – and your employer arranges the pension, means
less hassle and that you are less likely to put off making any pension
provision at all.

Do you have any pension provision at all?

NO
Consider investing in a stakeholder pension.

YES

Do you have a paid-up personal pension?

NO
Skip to the next question.

YES
You can often restart contributions; however, check:

- The charges of the pension plan – are they as low as the best stakeholders?

- How flexible/inflexible is your pension plan?

- What has the performance been like?

Generally you will be better off taking out a stakeholder, because stakeholders are flexible and low cost. You can have a stakeholder and a personal pension at the same time (provided you do not breach the maximum investment rules).

Consider transferring any pension built up in old personal pension schemes to the stakeholder, but consider:

- any penalties that are imposed for doing this

- whether the lower charges make up for these penalties

Do you have a deferred pension with a former employer?

YES
Then consider transferring this deferred pension to a stakeholder if it is a money purchase pension and the stakeholder charges are more competitive. If you have a final salary pension you should generally leave it where it is (unless you are worried about the financial health of the pension scheme). Pension scheme transfers are subject to strict investment rules and you must seek professional independent financial advice.

Summary

These are the general rules for people wanting to top up their pension. However, much will depend on your circumstances.

- If you want to boost your pension, choose a stakeholder. Most people change jobs fairly frequently and stakeholders give maximum flexibility.

- If you are a member of a company scheme choose a stakeholder first and then an AVC to maximize your contributions.

- However, if your employer contributes to the AVC – opt for that. It should be your best option.

- If you do not want to be forced to buy an income (annuity) when you retire, choose a tax-free savings scheme such as an ISA.

- Make the most of tax relief on offer today – it may not be around for ever.

However, also take into account how charges vary from scheme to scheme, what happens if you leave your job and your investment choice. Apart from flexibility and investment limits the choice depends on benefits and charges.

10 Maximizing Your Pension On Retirement

You may think there is little you can do with your pension once you have reached retirement: you can no longer invest any more money in it, can no longer hope that the money you have invested grows more rapidly and may no longer be earning any money to set aside more for your future. However, you can make a significant difference to your standard of living by making the right decisions when you retire.

Your main choices are:

A Lump Sum v. Income

Although taking a lump sum from your pension when you retire will reduce the amount of pension income you receive it is not always an unwise decision. Employees in money purchase employer schemes and with personal or stakeholder pensions can take a maximum lump sum of 25 per cent of the fund. Employees in final salary schemes can generally take a maximum of one and a half times final salary as a tax-free lump sum. However, it is proposed that from April 2004 a 25 per cent limit will apply to these schemes as well.

Investments v. Pensions: You could make better use of the money if you invested it instead of using it to buy an annuity or taking the maximum pension from your occupational scheme.

While annuity rates tend to be higher than savings rates, they have still been beaten, historically, by the stock market. Use £50,000 to buy an annuity and you may get an income of £3,000 a year (depending on the type of annuity and your age). Invest the same amount in the stock market and if your portfolio rises by 10 per cent you would have a return of £5,000 (this is before tax but is below the capital gains tax threshold). You could either take your profits to boost your income or watch your money grow and buy an annuity with a larger lump sum later on.

However, as recent share price falls have proven, if you invested your money in shares rather than using it to buy an annuity you would be significantly worse off. In the current market this is a high-risk option. Also, if annuity rates fall further you could find that you are hit twice – once by the value of your investments falling and secondly by receiving a lower annuity rate.

Pensions Restrict Your Choice: One reason for taking the maximum lump sum is to spread your risks of investing and to get a wider choice of investments. You could, for example, use the money to invest in a buy-to-let property or to pay off borrowings to reduce your need for so much income.

If you forgo taking a tax-free lump sum these options will not be open to you.

Your Pension May Die With You: If you die after buying an annuity all the money you invested in it (less any income you have already received) is lost unless you pay extra for a spouse's/partner's or dependant's pension. Even then your widow/widower may only get half of your pension. Or you can buy a guarantee that the annuity will pay out for at least five years – but it will still be far less than the 15 or 20 years you could have expected.

The same applies to company schemes. Your spouse gets half your pension. However, if you are not married or widowed and have no dependants your pension will usually die with you. So you may have worked hard all your life to build up a decent pension and then find that because you die shortly after retirement it is very poor value.

The pensions Green Paper proposes a new value-protected annuity so that if you die before age 75 some of the capital that has not yet been paid out can be paid to your dependants (instead of the annuity dying with you). This payment would be equal to the difference between the amount paid for the annuity and the stream of payments already made under the annuity.

You Can Leave a Lump Sum To Whomever You Want: There are restrictions on what you can do with your pension from a company scheme or income from an annuity. These pensions can only be used to provide a widow/widower's or dependant's pension and with some annuities a partner's pension. You cannot – for example, pass on some wealth to your children in the form of a lump sum.

With a Lump Sum You Are Not Locked Into Low Interest Rates: With a lump sum you are not locked into today's low interest rates and therefore annuity rates (although this is not a problem if you are in a final salary scheme). You could keep back a lump sum and use this to buy an annuity at a later date if rates improve. However, a word of caution – rates could move down, not up as they have done in the past.

Pensions Are Taxed – Lump Sums May Not Be: Pensions paid from an annuity or employer pension scheme are subject to tax (unless your total income falls below the tax threshold). However, your investments may not be. You can invest up to £7,000 in a tax-free ISA each year (£14,000 for a married couple) as well as money in National Savings products.

However, a Pension Is Certainty: The advantages of using all or most of your fund to buy an annuity or boost your occupational pension (rather than taking the maximum lump sum) are:

- You are guaranteed an income for life. Your money is not at the mercy of the stock markets and is not affected by future changes in interest rates.

- You will not be tempted to spend the money – leaving you with less to live on when you get older.

- Any money you have saved or invested may be subject to inheritance tax whereas your pension will not be.

New Rules for Small Funds: More than four in ten annuities purchased are far less than £10,000. The government recognizes that for those with small aggregate funds it can often be uneconomic to have to convert their funds into income. Therefore the government is proposing to introduce a valuable concession to allow small funds to be paid as a lump sum rather than as an income stream – a process known as commutation. Pensioners over 65 whose total matured pension funds from all sources amount to no more than £10,000 would be able to take them, if they wished, as a lump sum.

A similar facility will be available for people with severely reduced life expectancy who will, with appropriate medical evidence, be able to withdraw all the value of their pension fund as a lump sum. This serious ill-health commutation is available currently in some types of scheme but will, in future, be available in all types.

So should I take the maximum lump sum?

On balance, yes. Annuities are only good value for money if you live to at least 82 according to Legal & General. The company says with an average pension fund of £23,000, 82 is the age pensioners would have to get to before an annuity would prove to be the better bet than investing the money in a building society – and that's even at low interest rates of 4 per cent.

However, if you live a long time, you may be grateful for your annuity. Consider Legal & General's research, which claims out of every 1,000 men retiring at 65 and buying an annuity, 304 will be alive to celebrate their 90th birthday. There is even more food for thought in the fact that for every 1,000 women buying an annuity at 60, a staggering 499 will live beyond 90.

An Annuity Today v. an Annuity Tomorrow

This section does not apply to most employees in final salary schemes unless they transfer to a personal pension before retirement to alter the way they receive benefits. If they do this they will, however, be giving up a guaranteed pension for an uncertain future so it is not usually recommended.

Most people in employer money purchase schemes can exercise their right to shop around for the best annuity rate. There are usually conditions – you must buy a five-year guarantee and a spouse's pension, which will eat into your pension income. It is possible to switch to a personal pension or an income draw-down plan to restructure the way you receive your benefits on retirement as well as giving you the flexibility to retire earlier or later than your employer's scheme allows.

Although you must purchase an annuity with at least 75 per cent of the pension built up in a:

- personal pension

- stakeholder pension

- money purchase scheme

- additional voluntary contribution (AVC) scheme

you do not have to do so until you reach 75.
In the meantime you can:

- Depending on the scheme, continue to contribute so your pension grows further.

- Invest the money and take an income from this investment equivalent to the amount you would have received if you had purchased an annuity. This is known as income draw-down (this is explained on page 253).

The advantages are that:

- You can buy an annuity when you are older – the rates will be better as you do not have such a long life expectancy.

- You can end up richer – but only if your money is invested well. There are no guarantees that you will not end up worse off.

- You can buy an annuity if and when interest rates are higher. Annuity rates are based on gilt yields, which in turn are linked to interest rates. Should interest rates rise above their current low level you could be better off. Once again, there are no guarantees.

- If you die before purchasing an annuity, your entire pension fund goes to your estate and is not taxed. This may be more favourable than if you do not delay buying a pension because if you die after purchasing an annuity, your spouse usually gets a maximum of 50 per cent of your pension and then only if you purchased a spouse's pension (these will usually be provided automatically with a money purchase scheme).

However:

- Annuity rates could fall further. They fell by 12 per cent over the year to January 2003.

- If you invest your money you will have to pay charges – and you generally need at least £40,000 to make this option worthwhile.

- Your money is at risk – if stock markets fall so will the value of your investments.

- New, limited period annuities to be introduced from 2004 will get round this dilemma. People retiring will be able to buy a three- or five-year annuity initially, and delay buying a life-time annuity until a later date.

Different types of annuity and their relative merits as well as the subject of income draw-down are discussed in greater depth on page 253.

What is the best option for me?

If you want more flexibility and are prepared to take an element of risk, then take the maximum tax-free lump sum allowed.

If, however:

- you do not need the lump sum (to repay a mortgage, for example)

- you have other savings, investments and sources of income

- and have used up your tax-free ISA allowances

you will generally be better off opting for a lower lump sum and taking the certainty of a larger pension.

Remember, this is the rest of your life you are gambling with.

Rules for Contracted-out Pensions

If you contracted out of the state second pension (SERPS followed by S2P), that part of your pension fund must be used to purchase an annuity at the age of 60 for women (due to increase to 65) and 65 for a man. These rules may change in the future so you can take both penions at the same time.

If you contracted out through a money purchase occupational scheme, this pension is known as the guaranteed minimum pension and must be inflation-proofed AND provide a spouse's pension.

IMMEDIATE VESTING

This is when you invest a lump sum into a pension, get tax relief and then withdraw your 25 per cent tax-free lump sum at the same time. It is an option available to: people over 50 who are employees, self-employed, or even already retired.

Basically, you can invest a gross premium of £10,000 of which £4,000 is tax relief (if you are a higher-rate taxpayer) so it has only cost you £6,000 – you can then take £2,500 out as a tax-free lump sum leaving you with £7,500 invested – still more than your pension has cost (although this is a simplistic calculation that does not take into account charges – it illustrates how financially advantageous this option can be).

Most stakeholder providers allow immediate vesting without any conditions. Some impose qualifying periods ranging from one day to one month or even one year.

By investing a large lump sum just before you retire you can therefore boost your pension pot and benefit from tax relief.

CONTINUE INVESTING

If you have sufficient capital or income you can continue to invest in a pension AFTER you retire. The stakeholder rules allow you to invest up to £3,600 a year and receive tax relief even if you are no longer working. If you are planning to work part-time after retirement you may be able to contribute more than this. See Chapter 14: On Retirement for advice on working past retirement age.

ANNUITIES

When these are purchased with the proceeds of a pension fund they are known as 'compulsory purchase' annuities. They provide you with an income for life.

After choosing the right pension, choosing the right annuity is the second most important decision you must make.

What is an annuity?

It is an income for life obtained from the proceeds of your pension fund. Annuities are provided by life insurance and other specialist companies and can be sold by a range of advisers. You are advised to buy from an adviser who specializes in this area and you can shop around for the best deal rather than simply buying the annuity from the salesman or the company who sold you the pension in the first place.

Who must purchase an annuity?

- members of money purchase employer pension schemes

- investors with stakeholder pensions

- investors with personal pensions

- people with additional voluntary contributions (AVC)

- people with free standing AVCs (FSAVC)

- people with S32 Buy-out (S32B) plans

However, not all of these people can shop around. With AVCs and money purchase schemes it depends on the scheme rules.

How much income will the annuity provide?

The larger your pension fund, the larger your pension.

The annuity rate (what income you will get from this fund) depends on a number of factors:

- annuity rates at the time of retirement or when you purchase the annuity if this is later

- your age

- your sex

- your health and past health

- whether or not you smoke

- whether you want to protect your pension against the ravages of inflation

- if you want a guarantee that you don't lose out because you die shortly after purchasing the annuity (you can buy a five-year guarantee)

- if you want a spouse's pension

- if you want to take some investment risk and buy newer styles of annuity

Basically, the higher the risk you will die shortly after retirement, the higher the income you will get. Older men who smoke and have had a past history of heart problems can expect a much higher income than a 60-year-old non-smoking woman. This is because the company will have to pay her – in all probability – a pension for much longer than the man because women have a longer life expectancy.

The more protection you want – against losing out if you die, against inflation, against your spouse missing out on your pension – the higher the annuity costs and therefore the lower the income.

People with a poor health history and smokers should ask for what is known as an impaired life annuity. So, if you

- smoke 10 or more cigarettes per day and have done for the last 10 years

- suffer from ill health or have had any previous illness or major surgery which is likely to reduce your life expectancy including:

  - *diabetes*

  - *liver impairment*

  - *hypertension which cannot be controlled by medication*

  - *a heart condition*

  - *cancer*

then you can expect an enhanced annuity rate – a higher income. Do not forget to include your spouse's or partner's health history when applying for an annuity as this too could increase the income you receive.

Another type of annuity is the socio-geo-economic annuity. If you are in a manual occupation or if physical labour accounts for a large part of your work, and you live in certain areas of the UK, you may qualify for this annuity, which tends to offer a higher annuity rate than the top standard annuity rate available.

How can I boost this income?

Shop around – you can get 30 per cent more by simply checking out the alternatives. Everyone should now be informed that they have a choice – known as an open-market option. These rules only apply to stakeholder and personal pensions. The pensions Green Paper proposes extending the rules to defined contribution (money purchase) occupational schemes.

The difference in rates can vary widely. It also depends on what extras you buy. See Choosing an Annuity on page 248.

Does it always pay to shop around?

Not always. The annuity offered to you by your existing pension provider may be the best deal, particularly if you bought a personal pension with a guaranteed annuity rate (GAR). These are hard to beat and if you opt for the open-market option you will give up this guarantee. Your ability to shop around may depend on your scheme rules if you are a member of a money purchase employer's scheme or contribute to an employer's AVC scheme.

Warning: Check before shopping around if you have a GAR. If you have one, retire on the stipulated date to take advantage of the guaranteed rate, which will usually be far higher than rates on offer today. If you chose to waive your right to a GAR you may be offered an additional income to make up for the reduced annuity.

The Financial Services Authority (FSA) has produced a fact sheet on people's options. Firms can use this to explain choices to their customers. It contains a decision tree to help a consumer decide on the type of annuity that would suit him or her (or decide whether to seek independent financial advice if their circumstances are more complex or difficult). From 2003, FSA comparative tables will be available on annuities. The tables will enable customers to compare annuity rates by provider for the most popular types of annuity product to help them get the most from shopping around.

What if I change my mind?

To put it bluntly, tough. Once you purchase an annuity that is it – you are stuck with it for life. You cannot decide after a year or so to switch to a different or better deal. You will, however, be given details of your rights to cancel should you change your mind upon purchase. The one exception is with income draw-down. You can in theory switch to another provider. New limited-period annuities to be introduced from 2004 will allow you to buy an annuity for three to five years and then choose another with the remainder of the fund.

What if I need to buy more than one annuity?

You may be able to combine the proceeds of various pensions into one annuity. However, this will depend on the types of pension. As the annuity rate is not affected by the size of your investment, there is no incentive (as there is with a savings account, for example) to pool your money. In fact, you will probably be better off keeping them separate. You then have the maximum flexibility over when to purchase the annuities and what benefits they offer.

You can also phase-in your income so that you receive different amounts at different times (quarterly, six monthly or annual annuities paid in arrears offer far better rates than annuities which pay income monthly in advance).

Why do annuity rates vary?

As we have already discussed, the annuity rate you are given depends on your life expectancy – which in turn is based on your age, sex and health – and the benefits you want to buy – a spouse's pension, inflation proofing, etc. However, the economic environment is also significant. Annuities are investments. The income they pay reflects the income they can afford to pay. When gilt yields (the return from government bonds) is at a low, annuity rates also fall.

This can dramatically hit the value of your annuity. For example, a male, aged 65, with a pension pot of £100,000 would have been able to achieve an annual annuity income of around £15,000 ten years ago. Today, the same man would only be able to secure an annual annuity income of about £8,000 a year.

Different Types of Annuity

Standard Annuities

These are the most popular because your income is guaranteed for the rest of your life. Once you know the benefits you want to take, the annuity is selected purely on price – the annuity provider paying you the highest pension income. You will be paid an annuity rate – for example, 6 per cent. If you have a £100,000 pension fund your annual income will be 6 per cent of this or £6,000.

They also carry no risks (other than that the annuity company goes bust). See How Safe Is My Annuity? on page 252.

Investment Annuities

With-profits Annuities: These carry some risk. They are relatively new and were launched when interest rates were low and stock market returns high and aim to provide income growth through steady investment performance. Bear in mind that the income from some with-profit annuities can go down as well as up so you could get poorer not richer as you age.

Some of them have a guaranteed minimum income level below which the annuity income can never fall.

Conventional With-profits Annuities: These have no guarantees, but you can select a level of first-year's income at the lower end of what you expect the bonus to be. Each year the provider will declare the bonus level it has achieved in the preceding year. If the total bonus is less than your anticipated bonus level, your income will be reduced for the next 12 months to reflect this fall. Obviously, if your provider achieves better results and the total bonus is greater than your anticipated bonus level, your income would be increased for the next year.

The annuity is linked to the investment performance of the insurance company, although with-profits funds are designed to smooth out investment returns in a volatile market. Some with-profits funds were harder hit by recent stock market falls than others so you need to check the financial strength and stability of the insurance company and its fund, and its ability to give good future growth.

So you have no certainty and your income will vary on an annual basis – and may sometimes fall as well as rise.

Note: Any protected rights benefits (the benefits that replace the state second pensions (SERPS or S2)) cannot be taken from with-profit or investment-linked annuities. They must be taken from a guaranteed conventional annuity.

Guaranteed With-profits Annuities: These are similar to the conventional with-profit annuities, but have minimum income guarantees, which in some instances will never be less than the starting income. Some providers have also scrapped the requirement to select an anticipated bonus level and have modified the bonus structure in order to simplify the product. However, the annuity is still linked to investment performance.

Warning: As with-profits annuities are complex investments and carry a degree of risk you should seek independent financial advice before making any decision.

Despite the bonus cuts suffered by with-profits annuities, some advisers recommend they may still be better than conventional annuities.

The assumed bonus – the amount needed to provide an income equivalent to that paid by a conventional annuity is now just 3 per cent. However, there is a risk. Bonus rates can vary and if the insurer goes under, the annuity is less protected. With conventional annuities 90 per cent of the income is protected if the worst happens.

Although once purchased, you cannot then change your mind about your annuity – it is a once-in-a-life decision – some with-profits annuity providers do allow you to switch to their standard annuity under certain circumstances. You cannot, however, move to another provider or switch back into a with-profits or unit-linked annuity.

Unit-linked Annuities: These are the riskiest of all. Your income may fluctuate and your investment is completely linked to the stock market – there is no ironing out of fluctuations as with a with-profits annuity.

These are only suitable for younger retirees who are prepared to gamble that stock markets will recover faster than the rates they can expect to get from a conventional annuity. Only a few providers offer this type of annuity. Generally, if you want this option you need to have other sources of retirement income, and not rely on this as a main source of income in retirement.

You should seek specialist independent financial advice and ensure it is ongoing so that you can change your investment strategy to maximize returns and minimize losses.

The annuity provider works out an income it will pay based on age and the size of your pension fund. This then buys units of the pension fund or funds and the value of these units fluctuates in line with market conditions. You can choose an anticipated growth level and take a gamble that investment performance will be higher than this. If it is not, your income will be cut.

Some unit-linked annuities allow you to choose your investments (these are known as self-invested annuities). However, they are riskier and invest directly in shares, gilts and unit and investment trusts. Once you reach 75 you can no longer self-invest.

Choosing an Annuity

In addition to the type of annuity (most will be standard annuities) you have other choices to make.

- when to buy it – the older you are the higher the income (see INCOME DRAW-DOWN on page 253)

- inflation-linking or other pension increases (or a flat rate annuity)

- pension for a spouse

- guarantees – should you buy some protection so that your annuity continues to pay out should you die in the first five years

Your choices will affect the income you receive. The tables below show the best rates on offer at the start of October 2002 and how your age, sex, whether or not you want a spouse's pension and the type of annuity you purchase affects your pension income. You may get up to £1,000 less each year by failing to shop around.

Best annuity rates for a £100,000 fund – no inflation linking.

Male, 55, single life	£6,139	Female, 55, single life	£5,825
Male, 60, single life	£6,912	Female, 60, single life	£6,363
Male, 65, single life	£8,061	Female, 65, single life	£7,195
Male, 70, single life	£9,839	Female, 70, single life	£8,289
Male, 74, single life	£11,809	Female, 74, single life	£9,627
Male 55, female 55, joint life	£5,854	Male 60, female 60, joint life	£6,293
Male 65, female 65, joint life	£7,019	Male 74, female 74, joint life	£9,355

Best annuity rates for a £100,000 fund – pension to rise by inflation (RPI)

Male, 55, single life	£4,270	Female, 55, single life	£3,942
Male, 60, single life	£5,005	Female, 60, single life	£4,526
Male, 65, single life	£6,051	Female, 65, single life	£5,330
Male, 70, single life	£7,819	Female, 70, single life	£6,444
Male, 74, single life	£9,789	Female, 74, single life	£7,656
Male 55, female 55, joint life	£3,872	Male 60, female 60, joint life	£4,442
Male 65, female 65, joint life	£5,232	Male 74, female 74, joint life	£7,554

All payments are monthly in arrears but are shown as the gross annual income amount, without a guarantee period and include escalation at RPI and spouse's benefit of 50% where applicable. Figures assume an annuity purchase price of £100,000. Figures supplied by The Annuity Bureau.

Although a pension for a spouse dramatically hits the amount you receive, it does at least guarantee that your pension does not die with you.

In addition, the following can affect what you receive as an income:

Frequency of Income

It is normally paid monthly but can be paid less frequently – quarterly, half-yearly or even annually. Income paid monthly in arrears is around 4 per cent less than annual in arrears according to the Annuity Bureau. For a male age 65 with £100,000 to purchase an annuity that can be the difference between £9,250 and £8,859 a year.

Whether Income Is Paid in Advance or in Arrears

If you take out an annuity and receive your payment the same day, you are being paid in advance. If you are paid a month later, in arrears. The difference in income is around 1 per cent. For a male aged 65 with £100,000 to purchase an annuity that can be the difference between £8,859 and £8,792 a year. You can opt for this to be with proportion (only suitable for those paid quarterly or less frequently). When you die the proportion would pay out a proportion of your annuity from the last payment until death.

Whether You Opt For a Guarantee

This guarantees to make payments for a guaranteed period even if you die within that period. This protects your pension if you die shortly after retirement and is suitable for those people who do not want their annuity to die when they do. You could also take this out to protect dependants (a spouse's pension will cover your spouse). The guarantee is expensive and could cost a man aged 60 1 per cent less income, aged 65 2 per cent less and aged 70 as much as 3 per cent. The rates are lower for women. The guarantee can either be for income to continue to the end of the five-year period or an equivalent lump sum to be paid.

Capital-Protected Guarantees

These will be available on annuities up to the age of 75 from 2004. On death, any remaining funds that have not been paid as income will be passed to the estate minus a 35 per cent tax charge. You will not be able to buy both a capital-protected guarantee or a 5- or 10-year guarantee, so you cannot buy a capital-protected guarantee and then switch. It will be possible to combine either a 5- or 10-year guarantee or a capital-protected guarantee with a spouse's permission.

Whether You Opt For an Escalating or a Level Pension

If you inflation proof, your starting pension will be lower. A 65-year-old man would receive 36 per cent less – a high price to pay. Bear in mind that a male aged 65 is likely to live for a further 19 years and a female aged 65 for another 22 years. According to the Annuity Bureau a 65-year-old man would be in his 80s before the total payments from an escalating annuity match those from a level annuity. So it is a gamble you must take. With inflation proofing you will preserve your spending power; even low inflation has an impact. After 15 years of inflation averaging 2.5 per cent, the buying power of £1,000 is just £684. On the flip side, if inflation is negative, however unlikely, your pension will decrease. You can also opt for limited price indexation – 5 per cent or inflation (the retail price index), whichever is lower – or a fixed percentage of up to 8.5 per cent a year. If you cannot afford full inflation proofing opt for a lower percentage.

A Spouse's Pension

Instead of your pension dying with you, an income – usually half your pension – is paid to your surviving partner for the rest of his or her life. You can choose anyone as your partner – unlike with most occupational schemes you do not have to be married and they can even be of the same sex. All that is required is the person's financial dependence upon you. The age of your spouse is the biggest factor affecting costs – particularly if your partner/spouse is significantly younger. According to the Annuity Bureau for a man aged 65 with a wife aged 62, the starting income would be around 14 per cent less than a single-life annuity if he chose a 50 per cent benefit for his wife. This income would fall to around 24 per cent less with a 100 per cent spouse's pension. Most couples, however, opt for an income between 33 per cent and 66 per cent.

Overlap

This is usually only available to retirees from company pension schemes where a five-year guarantee period and a spouse's pension are required. When the annuitant dies the spouse's pension starts immediately and – if death is within the guarantee period – the remaining guaranteed pension is also paid. Without overlap, annuities start paying the spouse's pension once the guaranteed period of pension finishes.

A Dependant's Pension

If you are not married, widowed, living with your partner or still have a dependent child (for example, one with special needs), you can provide a pension for this person – however, you will need to show financial dependency. This type of pension is expensive and not all annuity providers offer this as an option.

A New Choice

The pensions Green Paper has proposed limited-period annuities which will allow someone to use part of their pension fund to provide an annuity for a predetermined period.

How Safe Is My Annuity?

No one has been left out of pocket so far. However, annuities are not ring-fenced in a separate fund and, if their pension provider goes bust, they could lose money. However, in this instance up to 90 per cent of the money would be made up by the Financial Services Compensation Fund.

INCOME DRAW-DOWN

The main attraction is that on death the remaining funds (minus 35 per cent tax) pass to the surviving spouse or other named heir as a lump sum. With an annuity the funds die with you – unless you purchase a spouse's pension or a guarantee.

You are required to purchase an annuity by the age of 75 but in the meantime you can invest your pension fund in the hope that you will be better off as a result. This will be the case if:

- Your fund is invested well, giving a better return after charges than you have given up by not purchasing an annuity.

- Annuity rates when you finally buy an annuity have not fallen from the levels they were at your retirement.

However, few retirees can afford to leave their pension pot invested until they reach 75, so the rules allow you to draw an income from the pension fund, which is roughly equivalent to the income you would have received if you had purchased an annuity on retirement.

There are big risks with this option:

- You are swapping the certainty of a guaranteed income with the volatility of the investment markets.

- Annuity rates may not improve in future and could deteriorate.

- You will have to pay charges for investing your money which will eat into your returns.

This option is only open to those who can afford it, who:

- have at least £40,000 to invest

- have other forms of income (so do not have to rely on their income draw-down scheme)

- can delay purchasing their annuity for a long time – long enough for investment markets to improve and interest rates to rise

- do not need the income today, or may want to vary the income they receive

Even if you do not need the income today, you are required to withdraw a certain amount from your pension fund annually. What remains when you reach 75 must be used to purchase an annuity.

People who have very short life expectancy who fear they may die shortly after retirement or before age 75 may also consider the investment option, if they do not need to rely on this for their income, because the death benefits are more generous. Anyone who has not yet purchased an annuity can leave the entire fund to their relatives and are not restricted to simply providing a pension for their spouse. This amount will be subject to a 35 per cent tax charge – although it will not form part of your estate for inheritance tax purposes. If you have exceeded the inheritance tax threshold (£250,000 for the 2002/2003 tax year) your estate would have to pay a higher 40 per cent tax.

These schemes also put the investor in control, so you can choose where your money is invested. However, in general, these schemes are not a safe bet in the current environment.

Even if you delay purchasing your annuity for two years and this results in an extra £500 of income a year, you will have lost two years' income – for example, £10,000 – so will be far worse off. It could take you years to 'earn' this back from the extra £500 you get each year.

The Green Paper proposes that pensions can continue with income draw-down after age 75, but the arrangement after this age will become known as an 'unsecured annuity' and holders will no longer be able to pass on the remaining fund to their heirs. They will be able to buy a 5- or 10-year guarantee and a spouse's pension

– so an income can be provided but not a lump sum. Widows and widowers will also have the option of continuing with their spouse's income draw-down.

However, by removing the 75 age deadline, pensioners will get more flexibility and will not be forced to buy an annuity at a time when rates are poor or their investment fund has suffered a sudden downturn.

How do I know if it is a good idea for me?

Income draw-down schemes became popular when the stock markets were booming, but most pensioners who took them out are now nursing losses.

When considering the pros and cons, a specialist adviser will consider costs, expenses and risks before producing a critical yield comparison – this looks at what your investment will need to produce in order to match a conventional annuity. If you want to see how this works visit www.actuaries.org.uk and search for income draw-down. The technical notes are quite complex to understand, but do give a full picture of the factors you need to take into account.

For many people it will not come down to economics but how they feel. Generally, if you:

- have less than £100,000 in your pension fund

- want certainty in retirement

- are dependant on your fund for income

- are concerned about returns from equities

do not even bother to consider an income draw-down option.

PHASED RETIREMENT

The other alternative to buying an annuity with your pension fund is to purchase an annuity gradually over a number of years. This option, known as phased retirement, may be suitable for you if:

- You want to contribute to one of your pension plans to boost your long-term retirement income.

- You don't want to cash in all your pensions today when stock markets have still not recovered.

- You need to take some of your pension, but not all of it.

- You don't need to have all your tax-free lump sum today.

Phased retirement works by investing in a personal pension fund which in turn is divided into different segments. You cash these in as and when you need income. Each time you do so, you can take up to 25 per cent of that segment as a tax-free lump sum. You can, for example, cash in very few segments in the early years when, perhaps, you are working part-time. As with all personal pensions you must use the remaining fund to purchase an annuity by the time you reach 75.

The benefits, while similar to income draw-down plans, other than you do not have control over your investments, can be more tax efficient.

- Death benefits are more generous than with an annuity: the entire remaining fund can be left to your dependants. However, unlike with an income draw-down scheme, the entire fund can be left to your estate with no tax imposed.

- You can continue making pension contributions, and therefore receive tax relief, provided you are still earning a living.

There are still risks. Your fund remains invested and could still suffer from stock market falls (however, you can switch to much safer funds near or shortly after retirement).

Note: you can only take your tax-free cash entitlement each time you buy an annuity.

11 Pensions and Divorce

Britain has one of the highest divorce rates in the world. One in three marriages ends up in divorce and, apart from the emotional upheaval, separation from a partner can have drastic financial consequences. Both parties are often the poorer and the courts recommend an attempt to settle as amicably as possible to avoid escalating legal costs.

While most assets are fought over – including the house – until recently a man's second biggest asset – his pension – has been overlooked. This has left ex-wives much poorer because they tend to have very little in the way of private pensions.

If a wife has given up her career to run a home, raise a family and look after her husband, it is unlikely she has paid any pension contributions herself or has not done so for some time. If she goes out to get a job after the marriage breaks down it is likely to be low paid with little scope to build up her own pension rights.

According to statistics from the Department of Social Security, the average value of a man's occupational pension is £50,000, compared with £7,000 for women.

THE WELFARE AND PENSIONS ACT

In December 2000, the government recognized that the failure to take into account pension assets on divorce could lead to a real danger of increased numbers of women facing poverty in retirement.

The pension splitting law, the Welfare and Pensions Act, allows a spouse to take half the main breadwinner's pension (whether it is the husband's or the wife's) and allows them to plough it into their own pension.

How does it work?

The fund of the main breadwinner is 'debited' and a new pension fund for the other spouse is 'credited'. The pension scheme makes a cash transfer available so that the other spouse can start a new fund giving them a clean break from their partner. Some pension companies may allow the other spouse to set up a separate fund within the same scheme (an internal transfer) – or alternatively they could even transfer the 'credit' to a new scheme if they want to (an external transfer).

Of course, the spouse can only receive the benefit of the pension splitting when they reach an age of retirement themselves. However, under previous legislation they had to wait until their former spouse retired. So if a couple divorces at 40, the wife will not be able to take the pension until she retires (from 50 rising to 55 from 2010, for a personal pension or 65 with most employer schemes).

What was the previous legal requirement?

This law was complicated – an unsatisfactory system of 'offsetting' and 'earmarking' pension assets – that the courts used to employ.

Offsetting: The value of the pension fund was added to the total matrimonial assets, which were then divided up. The results were deeply unfair, leaving the wife in the position to walk away with a large amount of capital (albeit with no pension), while the husband could be left nearly penniless and still having to wait to reach a retirement age before he was able to draw out his own bit of the pension.

Earmarking: The courts used to set aside a portion of the pension to go to the ex-spouse to be activated when the fund was finally paid out. But in this instance, a different problem could arise: if the spouse with the pension rights died before retirement, the former partner could be left with nothing.

Both of these previous options were unsatisfactory, and people campaigned long and hard to introduce the pension-sharing law, but research shows there were just 367 sharing orders made in the last 12 months in 140,000 divorces.

Why are people still not taking full advantage of pension sharing?

The courts do not automatically enforce pension sharing – they consider it merely another option at the time and might only apply it to one third of couples who divorce each year.

Most couples are suffering from emotional stress during a divorce settlement, particularly when children are involved, and many find themselves wanting to sort out the housing issues first and are often concerned that if they bring the pension issue into the equation they could jeopardize negotiations and cause further delays. In other cases, spouses are simply unaware of just how valuable their former partner's pension is – although their legal advisers should recommend that they find out this information and include it as part of any settlement. They may feel that retirement is a long way off. This is no excuse not to consider the long-term future. Young women with children may not earn a sufficient salary to have enough to save adequate amounts for their own pension.

WHICH PENSIONS CAN BE TAKEN INTO ACCOUNT ON DIVORCE?

State Second Pension (SERPS/S2P)

Any pension built up in SERPS, now S2P, can be taken into account when deciding a divorce settlement. However, any entitlement to the basic state pension is not shared on divorce.

Personal/Stakeholder Pensions

These are the easiest to split as the money can simply be transferred to a separate pension or earmarked in a separate pot.

Employer Pensions

Specialist advice may be needed to determine the value. The spouse who is a member of the scheme may have a guaranteed pension if it is a final salary scheme, while the ex-partner may have to take on the risk of investing the money in a personal or stakeholder pension.

Top-up Pensions

Any scheme to boost the employer pension such as an additional voluntary contribution (AVC) can also be taken into account.

How are they valued?

The value placed on the pension – before it is divided – is the cash equivalent transfer value. However, this may be adjusted depending on the specific circumstances.

Should I transfer my share of the pension to my own plan?

You can do. However, if it is in a final salary scheme you may be advised to keep it where it is. You must seek advice from an independent financial adviser before doing so.

You may have to. Some schemes will not allow dual membership. Your share of the pension must then be given as an external transfer to another pension arrangement such as a stakeholder pension.

Divorce and State Pensions

If one spouse, during the marriage, paid insufficient contributions to build up an entitlement to the basic state pension (known as qualifying years) he or she can elect to use the former spouse's contributions for the years of the marriage. These will boost the basic pension given on retirement as people with insufficient National Insurance Contributions do not qualify for the full amount.

WHAT HAPPENS AFTER DIVORCE?

Former partners are no longer penalized if:

- their ex-partner dies

- they remarry

If the ex-wife (it usually works this way round) remarries she does not lose her rights to the pension from her former husband. Likewise, if her ex-husband dies she no longer loses out. Previously she could not claim his pension assets, now she is entitled to her own share. If her husband wishes to delay taking his pension, she can still take her share on time, on retirement age, or sooner if it is a personal pension. The member of the pension scheme (usually the husband) loses. He will have to make additional contributions to bolster his pension but cannot pay in more than 15 per cent of salary (higher if it is a personal pension) in order to make up for the sum given to his wife.

However, he may no longer have to pay for a spouse's pension when he retires.

WHAT HAPPENS IF I DIVORCED BEFORE THE LAW CHANGED?

There is little you can do now that the settlement has been made. However, bear in mind that you have lost out on a potential pension entitlement and make up for the shortfall by starting or boosting your own retirement provision.

12 The Pension Alternatives

Pensions may be tax efficient but they are also inflexible, unlike many other forms of investment which put the investor in charge. In addition, pensions are not so attractive as they once were. Following the recent stock market falls investors may be looking for alternative homes for their money. The mis-selling scandals, problems at Equitable Life, high charges, low annuity rates and restrictions on what you can do with your money on retirement, all make alternative investments look far more attractive than pensions.

Some workers may not want to wait until they are 50 – or 65 with employer schemes – to get their hands on their pensions, or they may want more flexible investments. Older workers may find pensions are not suitable because they do not have enough time to build up a significant pension on retirement, while younger workers may be looking for alternatives fearing that by the time they approach retirement the final salary scheme may be a thing of the past and the state retirement age could have increased to 70.

Life is less certain today. Gone are the days when you joined an employer from school or college and remained with the same employer for 40 years. Life's ups and downs and the high costs of housing mean that many younger workers are reluctant to invest in a pension – after all, the money is locked up until retirement and cannot be accessed in an emergency. Although some people would argue this is a good thing because it ensures that, whatever happens, at least they will have something saved for their future.

So what are the alternatives?

INDIVIDUAL SAVINGS ACCOUNTS (ISA)

These are flexible tax-free savings schemes which make an ideal alternative to a pension.

They will particularly suit people:

- who do not want to lock away their savings – younger workers, people with families who may need the money for other things, etc.

- who want to decide what they do with their money on retirement – with a pension the bulk of your fund (usually 75 per cent) must be used to provide you with a pension income, only a quarter can be taken as a tax-free lump sum

- who want to exceed the investment limits imposed on pensions

- who may want to take their money before retirement – for example, to pay off their mortgage and clear their debts

- who want to retire before age 50 (the minimum age allowed by pension schemes)

- who don't like paying high investment charges – ISAs (but not all) have some of the lowest charges for direct investment in shares

- who are very near retirement and want to keep their money in a savings account but not suffer tax on any interest

- who do not want to risk their money on the stock market.

- who don't want to have to buy an annuity when they retire in case they do not live very long

- who don't want to be locked into today's low annuity rates

- who don't want to risk retiring after the stock market has fallen (as it has done recently) and want to keep their options open

You should be aware that while ISAs are tax-free schemes they do not attract tax relief. So investors have to contribute £100 to invest £100, whereas with a pension they only need pay in £78 (as a basic-rate taxpayer) or £60 (as a higher-rate taxpayer) for £100 to be invested in their pension. However, with an investment such as an ISA, no annuity needs to be purchased so the entire sum can be taken tax free on retirement. As annuity rates are less generous for younger retirees (in their early 50s), ISAs could produce a better rate of income.

To sum up:

• With a pension you get tax relief – none is given on ISA investments.

• Both grow free of tax.

• You can only retire from age 50 with a personal pension – at any time with an ISA.

• You do not have to buy an annuity or take a pension with an ISA – you can do what you want with the money.

What Are ISAs?

ISAs enable savers to put their money into three different types of investment:

• Cash deposits. These are savings accounts offered by banks, building societies and other savings institutions. Some accounts may be more complex than others in that they may have tiered rates (a higher rate of interest is given, the more money is invested) and notice periods (so investors cannot get access to their cash instantly without incurring an interest penalty).

• Stock-market based investments. These can include unit trusts, investment trusts, open-ended investment companies, government bonds or gilts, corporate bonds and individual shares.

- Life insurance investments. There is no life cover as part of these investments, instead they are investment funds run by life insurance companies.

ISAs are free of income tax and capital gains tax and ISA investments do not have to be declared on tax returns.

The Tax Rules

The income tax rules are:

- Interest on cash deposits (savings) is free of tax.

- Dividends from UK equities receive a 10 per cent tax credit for the period to 5 April 2004 (they will suffer this 10 per cent deduction after 2004) and higher-rate taxpayers will have no further liability to tax.

- Corporate bonds (fixed interest distributions) receive interest gross of tax at 20 per cent.

The ISA provider will claim back all the income tax for investors, who do not have to do a thing.

After 5 April 2004, ISA investments that earn dividends will attract tax on these dividends which the ISA provider will pay. There will still be no personal liability to income tax or capital gains tax for ISA investors.

The capital gains tax rules are:

- All gains from any investment sold within an ISA are free of capital gains tax.

- Investors cannot offset any losses on ISA investments against gains made elsewhere.

The investment requirements are that:

- Investors must be aged 18 or over.

- Investors must be resident in the United Kingdom for tax purposes (or a Crown employee currently working overseas and treated as resident).

Investors cannot hold an ISA jointly with anyone else (so couples cannot have a joint account) or hold one on behalf of another person (so grandparents or parents cannot open an account on behalf of their grandchildren/children).

How Much Can Be Invested?

Each individual can invest up to £7,000 in each tax year (the tax year runs from 6 April to 5 April). This limit applies until April 2006 when it could be reviewed. Within this overall limit there are restrictions on the amount of money that can be held in each type of investment depending on the type of ISA that investors choose. Investors who do not have the full £7,000 need not worry. It is possible to open an ISA with as little as £1. Further investments can be made at any time – either as lump sums or as regular payments. Married couples each have an ISA allowance of £7,000 a year. That means a total of £14,000 can be sheltered from tax in each tax year by a couple.

The amount that can be invested in an ISA (within the £7,000 overall limit) depends on the type of investment and the type of ISA. There are three different types of ISA:

- maxi

- mini

- TESSA-only (you can invest the proceeds of a maturing TESSA into an ISA)

Maxi ISAs

These allow investors to invest the maximum ISA allowance of £7,000 with just *one* ISA provider. Investors cannot shop around for the best rates on savings and buy these from one provider and then find the most suitable investment fund and buy it from another provider. They have to buy all their investments from the same company. (There is an exception to this – see fund supermarkets on page 271.)

If investors buy a maxi ISA they cannot also have a mini ISA, but they can have a TESSA-only ISA.

Within the overall £7,000 limit, maxi ISA investors can invest:

- up to £7,000 in stocks- and shares-based investments

- up to £3,000 in cash savings

- up to £1,000 in life insurance investments

So an investor wanting to invest £2,000 in savings and £5,000 in share-based investments can do so with a maxi ISA because this does not exceed the £7,000 overall investment limit. Alternatively, the investor could put the whole £7,000 into stocks and shares.

Mini ISAs

Investors can have up to three mini ISAs provided each invests in a different type of allowable investment. So one could be a cash ISA, one a share-based ISA and one a life-insurance ISA. It is not possible to have two cash ISAs in the same tax year – even if the investor does not exceed the overall £7,000 ISA investment limit, and if an investor has a mini ISA, he cannot have a maxi ISA.

The maximum that can be invested in each type of investment through a mini ISA is:

- up to £3,000 in cash savings

- up to £3,000 in stocks and shares

- up to £1,000 in life insurance investments

Which Type of ISA Is the Most Tax Efficient?

Both types of ISA – maxi and mini – are free of income and capital gains tax, so there are no differences in the tax breaks. However, the different investment limits for each type of ISA mean that investors can invest more free of tax if they make a wiser choice. Investors who want to shelter more than £3,000 in a stocks and shares ISA should opt for a maxi ISA. With a mini ISA they can only invest a maximum of £3,000 whereas with a maxi ISA they can invest £7,000.

Investors who mainly want to invest in a cash savings ISA should look primarily at mini cash ISAs. While the investment limits for mini and maxi ISAs are the same for cash deposits, there is a wide choice of mini ISAs with some very good rates.

Maximizing the Investment Potential

Once you invest in an ISA do not cash it in. If you are unhappy with the performance switch it to another ISA but do not take your money out, if you do you will lose your ISA allowance for that year for ever.

If you invest £7,000 a year for 10 years, you can invest a total of £70,000, which could be worth £100,000 if invested well. This money will continue to grow tax free.

Cash in some of your investment and you cannot then reinvest without using up the current year's ISA allowance.

Even so, ISA investments can be cashed in at any time if money is needed in a hurry.

Choosing an ISA

The tax breaks of an ISA may be very appealing, but, investors should not let the tax tail wag the investment dog. There is no point investing in a tax-free savings account which pays 3 per cent interest if there is a taxable one paying 6 per cent, and the investor is a basic-rate taxpayer. He or she will be no better off.

To ensure that investors are not being seduced by a tax break at the expense of their savings, the government introduced what is known as the CAT standard. This stands for fair Charges, easy Access and decent Terms and conditions. The standard is voluntary and not all ISAs meet the CAT standard. The rules vary depending on the type of ISA.

For cash ISAs to be CAT-marked the ISA provider must:

- make no charges

- have a minimum transfer/investment of £10

- allow withdrawals within seven working days or less

- not pay interest that is more than 2 per cent less than the bank base rate

For stocks and shares ISAs to be CAT-marked the charges cannot total more than 1 per cent of the investment and the minimum saving must be no more than £500 as a lump sum per year or £50 per month.

For life insurance ISAs to be CAT-marked the charges must be no more than 3 per cent of the investment, there must be no penalty when the ISA is cashed in and investors must get back at least all the premiums they have paid in the three years or more before the date when the life insurance investment is cashed in.

However, opting for an ISA that meets the CAT standard is no guarantee that it is the best deal for an individual. Some cash ISAs, for example, do not meet the CAT standard because they have notice periods and minimum investments of £3,000. However, these non-CAT standard cash ISAs often pay the highest rates of interest. Some ISAs with low charges that do meet the CAT standard have a poorer performance than those with high charges and no CAT mark. It is better to get a 20 per cent return on the investment year-on-year and suffer a 3 per cent initial charge and a 1.5 per cent annual charge than to get a 5 per cent return with charges totalling just 1 per cent a year.

Choosing a Cash ISA

- Rates can fall – check if the ISA is CAT-marked, which will guarantee a minimum return.

- You can get a fix – fixed rates offer the greatest certainty, but you may not be able to access your money without giving as much as 90 days notice. This should not be a problem, though, if you are using your ISA for pension planning.

- The more you invest the better the rate – the best rates are usually only given to those prepared to invest the maximum £3,000 allowed.

You can check out the best ISA rates in personal finance sections published by newspapers such as the *Telegraph*, in specialist magazines or by searching on the internet at sites such as www. moneysupermarket.com. Do not be tempted to take the easy route and buy the ISA from your bank, the rate is unlikely to be the most competitive. Shop around first.

Choosing a Stocks and Shares ISA

- Past performance is no guarantee of future performance – look for an ISA with a consistently good investment track record rather than the latest investment fad. Sectors that perform spectacularly well often fall back just as fast – remember what happened when the dot.com bubble burst.

- Charges will eat into your returns. Think twice about investing in a fund with slightly higher charges than others. You are investing for the long term and even a 0.25 per cent a year difference in charges will add up significantly over ten or even 20 years. There can be two charges – the initial (from 0–5 per cent) and the annual (from 0.5–1.5 per cent).

- Investment choice is important – some providers only offer basic tracker funds which track a stock market index. However, if one market dips you will want the ability to switch to a different sector that is unaffected or hit less hard.

- Your existing investments. Each year invest the £7,000 allowed in a different fund or sector. You don't want to have all your eggs in one basket. Diversity is important.

Self-select ISAs

Investors who believe they can produce better returns than a fund manager, can make their investment decisions themselves. Self-select ISAs allow the investor to choose individual shares or even a combination of shares, investment trusts, unit trusts, open-ended investment companies, gilts and bonds.

Where Can I Buy an ISA?

ISAs are sold by:

- banks

- building societies

- fund managers/unit trust managers

- stockbrokers

- financial advisers

- fund supermarkets

- discount brokers

What Is a Fund Supermarket?

Although investors with a maxi ISA are usually restricted to buying all their investments from one ISA provider, there is a way for investors to purchase a range of different funds from different fund managers. Fund supermarkets allow investors to mix and match their stocks and shares ISAs. So instead of being restricted to the choice of funds from XYZ fund manager, the investor can select two or three from various fund managers from a choice of over a thousand and hold these within one ISA account. The added advantage is that fund supermarkets usually sell unit trust funds at a discount – rebating some of the commission they would other-wise have earned from the fund management company. However, this comes at a price. Individual investment advice is not given although most have lists of recommended funds. As a result these supermarket services tend to cater for the more sophisticated investor.

What Is a Discount Broker?

A firm of financial intermediaries (who may also be financial advisers) who sell financial products without giving any advice. Instead, they pass on to the investor some or all of the money that would have been deducted by the fund manager to pay for the salesman's commission. As they give no advice, their costs are lower and so they can afford to do this. However, they rarely pass on the annual commission paid to advisers (this is part of the annual charge you will pay) and still make a comfortable profit.

Note: Even if you buy your stocks and shares ISA direct from a fund manager the same charges apply – whether you receive advice or not. So why pay for it, if you are not getting it?

Although no advice is given, investors are usually given a list of recommended ISA funds and sometimes there are decision trees to help them make their investment selection. If, however, you are not comfortable in making your own choice, seek independent financial advice.

Reviewing Your ISA Performance

It is vital that you review your ISA investments to ensure that you are still getting value for money. The rates on cash ISAs can fall and the investment funds you selected five years ago when they were top performance may now have dropped to the bottom of the league tables. Investors who are not happy with the performance of their ISA should not be tempted, however, to cash in their investment, because they will lose the tax break. Instead, they should consider switching to another fund or another ISA provider. Only the same components of an ISA can be switched. So an investor cannot move a stocks and shares ISA into a cash ISA or vice versa. Transfers much be made directly from one ISA provider to another – investors cannot cash in their investment and then reinvest this money with a different provider.

Your Options on Retirement

You can do what you want: retire when you want; use the money for what you want; and you will not pay tax on it – unlike with a pension, which is taxed as income.

OTHER TAX-FREE INVESTMENTS

ISAs are the main alternative to pensions. However, they are not the only tax-free schemes and they do have strict investment limits (£7,000 a year). If you want to exceed these limits without suffering tax you can consider:

National Savings

It offers several schemes that are tax free. However, savers should not be seduced by the tax breaks. Some accounts pay very poor rates of interest. In some cases the total return can be beaten by investing in an alternative savings account even where the interest paid is subject to tax. However, higher-rate taxpayers may find that the 40 per cent tax saving makes these schemes competitive.

Savings Certificates

Both the index-linked and fixed-interest savings certificates are tax free. The minimum investment is £100 and the maximum in any one issue is £10,000. However, as new issues are made relatively frequently, investors have the opportunity to invest further amounts in each one. There is also no limit on reinvesting the proceeds of matured certificates. Fixed-interest certificates pay a guaranteed income over five years – hence, the term 'fixed'. Index-linked certificates, as the name implies, pay interest at a fixed percentage above the annual rate of inflation (the retail price index). Savers who withdraw their money before the term of the account is up (two or five years depending on the certificate) will suffer because reduced interest is paid, and no interest in some cases. No amount of tax breaks will make up for this. So savers need to be sure that they can hold their certificate for the required number of years.

Friendly Societies

These offer long-term investment plans (ten years minimum) which are tax free but restricted to a very small annual investment of just £270. They are a useful addition to a portfolio, but charges can be high, and they are very inflexible with investors suffering heavily if they cash in their plan early.

Tax-free Investments You May Already Have

If you have any tax-free investment that are no longer on sale, these should be included as part of your pension planning. Do not be tempted to cash these schemes in (unless you have to) as you will lose the tax breaks they offer for ever. Review their investment performance regularly because you may no longer be getting value for money. You should be able to switch your investment to a better-performing scheme without losing any of the tax advantages.

These schemes include:

Personal Equity Plan (PEP)

Although PEPs were withdrawn from sale on 6 April 1999, when ISAs were launched, they did not cease to exist. Any PEP investments made before that date can continue to grow free of tax, although no additional investments can be made.

PEP investments are restricted to stocks- and share-based investments. In that sense they are similar to stocks and shares ISAs. They ran for a decade and attracted £70 billion of investors' money – far more than is invested in ISAs. It is vital that investors do not forget about any money tied up in a PEP and review their investments regularly to ensure they are performing well. Transfers are allowed. All investors need to do is check there are no penalties or charges for switching and to check that the manager to whom they wish to transfer their holdings is willing to accept the transfer.

Remember, PEP investments are an addition to any ISA investments – so they increase the amount that can be invested free of tax.

Tax Exempt Special Savings Account (TESSA)

The TESSA was also withdrawn from sale on 6 April 1999 and replaced by the ISA, and once again existing investors could keep their tax breaks.

Any money invested in a TESSA can continue to grow tax free and investors with TESSAs taken out before 6 April 1999 can continue to invest regular amounts (up to set limits) until their TESSA matures at the end of five years. The maximum that can be invested over the five-year term is £9,000 (existing TESSA savers can invest up to £1,800 each tax year until the five-year term is reached).

Because of the five-year term, many TESSAs are now coming up to maturity. In 2001 alone over two million savers had £21 billion invested in maturing TESSAs.

Once the TESSA matures, investors have these options:

- take all the proceeds

- place the capital (not any interest earned) of the maturing TESSA into a TESSA-only ISA

- transfer the capital proceeds into the cash component of a maxi or mini ISA

Transfers into cash ISAs or TESSA-only ISAs must be done within six months of the TESSA maturing.

As with PEPs, savers who are unhappy with the performance of their TESSA (rates can be poor) should not cash in their account. Once they close their TESSA, the tax breaks these schemes offer are lost for ever. Instead, they should consider transferring their TESSA to another provider. However, check first if there are any penalties charged and that providers paying better rates accept transfers (not all do).

OTHER FORMS OF INVESTMENT

You do not have to buy shares and other equity investments such as bonds or gilts through an ISA – you can buy them direct. However, the charges are often higher. Over the long run you will usually be better off investing in an ISA than investing in the same investments without the tax-free wrapper. However, ISAs do have limits – a maximum of £7,000 can be invested in each tax year; although this will cover most investors' needs, some may want to set aside more for their retirement.

Shares are the main alternative to an ISA. Despite recent falls in stock markets historically they have produced better returns than savings accounts. However, bear in mind:

- You need to spread your risk. Buying individual shares is expensive so you may want to buy through a collective investment such as a unit trust or an investment trust.

- If you want advice it will be expensive. Cheap stockbroking deals are only offered on execution-only business, where no advice is given. For a full advisory service, some stockbrokers will require you to have at least £50,000 to invest.

- You will pay tax on the dividends (the income from shares) and on any profits (capital gains) at your highest rate.

USING PROPERTY TO BOOST YOUR PENSION

Your home is not only your biggest asset but probably also your biggest expense. During your working life you can make it work for you to help you plan for your retirement. Remember:

- Profits made on your main home are usually tax free.

- Any interest you save on your mortgage is tax free while any interest on your savings is usually taxed.

- The longer you borrow for, the more interest you will pay.

- The lower your monthly mortgage payments, the more money you will have to invest for your retirement.

- If you repay your mortgage more quickly you could retire early.

Making the Most of Your Mortgage

It has never been more vital to make the most of every penny. If you are prudent and have savings, investments and pensions you will have seen the value of these plummet as stock markets have tumbled, and now your endowment policy may no longer provide enough to repay your mortgage. At the same time, savings rates are at an historical low so you will not get rich sticking your cash in a bank or a building society.

So how can you make your money work for you?

- Stop paying the standard variable rate – the very least you can do is to remortgage to a better rate, but check first if there are any penalties for doing so.

- Opt for flexible facilities – you can then pay in a little extra each month to repay your mortgage more quickly (flexible mortgages allow this).

- Offset your mortgage and savings to get mortgage savings – combine all your financial products to make the most of them. Savings reduce borrowings and therefore reduce the interest you are charged, cutting the costs and reducing the term of your mortgage. Opt for an offset or all-in-one mortgage.

- Use your current account to save money. By paying your salary into your all-in-one or offset account you cut your total borrowings instantly, and therefore save interest. As the month goes on and you spend more, the amount you owe will rise, but you will still save money. The average earner pays over £1 million into his or her current account during his or her working life but is paid just over £40 in interest – what a pitiful return! You could save £4,000 by paying your salary into an all-in-one account. These are known as current account mortgages.

To find out how much you could save, visit www.charcolonline.co.uk, and to compare mortgages visit www.fsa.gov.uk/tables. By charging interest at a competitive rate on a daily basis (so you only pay interest on what you actually owe, unlike with a traditional mortgage which charges you interest on the amount owed at the start of the year) the savings add up so borrowers have the added bonus of paying off their mortgage more quickly. As a nation we could ⌐ billions of pounds by pooling our finances in all-in-one or o¬⌐ accounts with the average mortgage holder saving £12,000 according to Barclays.

However, if you want to take advantage of an all-in-one account, you have to change the way you think.

- Put all your eggs into one basket: it goes against the grain, but if you combine all your finances in one account, or linked accounts, any money you have in your current account and savings accounts then reduces the amount you owe on your mortgage and loans and in some cases credit cards. As you owe less, you pay less interest.

- No longer have savings: it is natural to want the comfort of a savings account. However, instead of earning the low rates of interest paid on savings accounts (3 per cent after tax if you are lucky) you effectively earn the much higher mortgage rate in an all-in-one account because savings are used to reduce borrowing. Because you are saving interest, not being paid interest, these savings are tax-free. If you need your 'savings' you simply increase your borrowing facility.

- Borrow more: having one big debt may seem daunting, but by putting all your borrowings into one large mortgage including personal loans, credit card debts, car loans and any other finance that costs you money, you will save money. The mortgage rate is by far the cheapest way to borrow. By picking the cheapest rate you can even borrow MORE and it will cost you LESS.

Not Just For Young Homebuyers

Although flexible and all-in-one accounts mainly appeal to wealthier, younger homebuyers, older homebuyers can benefit more because:

- They tend to have more savings.

- They have fewer drains on their finances (lower mortgages, children grown up).

- They generally want to be mortgage free as soon as possible.

- They have exhausted most other tax-free ways to save (although offset and all-in-one accounts aren't tax free, because interest is saved not earned you are effectively earning a much higher rate than in a savings account and earning it tax free).

The average UK mortgage borrower aged between 45 and 54 owes £55,800, has 9.5 years left to run on the mortgage, a current account balance of £1,640 and savings of £4,020. Put these into an offset account such as the one offered by Intelligent Finance and this could save them £6,530 compared to a standard mortgage.

Using Your Home as Your Pension

Many homeowners wrongly think that their property – which has risen in value dramatically over the last decade – will keep them in their old age. But you will still have to pay for somewhere else to live, and all property prices have risen. If you are prepared to trade down the property ladder to release some capital this can help fund your retirement. The alternatives are releasing equity from your home while continuing to live in it. See Chapter 14: On Retirement for further advice.

Investing In a Second Property

This has been a boom market. Share values have plummeted while property prices have soared so it is no wonder that increasing numbers of people are looking to bricks and mortar as an investment – often for their retirement.

Buy-to-Let

This is the most popular form of property investment. Homes are purchased generally with:

- a minimum 20 per cent deposit

- a buy-to-let mortgage

The theory is that the rental income from the property will then cover these mortgage payments as well as any other associated costs. A small profit may even be made.

On retirement, the options are to:

- Sell the property and once capital gains tax has been paid use the proceeds to fund retirement.

- Continue to rent the property and with the mortgage repaid use the rental income as an income in retirement. By this stage, the rental income could be substantial. Like other income it will be taxed (although you can deduct some associated costs, such as letting agent's fees, before your taxable profits from renting are calculated). As an example, if the property achieved a rental yield of around 7 per cent a year and was worth £150,000 that would give you an additional pension income of roughly £875 per month – or £200 a week. This will rise every year or so as rents tend to rise annually. You may only have had to invest £20,000 in this property in the first place so that is a substantial return.

There is probably no other pension that can give you an income for life of £875 a month (and rising) for a £20,000 investment.

Buy-to-let is not without risks.

- Property prices could fall.

- Mortgage rates could rise and the interest may not be covered by the rent, plunging you into debt.

- You may not be able to rent the property and will have to pay two mortgages.

- Your tenants may run off without paying you and take all your furniture/the cooker, etc.

The current market has overheated and supply has outstripped demand in many areas and people who have jumped on the buy-to-let wagon have found themselves with a financial drain not an asset.

However, you are looking long term – 20 years or even longer – so you must take a long-term view.

- Pick a property that you will still be able to let in ten years' time – so go for an area that is already established with strong demand (from students, for example). Up-and-coming areas may remain less desirable.

- Pick a property that is easy to maintain. You do not want large repair bills in five or ten years' time.

- Pick a property that is nearby. As you get older you will not want to travel large distances to keep an eye on your property.

The tax advantages

Little or No Income Tax Initially: As most of your rent will be eaten up with mortgage payments you will make very little profit and therefore suffer little or no income tax. Put the property into the name of a non-taxpaying spouse and it will be tax free.

Investors in buy-to-let properties are generally advised to charge around 30 per cent more than their borrowing costs to cover periods when there are no tenants and the costs of letting out the property (management fees, advertising costs, etc.).

Before arriving at their taxable profits they can deduct allowable expenses including:

- mortgage interest (but not repayments)

- service charges and ground rents

- letting agent's fees

- advertising costs

- managing agent's fees

However, the cost of furnishing a flat or house cannot be deducted as an allowable expense. Although this is not an issue for people letting an existing home which is already furnished, for new buy-to-let landlords it can represent a significant cost particularly as the better quality the furnishings (and therefore the more expensive) the higher the rent. Only wear and tear can be claimed (generally 10 per cent of the rent). To get round this restriction, landlords can rent the furniture and claim the full costs of renting it as an allowable expense.

Buy-to-let investors cannot claim the deposit paid on the property (generally at least 20 per cent of the purchase price) as an allowable expense. They can claim the interest they pay on a loan taken out to buy or improve the property. As a result, it pays to borrow as much as the individual can afford or is allowed.

✎ TIP

If a buy-to-let landlord makes a loss – for example, if the initial costs of furnishing a property and advertising it do not cover the costs of the mortgage – then they can use this to offset future rental profits by carrying the loss forward to the next tax year.

Capital Gains Tax at a Reduced Rate: The capital gains tax you pay on the sale of assets, such as second homes, is greatly reduced the longer you own the asset. The tax is paid on gains – basically the profit, or what you sold the house for minus the cost of buying it, the cost of any improvements and the cost of buying and selling it. The tax is paid at your highest rate on all gains over £7,700 (the 2002/2003 tax year figure) in any tax year. As most buy-to-let properties are owned for a long period your tax will be reduced as follows:

How Taper Relief Reduces the Equivalent Capital Gains Tax (CGT) Rate

Complete years after 5 April 1998 the asset was held	Percentage of gain chargeable (this is the taper)	Equivalent Basic-rate taxpayers	CGT rate Higher-rate taxpayers
0	100	20	40
1	100	20	40
2	100	20	40
3	95	19	38
4	90	18	36
5	85	17	34
6	80	16	32
7	75	15	30
8	70	14	28
9	65	13	26
10+	60	12	24

A whole year refers to any continuous period of 12 months – it does not have to coincide with a tax year. Fractions of a year are ignored.

So, even as a higher-rate taxpayer the maximum you will be charged in CGT is 24 per cent of the taxable gain, assuming like many buy-to-let investors you invest for at least ten years.

Buy-to-Let v. Shares

What makes buy-to-let more potentially profitable is the gearing (borrowing).

With a £20,000 deposit you can buy a £100,000 property and benefit from the income and growth on that full £100,000 whereas you can only buy £20,000 of shares with the same amount of capital. Even if property prices grow at a much slower rate than the stock market, the profits will be greater from buy-to-let. In this example, if property prices rose by 20 per cent over 5 years you would make a £20,000 capital appreciation from a £100,000 property. So your profits on your £20,000 deposit would be 100 per cent. To make the same amount from shares, they would have to double in value.

Also, two mortgages may be better than one. Even if the rental income only covers your costs, someone else is paying the mortgage and you benefit from the capital appreciation of the property.

Warning: Buy-to-let is not without its risks. If you cannot afford to pay two mortgages at times when you cannot find a tenant you could end up in serious financial trouble and lose both homes. Do your sums before investing.

Let-to-Buy

This is similar to buy-to-let only the other way round – you let your existing home and then buy another. For example, a couple own two properties, but want to buy a home together. They sell one property to raise the deposit for the marital home and keep the other property as an investment.

If you do decide to rent out your home and move to another, do not forget to add in the cost of moving, stamp duty and the deposit on the new home.

The advantages are:

- You can cash in on the rise in value of two properties – not just one.

- If two of you own properties and you want to buy together, you only need sell one home to find the deposit and you can rent the other out keeping it as an investment.

However:

- You need substantial capital – 20 per cent of the price of your existing property for a buy-to-let mortgage and around 5 per cent for your new home.

- If you are planning to rise up the property ladder you may not be able to afford a bigger home as some of your capital is tied up in your existing property and you may not have sufficient income to stretch to a bigger mortgage with less capital.

Where can I find out more?

The Association of Residential Letting Agents hotline – 01923 896 555 – can give you details of your nearest agents and send you a free booklet.

The Council Of Mortgage Lenders publishes two leaflets, *Buying to Let* and *Thinking of Buying a Residential Property to Let? A Check-List for Investing Landlords*. They are obtainable free of charge by ringing 020 7440 2255.

Alternative Investments

Some alternative investment indices have done far better than shares over the 10 years to the end of 2002 – mainly because of stock-market falls. The wine index (based on the *Decanter* magazine's value of a bottle of Mouton-Rothschild 1982) outperformed the FTSE by 295 per cent, average UK house prices outperformed by 33 per cent and antiques by 8 per cent. The conflicts in the Middle East sent the gold price soaring and the value of oil has increased. While these investments may seem to be a better bet than shares, remember that gold has proved a poor investment in recent years and most alternative investments are in unregulated areas so it is easy to get ripped off.

13 Planning Your Retirement

As the population ages, retirement gets longer and that has implications for your wealth, health, home and family.

Life expectancy for men and women at birth will have increased from 45 and 49 years respectively in 1901 to a projected 80 and 84 years by 2011. So you can expect 15 to 25 years of retirement. It is a long time, particularly if you have little money and spend your final years in poverty.

Many of us dream of a retirement spent cruising the world, playing golf, having friends and family to visit, going to the theatre and generally enjoying our golden years. However, if you do not plan your retirement carefully, these dreams will remain just that – dreams.

CHOOSING WHEN TO RETIRE

You generally need to choose when you are going to retire well in advance. When you take out a personal or a stakeholder pension, for example, you are required to give a planned retirement date – even if this is 40 years away. You do not always get a choice. Your employer's pension scheme will usually require you to retire at 65. Your retirement date may also be forced upon you because:

- You may be made redundant.

- You may be asked to take early retirement.

- Ill-health may force you to stop work.

So although your retirement date may not be set in stone, you need to plan well in advance, particularly if you are hoping to retire early

or to live abroad (these subjects are covered in greater detail below
and on page 294).

PLANNING TO RETIRE EARLY

Pension-tax rules allow you to retire from age 50 (55 from 2010) and
this is a pipedream many people have.

If you plan to retire early, you will need far, far more in your
pension fund to pay for what is likely to be 30 years of retirement
after only 30 years of employment. Even if you have built up a
£100,000 pension fund (over four in ten people retiring today have
just £10,000 with which to buy an annuity pension) you will get just
£4,000 a year in income (assuming it is inflation-linked) at 55
compared to £6,000 at age 65. So the chances are that you may not
be able to afford to retire at 50 unless you start planning this when
you are in your 20s. A male retiring at age 50 wanting a decent
income of £20,000 a year, rising by 3 per cent per annum, would
need a pension fund of almost £500,000 To fund a more indulgent
£30,000 a year, would require a pension fund of over £700,000. For
most people a wealthy and long retirement is unachievable unless
they have other sources of capital and income – for example, a large
cheque from the sale of a business or a second home.

If you still want to plan to retire at 50 or 55 read Chapter 9: How
To Boost Your Pension and Chapter 12: The Pension Alternatives.

Everyone Should Plan For an Early Retirement

Early retirement, however, is not always a choice. Fewer than half
of us do any paid work in the year before the current retirement
age.

If you are not working, you are not paying into your pension and
therefore you will get less when you retire, and you will probably
be dipping into your savings and investments, so once again you
will have less to live on when you retire. Your plans should take

into account the fact that you have a less than 50 per cent chance of working right up to retirement as a woman and only 33 per cent chance as a man.

The average age of withdrawal from the workforce is 62.6 for men and 60.4 for women according to the pensions Green Paper.

Do not assume you can make up for years of under-investment in your pension in your 50s and 60s when your mortgage has been paid off and your children have grown up. If you are forced out of the job market at an earlier age than anticipated, you will have no scope to meet your pension shortfall and will have the double whammy of having to make your reduced pension fund last longer than you planned.

PLANNING TO WORK PAST RETIREMENT

There are two reasons why you may decide to do this:

- Because you want to: over 20 years of doing nothing is just too grim a prospect for some people. They would miss work and still feel young and healthy enough to continue working.

- Because you have to: while some people are dreaming of retiring at 50, others are only just starting to plan their retirement. Getting to 50 with no pension planning is not as uncommon as you may think. The only way to ensure a decent pension, therefore, is to keep working for as long as possible.

A man who starts saving for his pension at 30 could double the amount he receives each year in retirement if he retires at 65 rather than 55.

Warning: If you go back to work for the same company you could find that any tax-free lump sum you received on retirement becomes taxable. If you are planning to do this, transfer your company scheme rights to a personal pension before drawing any lump sums. However, as from 2004, you will be allowed to draw your pension while taking a phased retirement from your employer or working past age 65.

Retirement and Tax

The bad news is that even after you retire you will still pay tax. The good news is that you can earn far more before paying tax and you no longer have to pay National Insurance Contributions once you reach state retirement age. While the basic personal allowance – the amount you can earn before paying tax – is £4,615 for the 2003/2004 tax year, once you reach 65 the allowances increase to:

£6,610 aged 65–74
£6,720 aged 75 years and over

In addition, existing retirees (those born before 6 April 1935) qualify for a married couple's allowance of £5,565–£5,635 depending on age.

However, these allowances are reduced by £1 for every £2 of income over £18,300, so if you earn a lot you may see no benefit from the age allowance. It will simply be reduced to the basic personal allowance for the under 65s. Your state and private pensions are part of your income and therefore taxable and included in this £18,300 figure.

The age 65 applies to both men and women even if the woman has a state retirement age of under 65. To qualify for an age allowance individuals must have reached the required age by the end of the tax year – not the start. Even people born on 5 April (the last day of the tax year) can still claim age-related allowances for the entire tax year once they reach 65.

The personal allowance for people aged 65 or over was increased by more than inflation in 2003/2004. In future, the increase in the allowance will be linked to the rise in earnings, not inflation, for the remainder of this parliament. This is an important concession as earnings tend to rise at a faster rate than inflation.

Pensioners who earn more than the £18,300 allowed for 2003/2004 should consider:

- Deferring taking their pension if possible (including their pension from the state) to reduce their income and therefore their tax liability.

- Deferring income to later years or switching to investments that produce capital gains rather than income so they can reduce their taxable income to below the threshold and make full use of their age allowances.

- Tax-free investments. Income from tax-free savings schemes including ISAs, PEPS, TESSAs, National Savings Certificates and the first £70 of interest from the National Savings Ordinary Account and some social security benefits including:

  - *council tax benefit*

  - *Christmas bonus for pensioners*

  - *widow's payment*

  - *attendance allowance and disability living allowance*

  - *war disablement pension*

  - *war widow's pension*

If one spouse earns more than the income threshold and the other does not, consider splitting the ownership of income-generating assets differently so that neither exceeds the limit.

Working Rights

At present if your employer tries to replace an older person with younger staff, they have no legal protection. However, in 2006 if the government implements a European Union directive prohibiting age discrimination, that could change.

Problems in recruiting trained staff or any staff at all have led to more employers introducing flexible retirement.

- They can raise or abolish their mandatory retirement date.

- Introduce a flexible window, during which employees can choose when to retire. This is the most popular option.

- A few offer greater flexibility by allowing employees to work part-time to reduce their workload and/or responsibilities gradually ahead of retirement, or after the normal retirement age.

You need to know what your employer currently offers and plans to offer. If it does not suit your needs you could lobby for change.

Note: The pensions Green Paper proposes to make it easier to work up to and past 65.

Pension Rights

Tax rules introduced in 1989 prevent people who want to stay working part-time for the same employer from drawing part or all of their pension to supplement their income. As a result, anyone who joined their employer's scheme after June 1989 and wants to continue working part-time can only draw their pension if they move to another employer. So some people can continue to work while drawing their pension while others (loyal employees) cannot. From April 2004 this situation will change and proposals currently being considered include the ability to take part pension and part salary between the ages of 50 and 75, even if you carry on with the same employer.

One concession has already been made. You can have gradual access to your pension through income draw-down schemes – by using your additional voluntary contributions (if you are in a final salary scheme) or your money purchase scheme to buy a pension from age 50 onwards even if you are still working. Although the tax rules have changed, your ability to do this will depend on your scheme rules. This is only an option for pensioners with at least £40,000 in their pension fund, and there are risks involved.

PLANNING TO BE DEBT FREE

Most people approaching retirement today have already paid off their mortgage. However, as more and more of us marry at a later age and start families in our late 30s, 40s or even 50s, more of us are still saddled with debts as we approach retirement.

The endowment scandal has also taken its toll. If you do not want to – or cannot afford to – make up for shortfalls in your endowment policy, it may not repay your mortgage on time, and the term of your mortgage may be extended until you reach – or even get past – your intended retirement age.

Once you retire, your income will be fixed, and you will want to make the most of every penny. So it is vital to clear yourself of debts well in advance.

Should I Pay Off My Mortgage Now?

Probably not.

- You may need your savings for a rainy day – once you have used them to repay the mortgage you may have none left.

- It is a bad time to cash in investments to repay your mortgage.

- Your mortgage repayments are likely to be relatively low and affordable. Will you put an equal amount into saving for your future?

A better option may be to remortgage to a cheaper rate and use the savings to pay off the mortgage more quickly, by keeping payments at the current level, and at the same time offsetting any savings against the mortgage balance using a flexible offset or all-in-one account. This will preserve your savings and leave you mortgage free at an earlier age, as well as saving you money in total interest costs.

Will I Ever Be Able To Stop Working?

This may be a concern, particularly if you have an endowment mortgage. Generally, advisers recommend that you do not bother to top this up. Instead, consider:

- remortgaging some of the loan to a repayment mortgage which is guaranteed to repay the mortgage at the end of the term

- moving to a cheaper mortgage rate and using the monthly savings to build up a savings reserve (to meet the endowment shortfall) or overpay on your mortgage each month so it is repaid more quickly

PLANNING TO RETIRE ABROAD

Retiring abroad away from the British weather to a country where the cost of living is far cheaper has its obvious attractions. However, the reality can often be quite different to the retirement you dreamed of when you were stuck at your office desk on a rainy day. If you are a seasoned international traveller you will know immediately if life abroad is going to be right for you. If, on the other hand, you have fallen in love with Spain on the back of a few holidays a year you should consider the following:

- Will you enjoy the climate all year round?

- Are you retiring to an isolated location, or will it be conducive to meeting new friends and creating a social life abroad? Are you near a local supermarket?

- Are you moving to a suitable property? Does it feel like you are hiking 10 miles to make it to the communal pool, or have you bought a house with too many stairs that will prove too challenging?

- Is the property in good condition? Builders are difficult to work with internationally, but if you rely constantly on foreign builders to keep your house in working order, not only could it prove costly, but the language barrier might mean you get a new sceptic tank instead of a boiler.

Your Finances

Pensions Abroad

UK state pensions are payable anywhere in the world. Around 900,000 pensioners in more than 200 countries are already claiming a pension overseas – and who can blame them? You will still receive your state pension on retirement (provided you have reached state pension age) if you live overseas. However, your pension may not be increased annually if you are going to live outside the European Economic Area (EEA) or if you reside within the EEA but are not covered by Economic Community (EC) social security regulations. Check well before retirement so that you can take this loss into account when choosing your retirement destination.

You may still qualify for winter fuel payments of £200 – even if you live in a sunny climate!

Tax While You Are Overseas

If you are going to live abroad permanently (to retire) you may be able to pay a lot less tax in addition to benefiting from a lower cost of living. This should be taken into account because it could substantially boost your standard of living.

Bear in mind that if you retire abroad you will still have to pay UK tax on income you receive from the UK, over and above your age-related personal allowance. But if you go to live in a country that has a double taxation agreement with the UK, you may be able to pay less tax. See the Inland Revenue leaflet *Income tax and pensioners* (IR121) for further information. This can mean that if you rent out your UK property, this rent will be taxed. You can, however, ensure that savings and investments escape tax by taking advantage of offshore banking. As you will no longer be resident in the UK you will no longer be taxed in the UK on your worldwide income (only on a UK income).

Welfare Benefits

You may be planning a wealthy retirement overseas but you should still consider what will happen should things go wrong. If you are going to another country in the EEA, or to a country that has a social security agreement with the UK, you may be able to claim some UK benefits or the benefits of that country. In addition, benefits you receive in the UK may also be affected by your move abroad. Each benefit has different rules and some UK benefits cannot be exported, e.g. housing benefit. For further information see the leaflet *Going Abroad and Social Security Benefits* (GL29) from the Department of Work and Pensions.

For countries within the EEA see the leaflet *Your social security insurance, benefits and health care rights in the European Community, and in Iceland, Liechtenstein and Norway* (SA29). The rules that coordinate member states' social security schemes also cover Switzerland. These are both available from the Department for Work and Pensions along with guides for other overseas destinations.

You can also find out more about your entitlements by requesting a leaflet called *Your Social Security Health Care and Pension Rights in the European Community* available from the DSS Overseas Branch, Newcastle upon Tyne NE98 1YX.

Choosing Your Destination

Sipping fine wines in the sun and inhaling the balmy air of foreign climes may sound like an idyllic retirement plan to most people but, unless it is carefully thought through, you might surprise yourself and find that it is not as suitable as you hoped. What works for a perfect two-week summer holiday trip might not be repro-duced around the clock three hundred and sixty five days of the year.

As an EEA national, you have the right to live in any EEA country. For non-EEA countries speak to the British Consul abroad and the foreign consulate in the UK.

Check Out the Facilities: It is important to remember that the facilities you may need when you retire initially may be very different from those you need twenty years down the line when you are not so mobile. A rustic house on top of a steep hill may look romantic while you are still into rambling, but it might not be so convenient if you have to struggle to buy a pint of milk.

Security: If you think you might feel vulnerable living in a remote area, perhaps you should consider living in a complex where there are always friendly neighbours around you to help out if there is a problem and where you will be sure to hear an English voice. Once again, think about your needs as you age – and perhaps what would happen if you were widowed and left on your own.

Friends and Activities: You may loathe the idea of moving abroad only to spend your nights stuck in a club with a load of ex-pats who do not integrate into the local community. However, it is much easier to create a social life abroad if you speak the same language. Get in touch with expatriate organizations in the country you plan to live in. The internet is a very good source of information if you search the Expatboards.

The Climate: You may be retiring overseas for no other reason than the weather – but remember, living in 90 degree Fahrenheit heat on a permanent basis might not be right for you. It could end up being 'too hot in the summer and too cold in the winter'; some coastal resorts can suffer from high winds. Renting first will give you a taste of the highs and lows.

Health Facilities: As you age, your health usually starts to deteriorate. Retiring abroad means you are intending to age abroad and, as a natural extension of this, there will be a greater chance you will need to use the local medical facilities at some point. Pensioners living in Economic Union (EU) countries are entitled to claim medical and health facilities that are available to the nationals of the country. These will include free dental care, sickness benefit and often free drugs. Pensioners can take advantage of the reciprocal agreement between EU countries and need to obtain form E211.

If you do not want to rely on the local facilities or there are gaps in the system, consider taking out a private health care policy. In countries outside the EC, such as in the United States, this is often a qualification for entry. As a pensioner it can be an expensive option and on average, for someone over the retirement age, can cost anything from £1,000–£2,000 a year even for basic cover, so you should budget for this at the outset. These expenses can be trimmed down sometimes but only at the cost of losing cover, so check out what you get for your money in a typical scheme.

You can find out more about your entitlements by requesting *Your Social Security Health Care and Pension Rights in the European Community* available from the DSS Overseas Branch, Newcastle upon Tyne NE98 1YX.

Before the big upheaval of the final move, it would be worth considering the following points:

Think About Renting First: Finding a location to settle down in abroad might take longer and be more difficult than you think. One village in Europe can vary enormously from the next, so you should think about renting abroad first before you buy – and rent out your accommodation in England before selling it. A three-month trial is probably long enough to discover if living abroad permanently is for you.

Can You Afford To Return? Property prices in the UK are far higher than in most overseas countries and have been rising at a more rapid rate than elsewhere. If you sell your UK home and then decide to return to the UK later on, you may find you cannot afford a comparable property because your overseas home has failed to rise in value at the rate of house price inflation in the UK. You may then be forced to live in greatly reduced circumstances.

Buying Overseas

When you do buy property abroad make sure you seek professional legal advice. You also need to meet certain legal requirements, such as registering with local authorities and applying for a residence permit (this should be done within three months of arrival in another EEA country).

You should also make a will. If you die intestate abroad this can cause great difficulties for your heirs; seek professional legal advice. You may require separate wills for assets and property held in the UK and in other countries.

Your local British Consul can provide a list of English-speaking lawyers who can assist you.

PLANNING YOUR TIME

Up until not so recently people would work to 64 and die at 69 with four years of retirement. If you retire now at 55 your average life expectancy is 79: that four years has stretched to 24 – a six-fold increase.

Think carefully. Could you be 'retired, retired' for that length of time or possibly longer as life expectancy increases? Planning for your retirement is not just about sorting out your finances.

Retirement is mandatory at a certain age for people who are in employment and voluntary for the self-employed. Whether it is at 58, 60 or 65, it brings some sudden changes and harsh adjustments for which many are little prepared. Overnight, you find yourself without work, without contact with your co-workers and without any goal to look forward to. You may also find relationships at home become strained. After being away from home for 40 or even 50 hours a week, you are stuck with your partner 24/7. This will be no problem if one of you spends half the day at bingo or at the allotment, but that is not how many of us plan to spend our retirement. Leisure activities can be expensive and you may also lack mental stimulation if you have been at work. The more active you keep, the better your chances of remaining physically and mentally healthy. So consider:

- voluntary work

- learning – the University of the Third Age has U3A groups around the UK that tackle anything from language learning to philosophy.

- hobbies

14 On Retirement

PRE-RETIREMENT CHECK LIST

As retirement looms you need to get more than your finances in order.

Health and Happiness

You cannot stop the ageing process but you can stop some of its worst effects from taking a toll on your body – and your mind. You should take care of your body, your diet and your lifestyle and keep yourself physically and mentally active. You also need to consider whether or not you continue to pay for any private medical insurance – the costs rise dramatically as you age. When you leave your employment you will lose out on any private medical insurance (although you can often continue with the scheme by paying the premiums yourself). On the plus side, certain health benefits – prescriptions, for example – will be free.

Your Home

Some 1.1 million elderly homeowners are seriously considering selling their homes and moving to smaller properties to provide a much-needed boost to their income, according to a recent survey by Key Retirement solutions. It found that a further 800,000 are thinking about using some form of equity release scheme to achieve the same result (these are discussed in greater detail on page 310).

If you are on the brink of retirement, the first element on your check list should be the suitability of your home. It could be that since the children have flown the nest, you should downscale and save on the costs of running an over-large house that is no longer right for you. Moving to a smaller property or simply relocating to a different area could mean you will be able to tailor your new accommodation to meet your needs.

- A smaller or newer home will be more economical to run and easier to heat and manage.

- You could move nearer to shops, the doctor, transport links – as you get older convenience will become more important

- You could move nearer to friends and/or family – with so much time on your hands you may want to be nearer people you know.

If you are fearful that mobility could soon become a problem, you could consider one-storey bungalows.

You might also choose to move to an area which has a higher ratio of other pensioners around. By sharing the same concerns, you can keep an eye on each other and increase your social life. Living within a helpful and watchful community could give you a feeling of added security and prevent a feeling of isolation. However, consider the upheaval, leaving familiar surroundings, leaving friends and neighbours and the costs.

If you feel a move will be inevitable at some stage, consider moving sooner rather than later – when you want to, rather than when you have to.

Alternatively, look at ways to cut the cost of running your home. Can you install insulation, draught proofing or double-glazing?

Think long term. If you need to replace the boiler later on, you may struggle financially. Perhaps you should invest in your home now, before you retire, rather than when you are on a fixed income.

Whatever your choice, you will have to prepare for the fact that there may be a time when you will no longer be able to physically do the things you did when you were younger. You might not be able to fix the broken tiles on the roof like you used to. Plan for this eventuality.

If you need adaptations or conversions for your current home, ask your local authority about grants. A renovation grant, a disabled facilities grant or a home repair assistance might help with the costs of the work. Before making any changes, talk to the Home Improvement Section or the Environmental Health Department at your local council.

Warning: Some elderly people choose to move in with family or friends. Talk to a solicitor if you are putting money into a home or paying for work to a house that is not entirely your own.

Take legal advice before signing property or assets over to your family. You may want to do so for tax reasons, but if you reach the point where you need nursing care, you might wish you still had your assets so that you could pay for private nursing care in your own home. There are also issues about inheritance tax and long-term care – see these sections on pages 306 and 314.

Bills and Overheads

The average cost of running a home is now £5,226 a year according to the Centre for Economics and Business Research. It found that household expenditure for retired people averages 38.6 per cent of their disposable income – far higher than for other age groups.

Before these costs become a burden, consider ways to reduce your household bills including:

- switching insurer – most offer discounted rates to older homeowners and older drivers

- switching energy supplier

- insulating your home to cut fuel bills

- changing your car for one that is more economical to run, tax and insure

- applying for any benefits you may be due such as council tax benefit

- opting for a different way to pay your telephone bill and/or signing up for discounts – you may find you are on the phone a lot once you retire

- pay by direct debit – it will help you to budget and you may qualify for a discount on your utility bills

ON RETIREMENT CHECK LIST

State Pensions

You should be contacted about four months before you reach state pension age with details of how you can claim your basic state retirement pension. Make sure that the Department of Work and Pensions knows your current address.

If you are four months or less away from state pension age and have not received your invitation to claim, call 0845 300 1084 (7 a.m.–7 p.m.).

Private Pensions

There is an estimated £6 billion 'lost' in former employer's schemes and more in personal pensions. Track down your pensions well before your chosen retirement date to ensure they know your current address. You need to confirm when you want to take your pension. If you are deciding to retire at 60, for example, but when you bought your personal pension you selected a retirement age of 65, you will need to notify your pension provider (and there may be penalties to pay).

Wills

If you have not made one before it is now time to make a will. Nearly two in three people in the UK die without a will, leaving confusion over who should receive any inheritance. As you get older, you have a duty to leave your spouse and children with as few problems as possible. And you can, while writing a will, look at ways to minimize or even eliminate your estate's liability to inheritance tax.

It is also important to make provision in case any beneficiary dies before the individual making the will. If they do, any gift that was intended for them will fall into the residue of the estate unless the will specifies that it should go to someone else. The residue is what is left over after all debts and expenses have been deducted and any gifts to beneficiaries have been given.

Some people have been caught out by not having their will witnessed properly or by failing to sign or date it. The legal requirement is that the will must be signed by the individual in the presence of two independent signatories who do not benefit from the will. All three signatories must sign in each other's presence.

The will should be stored in a safe place but not so safe that it cannot be found.

If you do not make a will, your worldly wealth will be divided according to the rules on intestacy. The rules depend on whether or not the deceased is married. If someone is married:

- Only the first £125,000 automatically goes to the spouse.

- If the estate is worth more than this and there are children, the spouse receives the first £125,000 and a life interest in half the remainder, as well as any personal effects. Their children (or their children's children if they are no longer alive) get the rest.

- If there are no surviving children, the deceased's parents will inherit half the balance in excess of £200,000 (with the spouse getting any personal effects).

- If there are no surviving children or parents, brothers and sisters of the deceased share in half the balance in excess of £200,000 (with the spouse getting the personal effects). If the brothers and sisters are no longer alive their children can inherit.

If the deceased was not married then:

- Any children inherit the entire estate with it shared equally between them or their issue.

- If there are no children, the deceased's parents inherit with the estate shared equally between them.

- If the parents are no longer alive, brothers and sisters or their issue then inherit.

- If there are none of the above still alive, first grandparents and, if they are not alive, then aunts and uncles or their issue then inherit.

If there are no relatives everything goes to the Crown.

Inheritance Tax Planning

The UK wastes £1.1 billion through poor inheritance tax (IHT) planning according to research from IFA Promotion. If you have not done anything about avoiding the tax so far, now is the time to do so.

- Once you have paid off your mortgage, your home will be worth more when calculating the value of your estate. That means more IHT.

- Once you take a lump sum on retirement this too will boost the value of your estate.

- If you plan now – and take advantage of the seven-year rule on inheritances – you can pass on a large amount to the next generation today, saving IHT in the future.

In the tax year ending April 2001, 1.1 million people were expected to have shared inheritances totalling £25 billion, with £1.4 billion of this going straight to the tax man. Yet, with a little financial planning, much of this tax could easily have been avoided. In fact, some accountants call IHT the 'voluntary tax' because it is so easily avoided. Anyone living in the UK is subject to inheritance tax on all their property owned worldwide, even if they have no assets in the UK and have lived abroad. However, many estates fall within the nil-rate band of IHT which means no tax is payable if the value of the estate does not exceed £250,000 for the 2002/2003 tax year.

The tax is paid on the value of the estate upon death. This includes:

- property

- bank and building society deposits

- shares and unit trusts

- investments, including tax-free investments such as ISAs

- cash

The following assets are exempt from IHT and not included when the value of the estate is assessed:

- all transfers between spouses

- normal expenditure out of income

- gifts made more than seven years before death

- pension fund savings

On death, IHT is levied at 40 per cent on all assets in excess of the nil-rate threshold (£250,000 for 2002/2003). Even non-taxpayers or basic-rate taxpayers will suffer 40 per cent tax on their estate if it exceeds the nil-rate band. This nil-rate threshold is increased each year in the Budget and is usually raised in line with inflation. But the full amount is not charged on gifts made within seven years of death. (Those made more than seven years before death escape IHT.) The reduced rates are:

One to three years	100% of the full charge at 40%
Three to four years	80% of the full charge giving an effective rate of 32%
Four to five years	60% of the full charge giving an effective rate of 24%
Five to six years	40% of the full charge giving an effective rate of 16%
Six to seven years	20% of the full charge giving an effective rate of 8%

It is the estate that pays the tax. It is deducted from the assets and must be paid before probate is granted (before the will is officially recognized). Any tax liability must therefore be agreed and paid before the beneficiaries receive any inheritance.

Reducing Your Tax Liability

The easiest way to reduce a potential IHT liability is to give away assets seven years before death, they then escape being included in your estate unless you retain an interest in them. You cannot, for example, give away your home to your children and continue to live in it. This will only work if you pay a market rent. Assets must be given outright – you must put the money into their account and have no say over how it is spent or give them an antique and accept they can sell it.

In addition, the following gifts and transfers are exempt:

- £250 to any number of individuals as small gifts each tax year.

- £3,000 per year given to an individual in any tax year.

- Gifts on marriage to a maximum of £5,000 from each parent (£2,500 by each grandparent or other relative and £1,000 by anyone else). The gift must be made before the wedding day.

- Gifts to charities, political parties and housing associations and for national purposes.

Transfers between husband and wife during their lifetime, or on death, are totally free of IHT. However, this often lulls people into a false sense of security. If the surviving partner inherits everything, the deceased partner has not made use of the IHT threshold – the facility to leave up to £250,000 (for the 2002/2003 tax year) tax free to their children, grandchildren or other beneficiaries. To ensure that this tax threshold is used to full advantage, any liquid assets such as savings, shares or mutual funds should be split between the two partners so that each can leave up to £250,000 to their children or grandchildren. This, however, is only of use if the surviving spouse would have sufficient income left.

You can also use an IHT avoidance scheme. These include:

- Loan trusts. You leave money to your spouse in exchange for an IOU. As you have made a loan, the value of the loan is deducted from your estate on death. With loan trust schemes offered by life insurance companies the individual makes an interest-free loan to the trust, which then invests this capital for growth (and up to 5 per cent income from this). Once the loan is made, it then falls outside of the estate for IHT purposes.

- Home reversion schemes. While these are not IHT avoidance schemes as such they work on the same principle. The loan reduces the value of the estate, but you get an income in the meantime.

- Leave half your home to your children. Put the property into a tenancy in common and on the death of the first spouse leave this half of the house to the children. When the second spouse dies only half the home is then liable to IHT.

- Discretionary trusts. The trust enables the first spouse to die and pass on up to £250,000 (the 2002/2003 allowance) to the next generation while still enabling the surviving spouse to benefit from the assets. The trust is taxed, with income taxed at 34 per cent, and any capital gains are also taxable.

- Other types of trust. life insurance and investment companies offer a range. With a reversionary interest scheme a series of investment bonds are held in trust outside the estate for IHT, but the individual can still receive regular annual payments to boost retirement income.

AFTER RETIREMENT

Running Out of Money

The main source of capital – and therefore a means of boosting your income – is your home. You can either:

- Sell it and move to a cheaper property.

- Sell it and rent (however, you will have the drain of rent on your income).

Or use it to raise some capital or an income.

Equity Release

Equity release or Home Income Plans enable you to release capital from your home – ideal for pensioners who are asset rich but income poor.

The soaring UK property market in recent years has left the over-60s living in properties worth an estimated £500 billion. Yet many pensioners are struggling by on £100 a week or less. No wonder demand for these schemes is growing rapidly as the population ages. The number of schemes taken out soared by 33 per cent in the first six months of 2002 alone.

Turning equity in your home into cash in your pocket is not

without risks. Although schemes vary, they generally allow you to either raise a capital sum or an income from your home in exchange for selling part of it. The company is paid its proceeds when you sell or die. So you can still sell your home (or the part you own) – for example, to move into a care home – later on.

Homeowners generally have to be in their 60s to be considered for these schemes. There are different types of equity release plan offered by a number of banks, insurance companies and specialist lenders.

Warning: Most schemes are outside the regulatory remit of the Financial Services Authority (FSA), the financial watchdog. Some will be covered by regulation in future but not all – so it is a case of buyer beware. Only equity release mortgages will be regulated from 2004, not home reversion plans. The pensions Green Paper is looking at proposals to create a level playing field for the regulation of these schemes.

Home Reversion Schemes

With these you sell part or even all of your property to a specialist company:

- They pay you less than that share of the property is worth (so you will not get 50 per cent of the market value for selling half your home).

- The money raised can either be given as a lump sum or used to buy an annuity income for life (or a mix of the two).

- How much you get will depend on your age and how long you are expected to live after signing the agreement. Older people receive more than younger homeowners.

- You have the right to continue living in your home until death. However, in this instance you will be a tenant rather than the owner of your property.

- You will, nevertheless, still be liable for the cost of maintenance and repairs.

- When the property is sold after your death or after you sell to move into long-term care, the home reversionary company will get a share of the proceeds, according to the share of the property you sold them. So they will benefit from the capital appreciation. They may have only paid you £30,000 for a share in the house but when it is sold they could get £60,000.

Some schemes guarantee that if the plan holder dies shortly after the scheme is set up, their estate will receive money for a minimum period, typically five years.

Home reversion schemes usually require a minimum property value of at least £40,000 and a minimum age of 60 plus.

Remember that if you release your equity from your home you are still responsible for insuring the house and for payment of all household bills.

Fixed-interest Plans

Sometimes known as interest-only mortgages, these allow you to borrow a relatively small percentage of the value of your house at a fixed rate of interest.

- The loan buys an annuity to provide an income for life.

- The annuity can pay some or all of the interest on the loan or the interest can roll up, increasing the amount you owe.

- The loan will reduce what is left when you sell your home leaving your family with little to inherit.

- However, you still benefit from any increase in the value of your home.

These schemes are not for everyone:

- Age: you should be at least 60 years old, preferably 70 or older. The older you are, the more income you will get.

- Property: your property must be in reasonable condition and you must have paid off your mortgage. The home income company will want to know it can sell your property and make a profit.

- .Benefits: you could lose your entitlement to state benefits if you receive an income from your home.

- Inheritance: your family will have less to inherit. Many children are, however, happy to see their parents enjoy a better standard of living. Check that the scheme has a guaranteed sum if you die shortly after taking out the plan.

Warning: These schemes can cause financial problems. Shared appreciation mortgages are the latest of these types of scheme to leave elderly homeowners worse off. Some borrowers are now facing interest equivalent to 67 per cent because of steep rises in house prices. With a shared appreciation mortgage (SAM), lenders bought an interest in the rise in value of borrowers' homes. It means that someone giving away 75 per cent of their home in exchange for a lump sum when the home was worth £100,000 could now have to pay £150,000 should they want to buy back the remaining interest, in addition to repaying any lump sum they received.

The Financial Services Authority will not assume regulatory responsibility for mortgage-based equity released plans until 2004 – you have been warned. Even then, there are no plans to bring home reversion plans – which involve selling part of your home immediately – under the same umbrella. They will not be regulated by the city watchdogs so you must be aware of what you are getting into.

Further Information

To protect the elderly, many providers of equity release schemes have joined a voluntary body called Safe Home Income Plans (SHIP) – call 0870 241 6060. Age Concern has produced a useful guide to *Raising Capital From Your Home* – call 020 8765 7200.

Explore the options before you need to, that way you will have more choices open to you should you need to release equity from your home.

The Alternatives

Sell part of your home to a child or your children. If they have some spare cash or can raise the finance they can in effect become their own home income company. You can raise money from your home and they will own a share of an appreciating asset (although they will have to pay capital gains tax when it is sold). In addition, the proportion they have purchased should escape IHT.

There is, however, a risk that if you fall out they could force you to sell up, or if your child goes bankrupt the courts could try to seize the asset.

Long-term Care

This can eat into any assets you have, leaving little for you to pass on to the next generation in the form of an inheritance. Under the current rules, anyone with assets of more than £19,000 (£18,500 in Scotland) must pay for all care apart from nursing care in full (other than in Scotland where personal care is also free) and the fees often exceed £20,000 or even £30,000 a year for constant nursing care and over £15,000 for residential care.

Only pensioners with capital of less than £11,750 in England and Wales and £11,500 in Scotland get all care free. Those with capital falling between the upper and lower limits, only get some assistance. The value of your home is not means tested for the first three months and a few homeowners may qualify for deferred interest loans. However, for most readers, it will be a case of selling up.

Despite the Labour government coming into power pledging to end the plight of elderly homeowners forced to sell their homes to finance long-term care some 40,000 homes are sold in a typical year to pay for care.

The proportion of people now aged 60 to 64 who own their own homes is 40 per cent higher than among people over 80 today, so the risk of losing your home will increase. It is estimated that the proportion of self-pay residents in care will rise from 33 per cent now to 45 per cent in the next few years. You will be subject to rigorous means testing to determine whether you should pay for this care and this will take into account your property, savings, investments and pensions. In effect you could be penalized for making prudent pension planning. There is a way round this.

Long-term Care Policies

You can buy an insurance policy to pay for these care costs. They are expensive, but not only do they provide financial assistance, they can also help in finding a nursing home.

According to IFA Promotion these are the questions you should ask before taking out a policy:

- What life expectancy will my cover be based on?

- Is there a plan that covers care in my own home?

- How much can I expect the monthly premiums to be?

- At what stage will I be entitled to claim?

- What range of services does your recommended policy include?

- What if I decide to retire abroad?

You are advised to seek independent financial advice before taking out one of these schemes.

Costs depend on your age. A man aged 65 can expect to pay around £60 to £90 a month for £1,000 a month of long-term care benefit and women a premium of up to £125 a month – so it is not cheap, particularly if you only claim the benefit for a few months. The younger you take out the insurance the cheaper it will be.

Giving Your Home To the Next Generation

If you try to get round the £19,000 rule, you are likely to run into difficulties. Local authorities are aware that the elderly may be tempted to pass on their wealth to the next generation in order to escape paying for long-term care. If you hand over your home to your children within six months of going into a care home they are likely to try to bill the new owners.

Most older people do **not** require care in care homes. If you pass on your property to someone else it is no longer yours, so you may not be able to sell it if you want to move to a smaller property or sheltered housing.

If the local authority decides that you have deliberately deprived yourself of capital to get free care, it can refuse your benefits.

You are advised to read *Transfer of assets, and paying for care in a care home*, Factsheet 40 from Age Concern.

15 Getting Advice

Choosing a pension is probably one of the most important decisions we will ever make in life. It should secure our future in old age so it is not a decision to be taken lightly. Yet choosing a pension is not an easy decision to make: they are complex; there are charges, tax breaks and performance figures to compare as well as a host of other features from flexibility to investment choice; there are hundreds of different plans on offer and they can often be difficult to understand.

If you do not feel confident to source the best plan by yourself, you should let a financial adviser, who will have the latest information and figures, do the shopping around for you.

Choosing the right financial adviser is crucial. Whom should you trust? Do they only sell the products of one company, and is that company any good? When they say they are independent are they genuine? Are they being paid a commission, and how will that affect their advice? Are they authorized to give you any advice at all?

Pension planning is not a one-off decision. As your circumstances change so do your pension options and needs, so it is important to review your plans on a regular basis.

Hiring an adviser is not an excuse to let someone else do the thinking and feeling for you. You need to be informed so you can have the security of knowing they are offering you a service and a product that will meet your financial needs. Despite all the regulation in the City, it is still a case of buyer beware. You cannot claim compensation if your investment performs badly or, with hindsight, if you realize you would have been better off investing elsewhere. If you buy the first product you hear about – for example, following a mail-shot to your home or a visit to your bank – and it turns out to be a poor deal, you will only have yourself to blame. Shopping around and understanding what you are buying is *your* responsibility although you do have rights and should expect:

- Firms to be financially sound and trustworthy.

- Salespeople and advisers who are competent.

- The information on which to base your decisions to be correct.

- Compensation if something goes wrong.

WHO OFFERS PENSIONS ADVICE?

Pensions are sold or provided by a wide range of financial organizations including:

- banks

- building societies

- life insurance companies

- fund management groups

- independent financial advisers

- actuaries

- stockbrokers

- accountants and solicitors

- some high street shops (like Marks & Spencer)

- trade unions

However, the type of advice given can vary.

Execution Only

This means no advice is given. You usually buy the product direct – even via the internet. Some companies do most of their business like this and can cut the costs of investment as a result. However, it is entirely up to you to determine whether their products are suitable.

The name execution only comes from the fact that it is you who decided to buy, while they 'execute' your decision. But beware. An unsuitable fund, or a poor performing company, can more than cancel out any money saved from a product's 'low' charges. You may want advice on how much you should contribute or which fund you should invest in.

Note: The low cost of stakeholder plans means that not all providers offer access to advice.

Tied Advice

People who represent a single organization, such as banks and building societies, are called tied advisers or company representatives. They are only able to offer advice on a limited selection of products. Therefore, they cannot advise you on whether these products are more suitable for you than those available elsewhere. Nor will they tell you that the pension has higher charges or poorer performance than other products on the market.

So while they may be able to advise you on which funds to invest in and how much to contribute to your pension, they will not shop around to get you the best deal. They may also not have the qualifications or experience to deal with complex matters such as the merits of transferring your fund from one occupational pension scheme to another (and they may be reluctant to do so as they will not earn any commission from it).

If the company does not have a pension product to suit your needs they should, in theory, tell you.

Company representatives are often referred to as life insurance salesmen, although their business card may give them a more fancy name such as financial consultant. They mainly work for the big insurance companies and banks. Tied agents include most of the major banks and building societies who started by having links with pension providers (mainly life insurance companies) but have now ended up taking them over.

Special Rules for Stakeholders

Although tied advisers can recommend only their company pension plans, there is an exception with stakeholder pensions. They can offer stakeholder pensions from other companies if it is possible to adopt them into their own company's product range. An adviser tied to this type of company can offer you the products of more than one provider.

Independent Financial Advice

One way to make sure you receive unbiased advice is to get it from an independent financial adviser (IFA) who should look at a full range of financial products and providers before choosing the best to suit your needs. Known as IFAs they are obliged to provide advice most suited to your personal requirements, and when financial products are recommended they must take into account the benefits provided, charges, flexibility, service and financial strength.

Most IFAs work for specialist financial advice firms, some of which are quite large; however, a few banks and building societies do offer independent financial advice, and so do solicitors and accountants.

Note: The Financial Services Authority (FSA) is abolishing the distinction between independent or tied (known as polarization), so check before buying how independent the advice will be.

Appointed Representatives

These may be either tied or independent, because they may be acting either as agents for a single-product company or as agents for a firm of independent advisers. You will need to check which sort they are.

Generic Financial Advice

To avoid the need to pay for advice, the pensions Green Paper proposes generic financial advice. For example, a financial health check that helps you decide which types of pension or investment are best for you. These will help consumers assess their financial position.

Which Is Best?

Recent polls of the type of advice most people would like to receive show, not surprisingly, that they think independent financial advice is the best. IFAs account for three quarters of all pensions sales and the majority of all annuities business. Bear this in mind:

- Almost 8 in 10 stakeholder sales are controlled by the top ten providers. So whether you go direct or via an adviser, you are likely to end up with a pension from one of these companies.

- Stakeholder charges are just 1 per cent or lower and not all plans pay commission. Will an IFA recommend those that do not pay a commission?

- When stakeholders were launched, Barclays, which did not have its own, sold the one from Legal & General and although its advisers were tied, the pension was identical to L&G's other than there was no annual management charge for the first three years – so investors may have been better off buying through the bank than through an IFA.

- Not all stakeholder providers offer advice – so if you want it you may have to go to an IFA and pay for it.

If your needs are for more than just the most basic stakeholder pension and you:

• want advice about contracting out

• want to know what to do with any existing plans

• want to know if you should consider transferring any pensions

You are recommended to seek independent financial advice.

All Change

The Financial Services Authority (FSA) will end polarization – rules which required advisers to be either tied or independent.
    It proposes that:

• Firms currently restricted to selling just one company's products to customers will, in future, be able to offer them more choice.

• Firms which continue to hold themselves out as 'independent' can do so provided they advise from across the market and offer their customers the option to pay by fee.

These changes are not likely to take effect until late 2003 or early 2004.
    However, the rules for stakeholder pensions have already been relaxed and firms can sell stakeholder pensions from other providers.
    The Financial Services Authority has also published proposals for a 'menu' for paying for financial advice instead of advisers being paid a commission from the pension company. The aim is to:

• reduce the potential for commission bias

• make consumers more aware of the cost of advice

• facilitate shopping around by consumers

In future, advisers are likely to be paid on a menu basis – receiving a fee based on a fee scale either per job or per hour. Consumers would be offered the choice of a fee, or given the choice of paying by commission. The consumer would be shown what commission the adviser normally charges set alongside average rates charged in the market.

One drawback to this proposal is that investors may be put off by the costs, even though they would probably be lower because most people are unaware of the costs they are paying today and often assume advice is free. No comparison would be made with tied agents. Often the most expensive financial products are sold through this channel. In addition, fees (most IFAs give consumers the option of paying a fee) have not, so far, proved that popular.

When fees are paid, the commission the adviser receives is either:

- rebated and paid into the pension

- used to reduce any fee that is charged with any excess paid directly to the investor

Once consumers see just how much commission will be paid into their investment product or rebated, fees may prove more popular.

Warning: Always check what type of advice you are going to get before sitting down with an adviser. If in doubt simply ask 'Whose products can you recommend – pensions from all the pension providers or from just one or two?'
See also How Can I Become My Own Adviser? on page 341.

HOW MUCH DOES FINANCIAL ADVICE COST?

Financial advisers are usually paid by either:

- a commission, usually a percentage taken out of the money you pay or invest

- a one-off fee, usually paid direct to the adviser

- a combination of commission and fee

When you are deciding which adviser to use, ask how they expect to be paid. Even those advisers who are paid by fees often give the first half hour of advice free, but check before you meet them.

I didn't know I had to pay for advice?

This is not surprising. Every time you buy an investment, some life insurance or even take out a mortgage, the adviser will usually be paid a commission, but as you are not charged and asked to pay a set amount you may assume that the advice is all part of the package and that it is free.

However, if an adviser is paid by commission, you ultimately pay this through the product charges. But charges are often the same whether you buy through an adviser or not – so it pays to take the advice.

How much will it cost?

You find this out – but only *after* a pension has been chosen for you (not before you agree to buy it) so you may not know how the commission compares. The commission could total £2,000 or more over a number of years, or be far less.

The alternative is to pay a fee, particularly if you want to guarantee unbiased advise which may mean no 'sale' for the adviser. This will be the case for pension transfers, for example.

Will a fee be cheaper?

Most IFAs charge between £40 and £200 per hour, although many will quote you a set fee for, say, arranging a pension. The fee is paid whether or not you decide to take the adviser's advice and, in most cases, VAT will be payable. Fees could be £1,000 for complex cases. In return, the commission on the product the adviser would have earned will be rebated and invested in your pension, used to offset the fee or given to you as a cash rebate. Some advisers even offer a mix and match arrangement, charging a smaller fee in return for some commission rebate, or other options.

To find out what's best for you, just ask your IFA.

Generally for small investments the fees outweigh the savings so you are better off with the commission system. For other cases it is a question of doing your sums.

If the fees are £500 but the commission rebated is £1,000 you will be £500 better off.

What if I don't receive any advice?

If you do not get advice, you get the commission back. Buy through a discount broker (these sell on an execution-only basis) and rebate the commission. If you know you want to buy a particular product, check out whether you can buy it cheaper through a broker than direct from the firm by ringing around.

FINDING AN ADVISER

Sadly, most people do not choose their financial adviser. Instead, they receive some direct mail, someone contacts them directly, their bank gets in touch or they are told to talk to an adviser by their employer. As the relationship with this adviser should be ongoing (if often isn't), because you should re-evaluate your pension provision on a regular basis, it is important that *you* choose an adviser you are comfortable dealing with rather than dealing with the first person who comes along.

Shop Around

Do not buy a pension from the first person you speak to.

- Your bank may seem very helpful, but how do you know they are offering you the best deal?

- The adviser you speak to may not be a specialist in pensions.

- The salesman could be in it for the money – selling you a pension and then not bothering to give you on-going financial advice or help.

There is nothing to stop you speaking to more than one adviser before making up your mind.

Personal Recommendations

This is one of the best ways to find an adviser. If someone you know and trust feels they have received sound advice and good service from an adviser, then this is better than dealing with someone unknown. However, bear in mind that your friend/colleague/relative may have been seduced by clever sales patter and it is not until they retire that they may find out that the pension they have been recommended has turned out to be a poor performer.

Ask if the relationship is ongoing and whether they receive regular communication from the adviser and regular reviews.

Evaluate Your Needs

If you know you want a stakeholder pension, do not need an adviser to shop around for you and have selected a shortlist of pension providers, there is little point in seeking financial advice (other than it can be helpful). You can deal direct or through a tied agent or a company representative.

If you want someone to search the market for the best deal and to give you advice on how much to invest, select an IFA.

If your needs are more complex involving pensions left with a former employer, several different plans, or you need advice on contracting out you should seek more specialist advice from:

- an IFA specializing in pensions

- a member of the society of pension consultants

- an actuary – they charge a fee and can deal with more complex calculations involving final salary schemes

Where To Find Out More

If you like the look of a particular pension plan, for example, after checking out the Financial Services Authority league tables at www.fsa.gov.uk, you may want to deal with just one company. In this case, you may be better off dealing direct or buying through a discount broker because the charges could be even cheaper. Details of discount brokers can be found at www.find.co.uk.

If you want to find an IFA you can ring IFA Promotion on 011797 11177 or the money management register of fee-based advisers on 0870 013 1925.

If you need more specialist advice on pension transfers or even on setting up a pension fund such as a small self-administered scheme (SSAS) if you run your own business, you can contact a member of the Society of Pension Consultants (SPC). Visit www.spc.uk.com and search for independent advisers who are members of the SPC in your area or contact 020 7353 1688. Hourly fees generally range from £95 to £255.

For even more complex matters you may need the help of a consultant actuary. The Faculty and Institute of Actuaries can help you search for an actuary to give you advice at its website at www.actuaries.org.uk – type in the type of advice you want and the area in which you live.

EVALUATING YOUR ADVISER

Is the adviser regulated?

All advisers and the companies they work for who are recommending pension plans must be authorized by the Financial Services

Authority (FSA) and they must abide by rules designed to protect their customers. To check your adviser or the company they represent is authorized you can phone the FSA Consumer Helpline on 0845 606 1234.

Is the adviser properly qualified?

All salespeople and advisers must have passed at least a minimum qualification, such as the Financial Planning Certificate, the Investment Advice Certificate, the Certificate for Financial Advisers or the Certificate in Investment Planning. A trainee must be supervised by someone who is fully qualified. To give some types of advice, for example, about pension transfers, the person must have extra qualifications.

To check whether a salesperson or adviser is properly qualified, write to:

Individual Registration
The Financial Services Authority
25 The North Colonnade
Canary Wharf
London
E14 5HS

Or you can fax them on: 020 7676 0017.

Advisers may need to have passed separate exams to give different types of advice. For example, only a few are qualified to give advice on pension transfers. So make sure you are dealing with someone who is qualified and authorized to give you the range of advice you need.

You will probably find the qualifications confusing. They are numerous. Some are just general examinations in financial planning, others are more specific and advanced. The list of initials after an adviser's name may seem impressive, but how do you know? All financial advisers are required to pass an exam known as the Financial Planning Certificate or FPC before they are allowed to see clients but this is a very basic exam. You will generally want to speak to someone who has more qualifications, particularly in the field of pensions. The FPC is rather like a challenging GCSE, and probably not as demanding as an A level. Are you going to trust your future wealth to someone with this level of knowledge?

IFA Promotion, the organization that promotes independent financial advice, keeps details of every major and relevant qualification awarded to IFAs and visitors to its website at www.ifap.org.uk, or callers to its hotline on 0800 085 3250, can ask whether an IFA possesses certain specialist qualifications.

Although letters after someone's name are no guarantee that their advice will be better than someone with no additional qualifications but years of experience, they are a guide.

Some of the main qualifications are

AFPC – Advanced Financial Planning Certicate
MSFA – Member, Society of Financial Advisers
ALIA (dip) – Associate, Life Insurance Association
FLIA (dip) – Fellow, Life Insurance Association
FSFA – Fellow, Society of Financial Advisers
ACII – Associate, Chartered Insurance Institute
FCII – Fellow, Chartered Insurance Institute

They may sound impressive, but MSFA, for example, simply means Member of the Society of Financial Advisers. It is equivalent to being an ALIA – Member of the Life Insurance Association. However, some of these members may be better suited to giving pensions advice because it offers a specialist advanced qualification in pensions. Some qualifications mean more than others, requiring the candidate to pass a number of exams and several years experience. Being a Fellow of the Chartered Insurance Institute (FCII), for example, requires the candidate to pass ten exams and have experience.

So ask what the qualifications mean.

You can really put the adviser on the spot by taking along a guide to the examinations and what the abbreviations mean produced by IFA Promotion. Call 0800 085 3250 for a copy.

Are You Comfortable Dealing With the Adviser?

To get sound financial advice you will need to give a lot of personal information – when you hope to retire, how much you earn, your attitude to risk, whether or not you plan to marry or remain married. If you do not feel comfortable talking to the adviser or feel under pressure to buy a product when you are still unsure, walk away. The same applies if you feel too intimidated to ask questions.

One in three people sold personal pensions stopped contributing to them within the first three years and often lost out substantially as a result. If they had been advised properly and had fully understood what they were buying, the commitment they were making and the consequences of failing to keep up their contributions, many would never have bought these pensions in the first place or would have opted for lower contributions that they could afford.

Never buy a long-term financial product if you do not understand what you are buying or the risks involved.

What To Expect From Your First Meeting

In order to decide whether the adviser suits your needs, there are a few questions you should ask at an early stage. The following have been supplied by IFA Promotion:

* How do you charge?
  IFAs can be paid by fees, which you pay, or commissions paid to them by product providers. Ask your IFA to explain the differences between fees and commission when you first meet him or her. Increasingly, more people prefer to pay fees.

* How long have you been in business?
  You may feel more comfortable with someone who has several years' experience.

- Will you let me speak to the company that is providing the product?
An adviser should feel totally confident and be willing for you to talk directly with the product provider involved.

- What qualifications do you have?
The benchmark qualification is the Financial Planning Certificate (FPC), and a competent adviser must hold all three components of this certificate or equivalent. Some advisers also have advanced level qualifications in their specialist areas, for example, pensions.

- Are you a specialist?
Many IFAs are all-rounders, but some may specialize in mortgages, for instance. However, some may not advise on certain areas at all, such as pension transfers. You may prefer to deal with an IFA who will not provide advice, but will set up your investment, protection, pension or other financial product on your behalf, often on a more cost-effective basis than you could arrange yourself.

- Who are you regulated by?
Advisers must be regulated by a recognized authority. The government has set up the Financial Services Authority (FSA) which succeeds the Personal Investment Authority (PIA) and the other Self Regulatory Organisations (SROs).

- Will I always see you or will other people in your company look after me as well?
In some larger organizations you may deal with several advisers. If you prefer the continuity of a single contact, you may feel more comfortable with a smaller organization.

How do I know the adviser is not being swayed by commission?

IFAs are obliged to give you 'suitable advice', so they have to look beyond the commission and take other factors into account –

investment performance, charging structures, your personal circumstances – before any recommendation can be made.

Put the adviser on the spot by asking:

- How many recommendations did you consider for me?

- How does the commission vary from product to product?

- If a company is offering you a very high commission rate on a product, are you prepared to take a smaller percentage?

What happens next?

All financial advisers are obliged to offer what is termed 'suitable advice'. This means they have to gain a full understanding of your circumstances and requirements before helping to choose any financial products (they will record your information so you can double check that they really have understood).

In addition, when recommending a product, all financial advisers have to provide written reasons why they think it is right for you. Again, make sure you are fully informed before committing yourself to anything.

In order to determine your needs and goals, the adviser will ask you many questions and it is up to you how much you tell him or her. This information will be written down and in many cases you will be asked to sign your name that the information is correct. Do bear in mind that, like a visit to your local GP, the more information provided, the more accurate the diagnosis or advice that will result.

Following the 'fact finding' initial stage, the financial areas you need to think about will be identified. If you are looking for a specific product, then one will be selected for you and you will get a full range of details in the key-features document.

Anyone giving you advice must make sure their advice is suitable. This means any product recommended must:

- fit your financial circumstances, for example, the amount you can afford, how long you can tie up your money, your attitude towards risk and your tax position

- help you achieve your goals, for example, if you want to protect your income if you fell ill, the product should meet this need

A tied salesperson generally sells the products of a single provider (but might sell the stakeholder pension of another provider). If the provider does not have a suitable product, the salesperson must tell you so.

Remember, you give up your right to suitable advice when buying investments or personal pensions if you buy without advice (in other words, on an execution-only basis).

MONEY LAUNDERING RULES

Before entering into a long-term investment (or even opening a bank account) you are required to provide proof of identity. This includes one of:

- a current full UK/EU passport

- a current full UK/EU driving licence

- a pension book/child benefit book

Plus proof of your address:

- a council tax demand for the current year

- gas/electricity/telephone/water bill

- bank/building society statement

Although it may seem like a hassle, you have to comply with these requirements. Your adviser is only asking for these documents because he or she is required to do so by law.

REGULATION AND YOUR RIGHTS

The Financial Services and Markets Act sets out a comprehensive system of regulation to protect your rights when buying most financial products (savings accounts, for example, are not covered by the Act and the city regulators are only just beginning to take over regulation of mortgages). The chief city watchdog is the Financial Services Authority (FSA). The law requires that:

- Investment firms must be trustworthy.

- People selling and advising about investments must be competent.

- You must be given certain information.

- You must be given suitable advice.

All firms must be 'authorized', in other words, have a licence to carry on investment business. To get and keep the licence, they must show the GSA or the other regulators to whom it delegates that they are financially sound, employ fit and proper people and conduct their business properly and fairly. If firms break the rules, they can be fined and even lose their authorization. Individuals who break the rules can be banned from working in the investment industry.

A firm can be authorized to do some types of business, but not others. For example, firms need special authorization to hold clients' money.

The FSA looks after your interests.

- It keeps a register of advisers who must be vetted, registered and have passed a minimum qualification before giving advice.

- It monitors the financial health of firms including life insurance companies.

- It lays down rules on how advice may be given, for example, the rates of return that must be used when projecting how an investment or pension will grow.

- It checks that claims made are not excessive – that advertising is not misleading, for example.

While you should be able to expect that the firm and adviser you deal with are financially sound, properly authorized and qualified and will not run off with your money, you have little redress about the quality of investment advice. For example, if you you are/were wrongly advised to leave your employer's pension fund you may get compensation. If your personal pension performs badly compared to another, you must suffer the losses.

So it is still a question of buyer beware.

How Should I Protect Myself?

The FSA has some useful tips:

Take accurate notes when you meet an adviser and keep them safe. They will be essential if there is a dispute later on and you want to complain or claim compensation. You can ask for a copy of the fact find and your application form.

DO make sure you understand the key features and/or other documents – ask questions if you don't.

DO shop around and compare different products to ensure you are getting the product which is the best value for you.

DON'T be embarrassed to ask questions.

DON'T be afraid to say NO, even if the adviser has been recommended by a friend, or has gone to so much trouble that you do not want to disappoint them.

DON'T sign anything until you are confident you fully understand it.

DON'T ever sign a blank form allowing the adviser to fill in the details later.

DON'T get carried away by promises of amazing deals.

Warning: If you decide to buy without taking any advice, you are responsible for your choice. If in doubt, get advice instead of buying direct:

- through a direct offer such as an advertisement
- via the internet
- by responding to a mailshot
- by buying through a direct company (by filling in a form or over the phone)

When you base your decision to buy on information printed in a mailshot, say, or on a website, you have the right to expect the information to be accurate and complete. If it turns out to have been wrong or misleading, you have the right to complain and seek compensation for any loss you suffered as a result.

Note: In many cases, you will buy stakeholder pensions without advice. Do not mistake information for advice.

What information should I keep?

If something goes wrong or you feel you have been misled, you will need to refer the information given to you before, when and after you bought your pension or annuity.

This is what you can expect to be given according to the FSA:

Information	When given	What it tells you
Status of salesman/adviser	At business premises in product advertisements on business cards on first contact	Whether salesman is tied or independent
Terms of business letter/ client agreement	At the start of the first meeting	Who regulates the firm, its status, what it sets out to provide, complaints procedure
Commission payments	With key-features document and/or illustration, also on request	How much the salesmen will get from the sale

Key features document	Before you sign the application form for the product that is being recommended	Product details: what you must pay and how often, charges, risk, investments, tax, etc.
Information	**When given**	**What it tells you**
Illustration	With key-features document	Based on set assumptions – what you might get back at end of investment
Cancellation rights	In key features document	Your right to change your mind

In addition, if you buy a stakeholder pension without advice, you should be given a decision tree to help you make up your mind. This should be given to you before the sales process starts or within a key-features document.

If you are going to invest in a with-profits investment you may also receive a guide to how bonuses are calculated.

What if something goes wrong?

In case you want to make a complaint, investment firms must have internal procedures and belong to an independent scheme. If an investment firm collapses, you are at least partially protected by a compensation scheme – but only up to a maximum of £48,000. With most products and services, the regulations give some protection if you are negligently or fraudulently advised to take out a product which turns out to be unsuitable.

Can I complain if I lose money?

Only if the firm has run off with your money. If you lose money because the stock market has fallen, you may feel like complaining but there is little anyone can or has to do. However, if your pension performs badly because someone has done something wrong – investing in the wrong fund, overcharging you, losing documents or poor service – and you lose money as a result, you may be able to claim compensation.

If the advice you received was negligent or wrong, you should also be compensated. So far, over £11 billion has been paid to employees wrongly advised to opt out of employer pensions and top up plans to personal pensions and Free Standing Additional Voluntary Contributions (FSAVCs) – compensation for the losses they suffered as a result.

What should I do?

The first step is to contact the firm which sold you the product, which must offer an internal complaints procedure. Only after you have exhausted that line can you take your complaint to an independent complaints scheme. Most financial firms belong to one of these.

An independent complaints scheme such as an ombudsman will:

- look at the details of your case

- ask for extra evidence if necessary

- decide whether your complaint is justified

- if it is justified, order the firm to put matters right

If necessary, all schemes can order the firm involved to make you a financial award (up to a maximum of £100,000 with some schemes).

If you need help working out which scheme to contact, call the FSA Consumer Helpline on 0845 606 1234.

Warning: All complaints schemes have rules, rules about what type of complaints they deal with and what you must do before taking your complaint to the scheme. Always ask for a copy of their guide to making a complaint and follow the rules to ensure your case is not rejected.

Ombudsman schemes will require you to:

- give the firm a chance to put things right

- go through the firm's own complaints procedure first

Only when you have reached a deadlock, with the firm saying (in writing) it cannot reach an agreement with you, can you go to an ombudsman. If it will not do this, you usually have to wait a couple of months for them to reply to your request for a deadlock letter.

Usually you can choose whether or not to accept the decision. If you do not accept the decision, you can take your case to court if you want to – but this is usually prohibitively expensive. Some schemes, however, bind you as well as the firm to the decision made – for example, the Pensions Ombudsman.

Whom do I contact?

The Financial Ombudsman Service (FOS)
South Quay Plaza
183 Marsh Wall
London E14 9SR
Tel: Helpline 0845 080 1800
Tel: Switchboard 020 7964 1000
Website: www.financial-ombudsman.org.uk

From 1 December 2001, the FOS replaced eight previous complaint bodies.

- the Office of the Banking Ombudsman

- the Building Societies Ombudsman

- Financial Services Authority Complaints Unit

- the Insurance Ombudsman

- the Investment Ombudsman

- Personal Insurance Arbitration Service

- the Personal Investment Authority (PIA) Ombudsman

- the SFA Complaints Bureau

For complaints regarding an employer pension scheme contact:

The Pensions Advisory Service (OPAS)
11 Belgrave Road
London SW1V 1RB
Tel: 0845 6012 923
Website: www.opas.org.uk

The Pensions Ombudsman
11 Belgrave Road
London SW1V 1RB
Tel: 020 7834 9144
Website: www.pensions-ombudsman.org.uk

Before making a complaint request the *FSA guide to making a complaint*. The free booklet can be requested from the FSA Consumer Helpline on 0845 606 1234 or can be downloaded at www.fas.org.uk.

Can I claim compensation?

If an authorized financial firm goes out of business and cannot pay the money it owes you, you might be able to get compensation from the Financial Services Compensation Scheme (FSCS) (see page 341). If the firm is not authorized you are not covered by the scheme, so check before giving any money to firms you are not sure about. The scheme may also pay compensation for bad advice or poor investment management if this took place after 28 August 1988. However, even if the loss is covered by the scheme you probably will not get all of your money back. The maximum it can pay out is:

- the first £30,000 of any valid claim in full

- 90 per cent of the next £20,000

This gives a maximum compensation of £48,000 – far less than many investors have in their pension fund.

What if a firm goes bust, what compensation do I get then?

When the FSCS became operational on 1 December 2001, it not only replaced the complaints and ombudsmen schemes listed earlier in this section, it also replaced the Investors Compensation Scheme, Policyholders' Protection Scheme, Deposit Protection Scheme and Building Societies Investor Protection Scheme.

Generally, anyone who has an annuity or pension plan will receive the first £2,000 in full, plus up to 90 per cent of the remaining value of their investment if their pension company goes into liquidation. The FSCS, in conjunction with the liquidator and with the help of an independent actuary, will 'value' your policy for purposes of compensation. So it may not be as high as you think. Specifically, the valuation may exclude any future bonuses – including the terminal bonus, which is often what attracts investors to policies in the first place.

Currently, the Financial Services Authority is monitoring the financial health of a number of insurers on a daily basis.

Whom do I contact?

Financial Services Compensation Scheme
7th Floor
Lloyds Chambers
Portsoken Street
London E1 8BN
Helpline: 020 7892 7300
Website: www.fscs.org.uk

HOW CAN I BECOME MY OWN ADVISER?

You Can Get Information Through the Following

Government Departments: For example, the Department of Work and Pensions has free leaflets on pensions and information on what your state pension will be; the Inland Revenue publishes free leaflets on the tax aspects of saving and investing.

Financial Services Authority: The FSA produces free, user-friendly booklets and factsheets and can help with general enquiries and complaints handling procedures.

Newspapers and magazines: Regular articles on savings and investment and lists of building society and bank interest rates in the personal finance pages of newspapers and in specialist magazines. But check the information given is up to date and accurate.

Websites: Web addresses are often listed in newspapers and magazines; follow links from one site to another, or use search engines to find key words relevant to the subject you are interested in. But check the information given is up to date and accurate.

Libraries: Most libraries have a range of books and magazines on financial services, including Consumers' Association publications and government leaflets. They can also give you details of local advice agencies and help you get information from the internet.

Trade Associations/Unions: These often provide free information to help people understand different types of investment and saving.

Individual firms: Most banks, building societies and pension and life insurance companies produce free leaflets. But remember, they want you to buy their products.

Generic advice: The pensions Green Paper proposes a new form of generic financial advice. Non-specific advice in the form of financial health checks to help individuals make up their own minds.

The Financial Services Authority (FSA) has already developed aids to help those who do not have access to advice to make informed choices. These include decision trees for stakeholder pensions (*www.fsa.gov.uk*) and comparative tables to allow consumers to compare products.

The Department of Work and Pensions (DWP) has launched a digital television pilot with a number of providers over the last few months. This provides impartial information on pensions to customers who are approaching or planning for retirement, as well as to customers who are already in retirement. It is also working with the Pre-Retirement Association and large employers to launch a web-based financial education package, due to be launched in 2003.

In addition, the DWP has, since January 2001, distributed more than two million pension guides.

An on-line retirement planner: The Association of British Insurers and the FSA have recently launched a 'ready reckoner' at *www.pensioncalculator.org.uk* to enable people to estimate the total state and private pension they might receive in retirement.

16 Where To Find Out More

The Financial Services Authority (FSA) produces the following free guides, which are available from the consumer helpline on 0845 606 1234.

FSA guide to saving for retirement – starting to save
FSA guide to saving for retirement – Reviewing your plan
FSA guide to topping up your occupational pension
FSA guide to contracting out
FSA guide to risks of pension transfers
FSA guide to the risks of opting out of your occupational pension scheme
FSA Factsheet: Retiring soon – what you need to know
FSA guide to annuities and income withdrawal
FSA guide to financial advice

The Department of Work and Pensions has several useful guides. They are available by calling 0845 731 3233. The line is open 24 hours and calls are charged at local rates. Alternatively visit www.dwp.gov.uk or www.thepensionservice.gov.uk.

A guide to your pension options (PM1)
State Pensions – Your guide (PM2)
Occupational Pensions – Your guide (PM3)
Personal pensions – Your guide (PM4)
Pensions for the self-employed – Your guide (PM5)
Pensions for women – Your guide (PM6)
Contracted-out pensions – Your guide (PM7)
Stakeholder pensions – Your guide (PM8)
State pensions for carers and parents (PM9)

IFA Promotion, the organization that promotes independent financial advice, produces several guides. Call 0800 085 3250 or visit them at www.unbiased.co.uk.

Thinking about your pensions?
The financial practicalities of bereavement
Time to think about inheritance tax
Thinking about your mortgage
Thinking about your ISA
Thinking about your tax efficiency
Thinking about your investments
Thinking about independent financial advice?
Surviving an economic downturn
Surviving on savings when rates are low
A guide to IFA qualifications

Factsheets available include:

- Long term care

- Feel free to ask how IFAs make their money

- Confused about endowments?

- Equity Release – The ins and outs of unlocking money from your home

- The pensions debate – What are your options?

The Inland Revenue, contact the Inland Revenue (Savings, Pensions, Share Schemes) orderline on 0115 974 1670 or visit www. inlandrevenue.gov.uk. General leaflets are available on 0845 9000 404. They publish the following leaflets:

- IR121 Income tax and pensioners

- IR143 Income tax and redundancy

- IR78 Looking to the future. Tax reliefs to help you save for retirement

- IR2 Occupational Pension Schemes

- IR3 Personal Pensions (including Stakeholder Pension Schemes)

- IR110 A guide for people with savings

Help the Aged offers a range of information and advice leaflets ranging from claiming benefits to home security. Ring the main office for England 020 7278 1114, for Scotland 0131 551 6331, for Wales 02920 415 711 or for Northern Ireland 02890 230666 or visit their website at www.helptheaged.co.uk. Financial information leaflets include:

Paying for Residential Care
Paying for Residential Care: Problems with Local Authority
    Funding
Bereavement Benefits
Thinking About Money
Equity Release Plans
Attendance Allowance
Can You Claim It? Advice on Welfare Benefits
Questions on Pensions
Pre-paid Funeral Plans
Claiming Disability Benefits
Check Your Tax
Individual Savings Accounts
Managing a Lump Sum
Your Guide to Making or Changing Your Will

Age Concern publishes a range of factsheets – to request one call the information line free on 0800 00 99 66 or visit www.ageconcern. co.uk. The leaflet numbers are printed below. Note: some leaflets are different for Scotland.

15. Income tax and older people
16. Income related benefits: income and capital
17. Housing Benefit and Council Tax Benefit
18. A brief guide to money benefits

19. The State Pension
21. The Council Tax and older people
25. Income Support (Minimum Income Guarantee) and the Social Fund
34. Attendance Allowance and Disability Living Allowance
7. Making your will*
14. Dealing with someone's estate*
22. Legal arrangements for managing financial affairs*
10. Local authority charging procedures for care homes*
20. NHS continuing care, free nursing care and intermediate care
24. Direct Payments from social services
29. Finding residential and nursing home accommodation
32. Disability and ageing: your rights to social services*
38. Treatment of the former home as capital for people in care homes
39. Paying for care in a care home if you have a partner
40. Transfer of assets and paying for care in a care home
46. Paying for help at home and local authority charges
2. Retirement housing for sale*
8. Moving into rented housing*
12. Raising income or capital from your home
13. Older home owners: financial help with repairs and adaptations*

*There is a separate factsheet for Scotland.

USEFUL CONTACTS

To request a state pension forecast: The Retirement Pension Forecasting and Advice Unit: 0845 3000 168.

For general information on state pensions including increased retirement ages for women: The Pensions Info-Line: 0845 7 31 32 33; the Department for Work and Pensions public enquiries: 0207 712 2171

To claim your state pension: 0845 300 1084

To check an adviser is authorized: FSA Consumer Helpline: 0845 606 1234.

To check an adviser is qualified: Write to:
Individual Registration
The Financial Services Authority
25 The North Colonnade
Canary Wharf
London
E14 5HS
or fax: 020 7676 0017

To find an independent financial adviser: IFA Promotion: 011797 11177

To find an independent fee-based adviser: The Money Management Register: 0870 013 1925

To find a specialist pensions adviser: Society of Pension Consultants: www.spc.uk.com or 020 7353 1688

For advice on your private pension: The Office of Pensions Advisory Service: 0845 60 129 23

For advice on your employer pension: The Occupational Pensions Advisory Service: 020 733 8080

To trace a missing pension: The Pensions Tracing Service: 0191 225 6316

To complain about your employer's scheme: The Occupational Pensions Regulatory Authority (OPRA): 01273 627 600

To find out if a stakeholder pension is suitable for you: The FSA stakeholder pension decision tree: www.fsa.gov.uk or 0845 606 1234

To compare personal and stakeholder pensions: www.fsa.org.uk/tables

For tax information if you are moving abroad: Centre for non-residents helpline: 0845 0700 040

For information about pensions, widow/bereavement benefits, incapacity benefits if moving abroad: The DWP Liaison Unit: 0191 218 7777

For forms and leaflets about inheritance tax: IR Capital taxes orderline 0845 234 1000, helpline: 0115 974 2400, helpline for Scotland: 0131 777 4050/4060

For information about contracting out: National Insurance Contracting Out helpline: 0845 234 1000.

For information about buy-to-let: The Association of Residential Letting Agents: 01494 431 680

For information on equity release: Safe Home Income Plans (SHIP): 0870 241 6060

To find a solicitor to help make a will: The Law Society of England and Wales: 020 7242 1222; the Law Society of Scotland: 0131 226 7411 or www.make-a-will.org.uk

OTHER USEFUL ADDRESSES

Financial Services Compensation Scheme
7th Floor, Lloyds Chambers, Portsoken Street, London E1 8BN
Helpline: 020 7892 7300

The Office of the Pensions Advisory Service (OPAS)
11 Belgrave Road
London SW1V 1RB
Tel: 0845 6012 923
www.opas.gov.uk

The Pensions Ombudsman
11 Belgrave Road
London SW1V 1RB
Tel: 020 7834 9144
www.pensions-ombudsman.org.uk

Age Concern
Information Line
Freepost (SWB 30375)
Ashburton
Devon TQ13 7ZZ
Tel: 0800 00 99 66
www.ageconcern.org.uk

The Association of Retired and Persons Over 50
Greencoat House
Francis St
London SW1P 1DZ
Tel: 020 7828 0500
www.arp.org.uk

Help the Aged
Senior Line
207-221 Pentonville Road
London N1 9UZ
Tel: 0808 800 6565
www.helptheaged.org.uk

Index